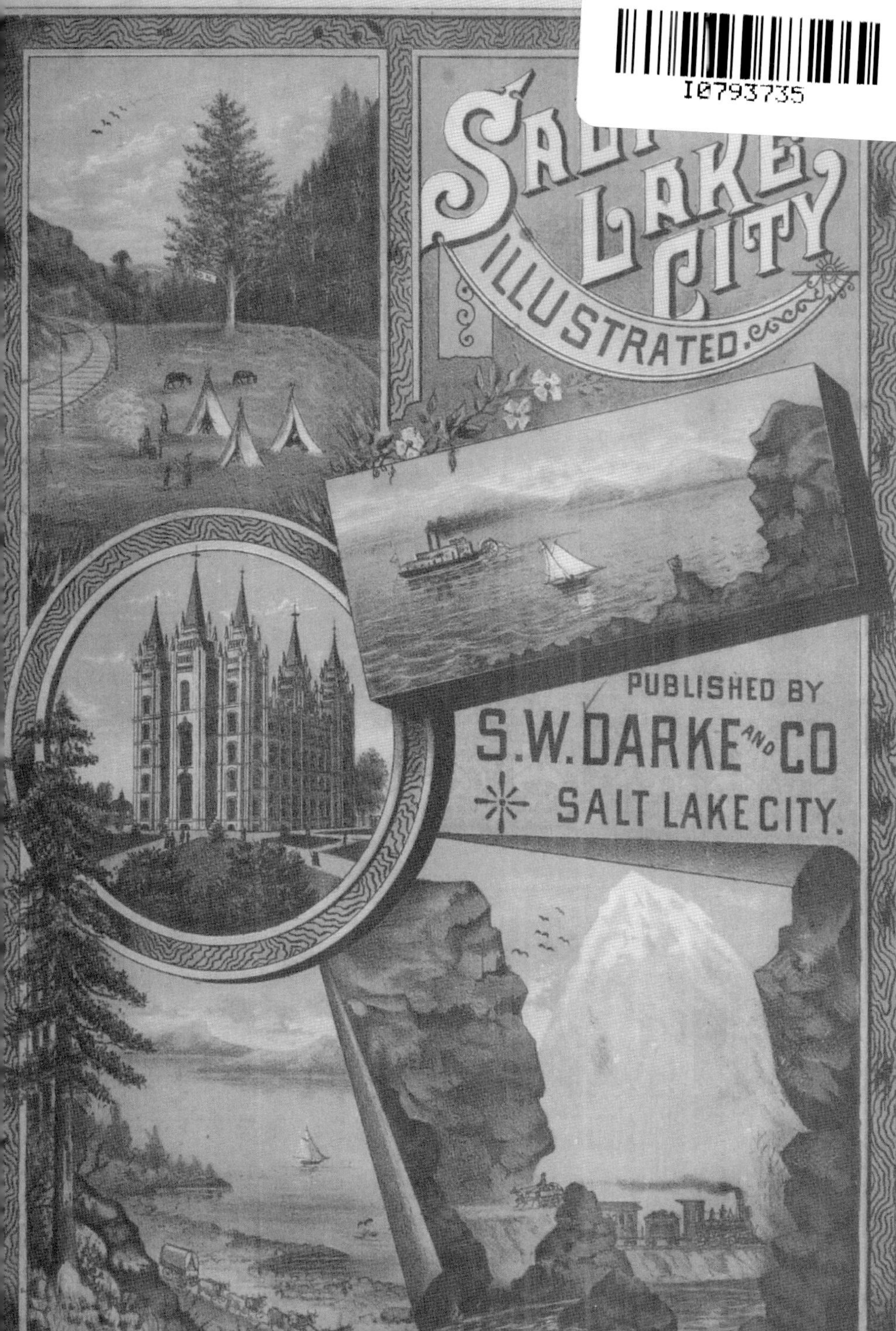

AUG. GAST BANK NOTE & LITHO. CO - ST. LOUIS & N.Y.

Marula

An imprint of Arcadia Publishing

Salt Lake City
by Sidney W. Darke and Co.

A Marula Historical Reprint
Originally published in 1887

Published by Arcadia Publishing
Charleston SC

ISBN 978-0-7385-9481-1

Printed in the United States of America

For all general information contact Arcadia Publishing at:
Telephone 843-853-2070
Fax 843-853-0044
E-mail sales@arcadiapublishing.com
For customer service and orders:
Toll-Free 1-888-313-2665

Visit us on the Internet at www.arcadiapublishing.com

The Noted Establishment for the Regulation of Low Prices.

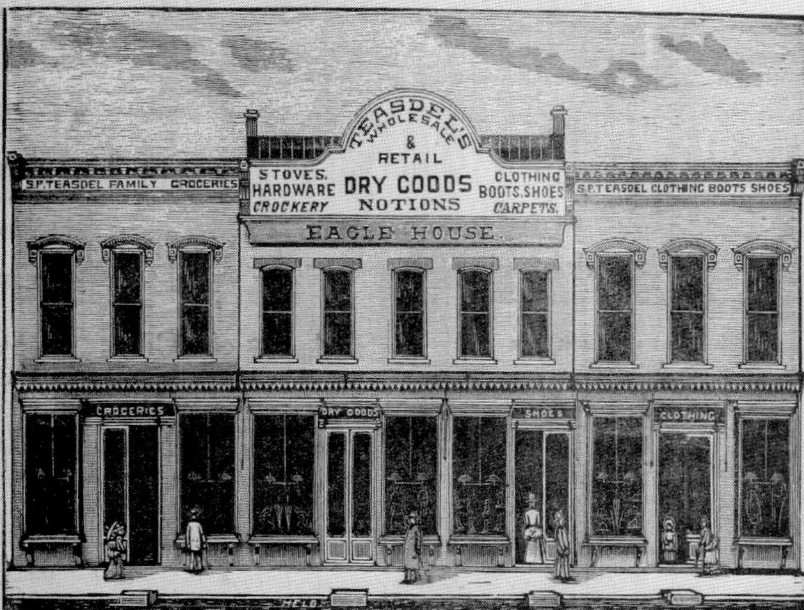

S. P. TEASDEL,

Importer, Wholesale & Retail Merchant.

WHOLESALE AND RETAIL UTAH DRIED FRUITS,

Dry Goods, Family Groceries, Flour & Provisions.

St. John Kirkham's & Co's. Boots and Shoes,
White Granite Crockery & Earthenware,
Tumblers, Glassware and Lamps,
Rathbone Cooking and Heating Stoves,
Ingrain and Three-Ply Carpets.

Men's and Boy's Clothing,
Floor Oil Cloths and Mattings,
Men's and Youth's Fur & Wool Hats,
Family Hardware & Farming Implements,
Etc., Etc.

THE BEST HOUSE IN UTAH FOR FARMER AND FAMILY TRADE——

——SEND FOR OUR PRICES BEFORE PURCHASING ELSEWHERE

S. P. TEASDEL,

SALT LAKE CITY.

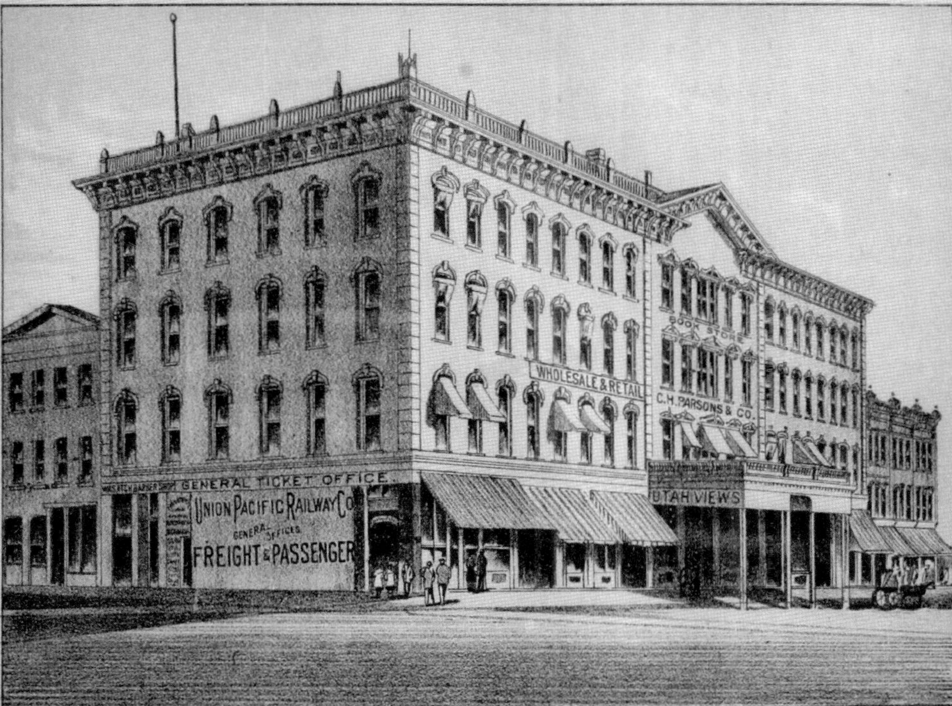

GROESBECK BLOCK.—FEDERAL COURT ROOMS AND POST OFFICE.

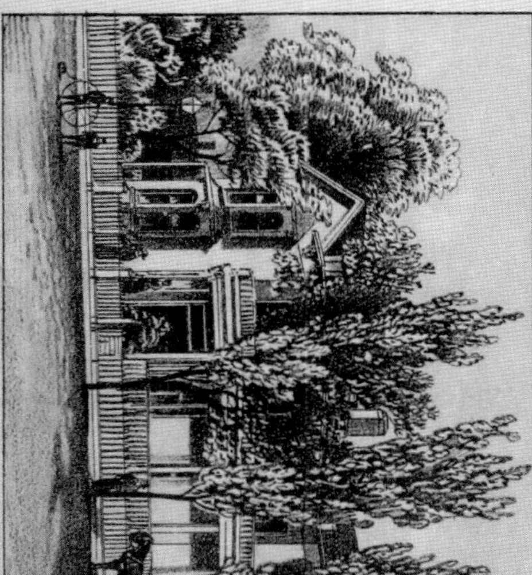

RESIDENCE OF HOWARD SEBREE.

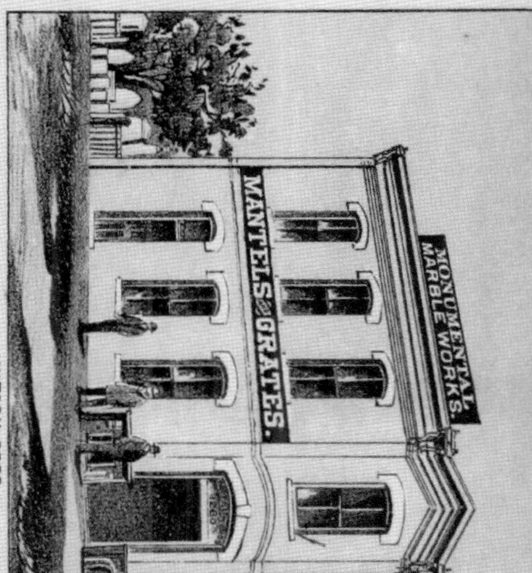

WATSON BROS.

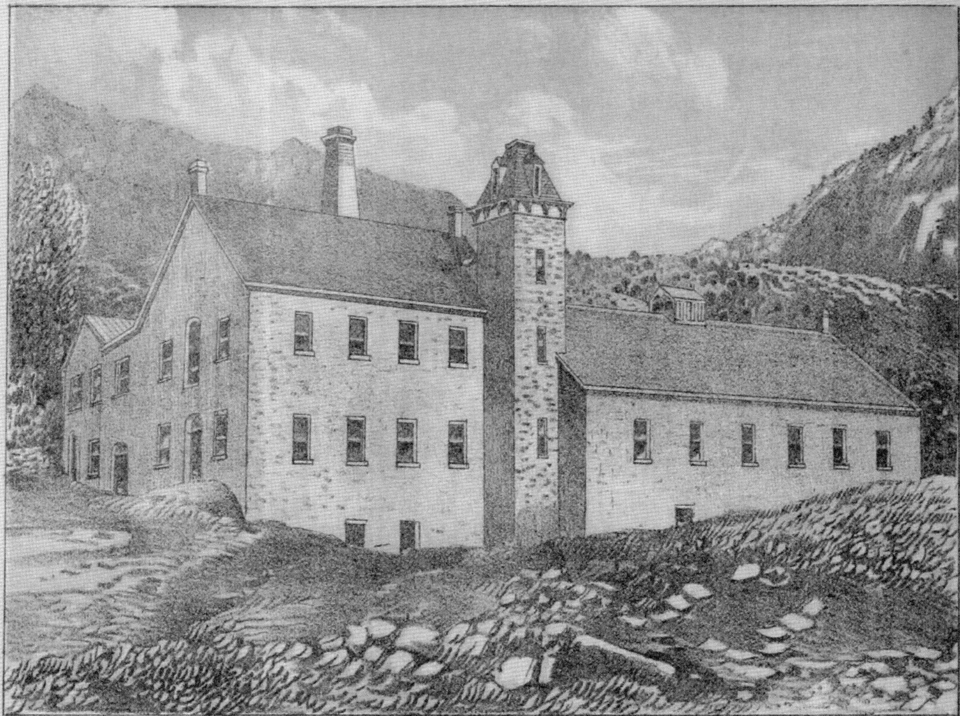

DESERET PAPER MILLS.

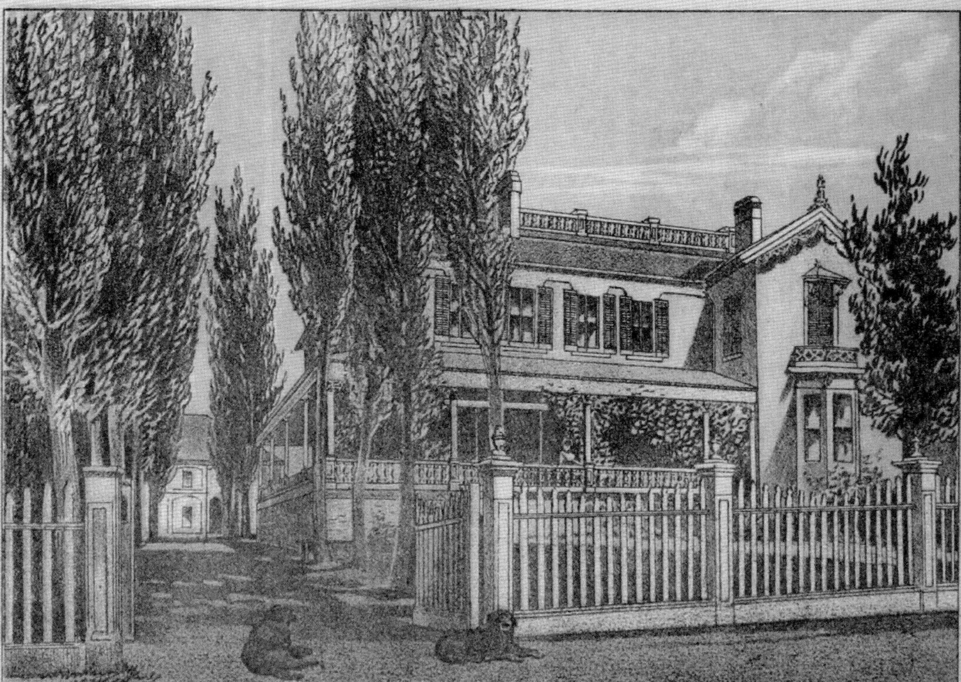

RESIDENCE OF MATTHEW CULLEN.

CONTINENTAL HOTEL,

The Leading Hotel of Salt Lake City

CORNER OF WEST TEMPLE AND FIRST SOUTH STS.

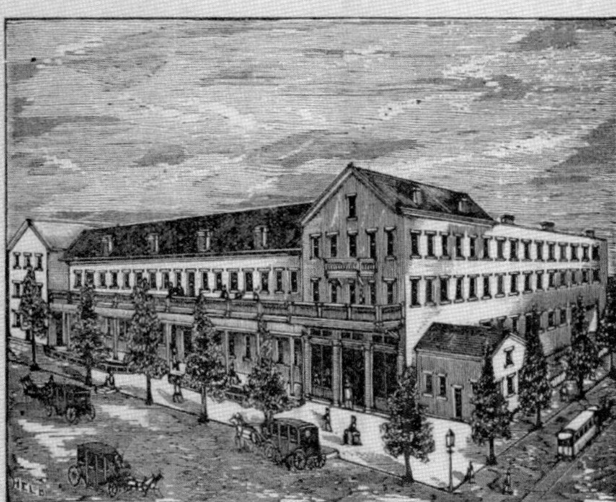

THIS House contains 125 Rooms, all well lighted, each apartment being at least 12 x 6 feet. It was re-opened on the 20th of January last, after being elegantly refurnished and thoroughly renovated throughout. All modern appliances for the convenience of guests are to be found here, including electric call-bells, telephone, electric and incandescent light, etc., etc.

THE CUISINE IS THE BEST THE WEST AFFORDS

The *chef* having the reputation of being unexcelled in his art west of the Missouri.

Tourists, Excursion Parties and Travelers Generally

Who purpose stopping in Salt Lake are respectfully invited to call.

J. H. & F. M. VAN HORN,
Proprietors.

VALLEY HOUSE,

ONLY HOTEL OPPOSITE TEMPLE AND TABERNACLE.

SALT LAKE CITY.

HEADQUARTERS FOR TOURISTS.

Horse Cars Pass Hotel to all DEPOTS and Points of Interest.

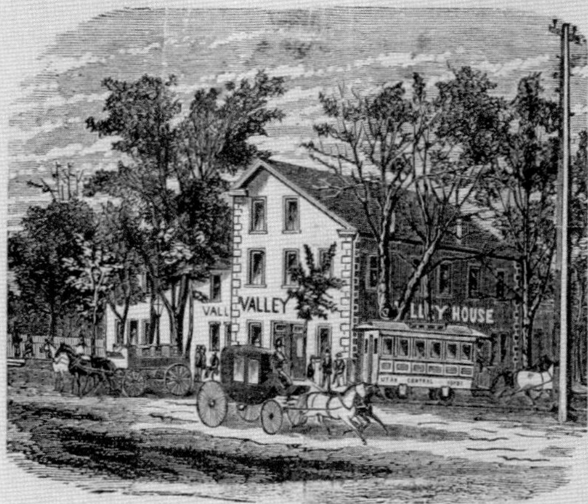

Three Commodious Cottages connected with Hotel. Baths and all modern conveniences. Refitted and refurnished throughout. Rates, $1.50 to $2 per day; Special rates to large parties.

HUBERT L. HALL, Prop.

illiam White. ohn H. White. — Wm. L. White. David H. White.

WHITE & SONS,

Butchers & Cattle Dealers

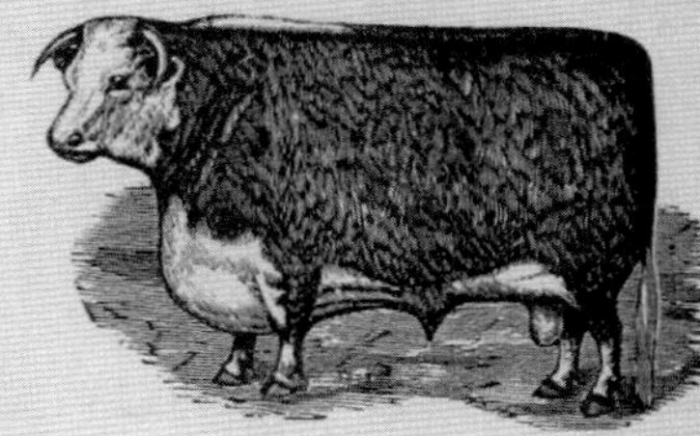

Buy and sell Cattle, Sheep, Hogs, Large Game in Season, and everything connected with the business. Packers of Strictly Choice UTAH RAISED PORK, Smoked Hams, Breakfast Bacon, and dry Salt Sides. All kinds of Sausage, Home Rendered Lard, etc., etc.

SHIPPERS OF LIVE CATTLE AND IMPORTERS OF DRESSED MEAT.

Dealers in Thoroughbred Hereford Cattle.

38 W. FIRST SOUTH STREET,

SALT LAKE CITY.

H. PEMBROKE

Will Send to your Address, postpaid, any of the following BOOKS, relating to the Mormons:

Salt Lake City, Illustrated,	30c.
Are We of Israel?	25c.
Album Views of Salt Lake,	50c.
Items of Church History,	15c.
Book of Mormon,	$1, $1.25, $1.75, $2 50, $3, $3 25
Voice of Warning,	50c., $1, $1.25, $1.65.
Spencer's Letters,	$1, $1 10, $1.25, $1.60, $2.25.
Does the Bible sanction Polygamy?	25c.
On Marriage,	5c
Doctrine and Covenants,	$1, $1.25, $1 75, $2 50, $3, $3.25.
Key to Theology,	50c., 75c., $1, $1.50, $1 60, $2.
Catechism for Children,	30c., 25c.
The Utah Pioneers,	10c.
The Spaulding Story,	25c

BOOKS

Das Buch Mormon, cloth,	(German,)	$1.25
Gesangbuch d. Heiligen d. l. Tage,	"	1.00
Ein Stimme der Warnung,	"	.50
Die Koestliche Perle,	"	50
Le Livre de Mormon, (French,)		1.50
An Englishwoman in Utah,		$1.00
Mormonism Examined.		.30
Our Constitutional Rights,		.25
In the Toils, or the Martyrs of the Latter Days,		1.00

Handbook on Mormonism,	25c.
The Myth of the Manuscript Found,	25c.
Handbook of Reference,	50c.
History of the Mormon Battalion,	$3.
The Tennessee Massacre,	25c.
Startling Revelations for Saints and Sinners,	50c.
Heroines of Mormondom,	25c.
The Martyrs,	50c.
Why we Practice Plural Marriage,	25c.
Mountain Meadows Massacre and Supplement,	25c.
Early Scenes in Church History,	25c.
Orson Pratt's Works,	75c.
Mormon Doctrine,	25c.
Unlawful Cohabitation,	25c.
Blood Atonement,	25c.

SPECIMENS OF NATURAL SALT, EVAPORATIONS OF THE GREAT SALT LAKE, FROM 50C. TO $1, POSTPAID.

72 Main Street,

SALT LAKE CITY.

Mormon Church.

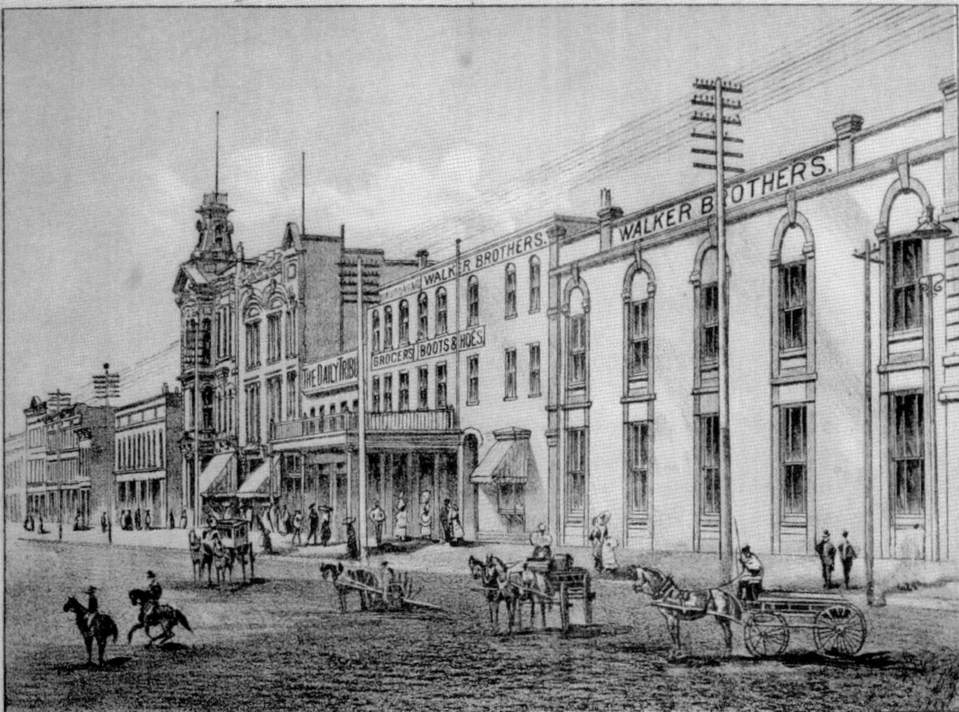

NORTH SIDE SECOND SOUTH STREET, LOOKING WEST FROM MAIN.

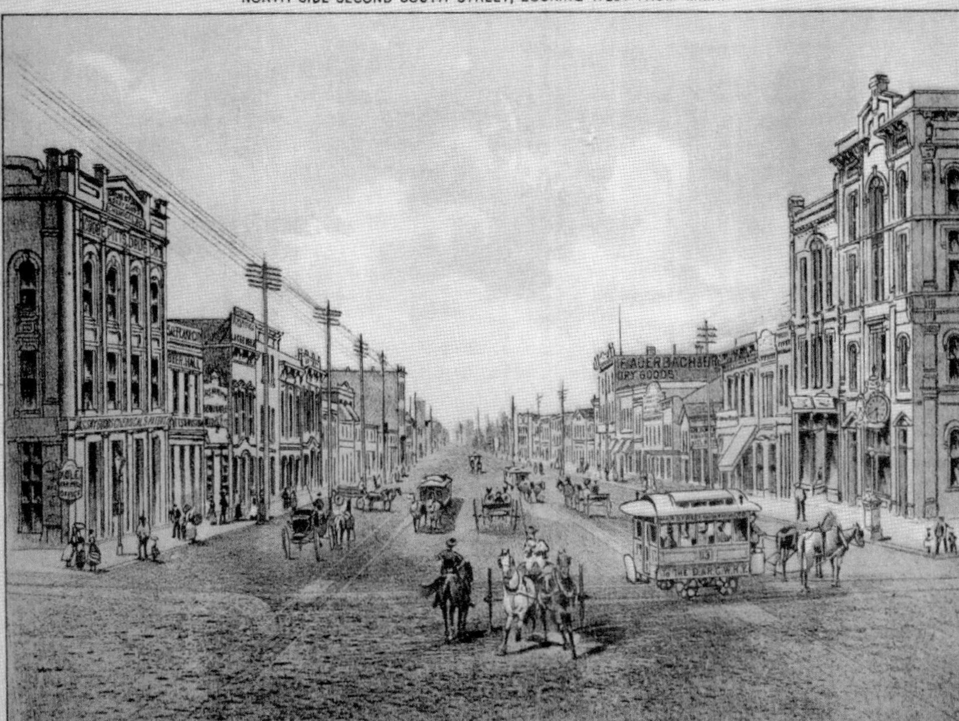

MAIN STREET FROM FIRST SOUTH, LOOKING SOUTH.

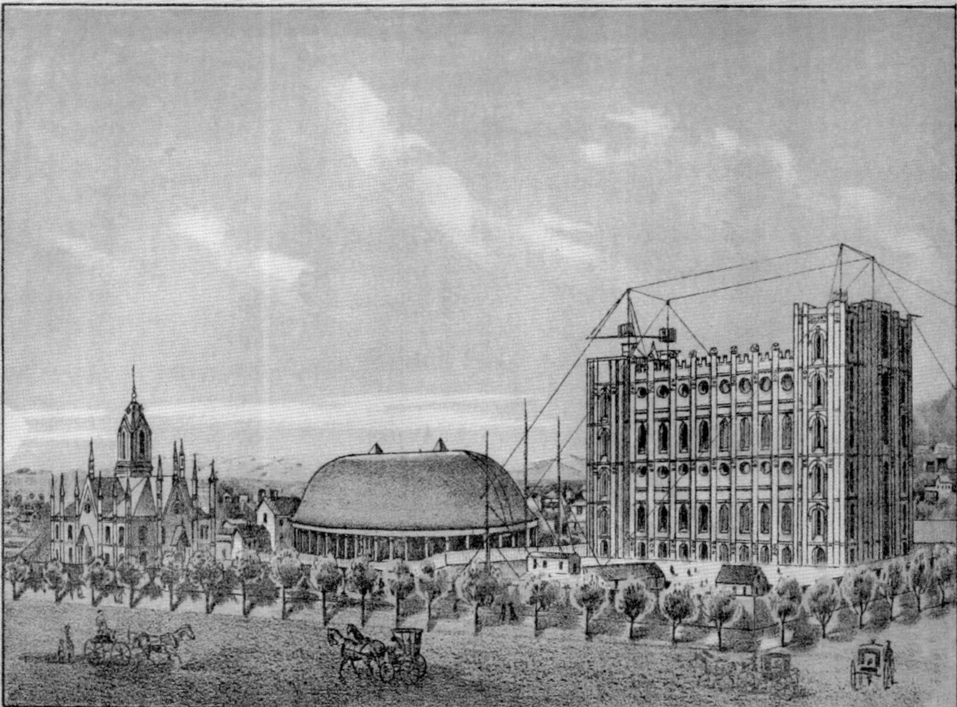

TEMPLE BLOCK.

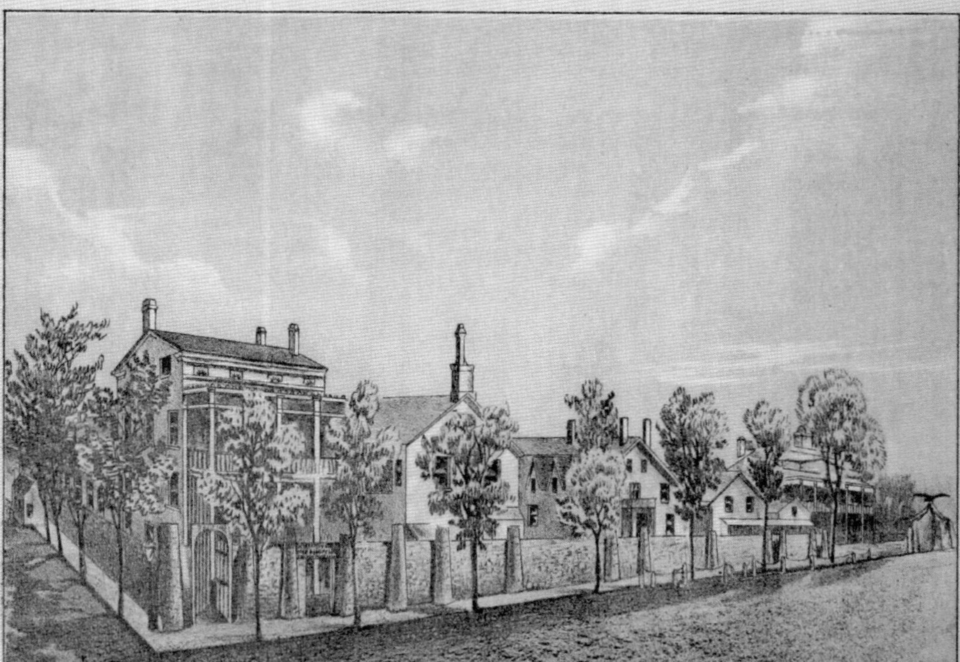

DESERET NEWS, LION HOUSE AND BEE-HIVE HOUSE.

SALT LAKE CITY.

UTAH.

WITHIN the memory of the present generation the map of North America represented the region now covered by the Territories of Utah, Wyoming, Arizona, the State of Nevada and the western part of Colorado, as the Great American Desert. In fact, until the explorations of Bonneville and Fremont, little if anything was known of its character. As early as 1833, Captain Bonneville had trappers on Green River—a tributary of the Colorado— and in July of that year he sent a party from that point westward, to explore this vast region. Passing down what is now called Ogden River, they discovered the Great Salt Lake. Colonel Fremont came afterwards, in 1842, and remained exploring in and around the Great Desert until 1846, but save for these travelers, the country was visited only by trappers and hunters. The advent of civilization into the Great American Desert was on the arrival of the Mormon Pioneers, after their exodus from Nauvoo, in Illinois. On the 21st of July, 1847, Orson Pratt, Erastus Snow and George A. Smith, accompanied by six or seven others, the *avant couriers* of the main body, rode into Great Salt Lake Valley, to a point west of the mouth of the canyon then called "The Golden Pass," and now known as Parley's Canyon. They found the mountain streams pure, springs abundant, and luxuriant grass covering the river bottoms, but the dryer places were infested with large crickets; they also discovered some sulphur springs, and were impressed with the idea that the soil generally was unfit for cultivation. This they had been led to expect, as the opinion of the trappers who had visited this region, was, that the country was unfitted for agriculture. Colonel Bridger, himself an old trapper and mountaineer, is credited with having offered a thousand dollars for the first bushel of grain or ear of corn raised in the Valley of the Great Salt Lake. Major Harris, also an old traveler in Oregon and California, spoke unfavorably of the country as a place for settlement. Until lately, the historian has done but little either in examining into or describing the history of Salt Lake City—why, is conjectural. For it is a history replete with early adventures of Indian depredations, of privations, suffering and of marvellous success. A tale of men with hearts of oak and nerves of steel, who were truly pioneers—who made roads, leveled canyons, built bridges, and brought seeming improbabilities within the range of possibility. On the 24th of July, 1847, the main body of Mormons, numbering about 143 men, arrived in the valley, with President Brigham Young at their head. Plowing and planting immediately began. The very dry ground was irrigated by damming up one of the creeks, a trench being dug from it to the land designed to be watered. During the night the whole tract desired to be cultivated, was irrigated. Thus began in Utah the system of irrigation to which the wealth, the beauty and the habitability of Utah is due almost wholly to-day. It has been the salvation, the very making of the Territory. So Salt Lake City—the half-way house of California, the oasis, the rest midst the desert, the embryo empire of the intermountain region was founded. About a week after the arrival of this party—the main body of the pioneers—a detachment of the Mormon Battalion—arrived, with some others, thus increasing the number in the camp to about 400. Within a month after their arrival the colonists had laid out a fort, built twenty-seven log houses, plowed eighty-four acres and planted them with corn, potatoes, beans, buckwheat, turnips, etc., and had manufactured 125 bushels of salt. The new settlement was called the "City of the Great Salt Lake" or "Great Salt Lake City," as it soon became named. In the month of June, 1848, the fields were invaded by the crickets, which came from the mountains in vast numbers and steadily advancing on the growing crops, began to devour them. The people were powerless against this enemy, and it appeared as though starvation was inevitable, when, to their great relief, perhaps half the crops were saved by an immense flock of sea gulls which suddenly appeared upon the scene, and ravenously devoured the crickets. These gulls are supposed to have come from the Gulf of California. Within a year the population had increased to about seventeen hundred, 450 buildings had been erected, three saw mills and a flouring mill. During the winter of this year the mercury is recorded as having gone as low as thirty-three degrees below zero, Fahrenheit. A faint idea of the scarcity of provisions in the settlement may be gained from the fact that a peck of potatoes sold for five dollars, and was considered cheap. The first post office in the city was opened in March, with Joseph L. Heywood as postmaster. In the months of May or June, 1849, parties from the east, *en route* for the California gold mines, first arrived, they brought with them all kinds of merchandise, wagons, tools and farming implements, which they gladly disposed of at a cheap rate in exchange for provisions. During the Spring and Summer a State Constitution was adopted, and A. W. Babbit, Esq., sent as Delegate to Congress, asking for admission into the Union. A year later, Captain

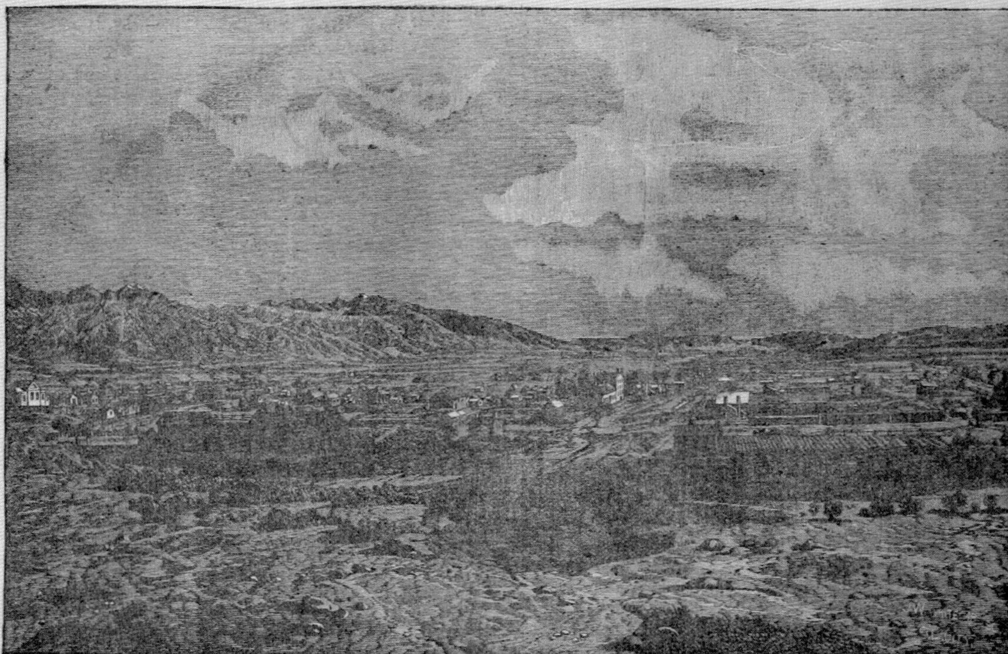

Stansbury, who had been for some time engaged in a topographical survey of the Great Salt Lake, completed his explorations. Parties had already commenced to branch out from Great Salt Lake City, and settle what are now Davis, Weber, Utah, Tooele, Juab and Sanpete Counties. In December of this year the first Sunday School was established. In consequence of the scanty harvests breadstuffs and other provisions became very scarce, and many people were compelled to eat raw hides, and dig segos and thistle roots to sustain life. Much suffering was avoided, however, by those who had provisions, generously but of course sparingly, dividing with those less fortunate. The Indians from the first were annoying and troublesome, and in February, 1850, the colonists generally were called on to assist the handful of pioneers settled in Utah County, in defending their homes from the depredations of Ute Indians. A battle was fought close by what is now called Provo, in which several were killed on both sides. There was, from this time on, for several years, a recurrence of these Indian troubles, so much so that Governor Brigham Young issued a proclamation ordering the Territorial Militia to be kept in constant readiness for marching against the Red Men. In all the Indian wars the people of this city were called upon to contribute to those needing it, by both men and means. In June, 1850, the *Deseret News* was published; the issue was a very small-sized paper at first, and appeared semi-occasionally, sometimes on wrapping paper, on account of the then great distance from supplies — being "a thousand miles from anywhere." On January 11, 1851, Great Salt Lake City was incorporated, with Jedediah M. Grant as Mayor, and in February, Brigham Young took the oath of office as the first Governor of Utah Territory. During the Spring school houses were built in most of the wards. There were now about 30,000 inhabitants in Utah Territory, of which nearly 5,000 were residents of this city. The Great Salt Lake, which now has a world wide reputation, was at that early period, recognized as a health resort, and on the 4th of July, the inhabitants of the city celebrated the Nation's birthday by an excursion to Black Rock and a bathe in the briny waves. On September 22, the first Legislature of Utah Territory convened in Great Salt Lake City, and in November the University of the State of Deseret was opened. On January

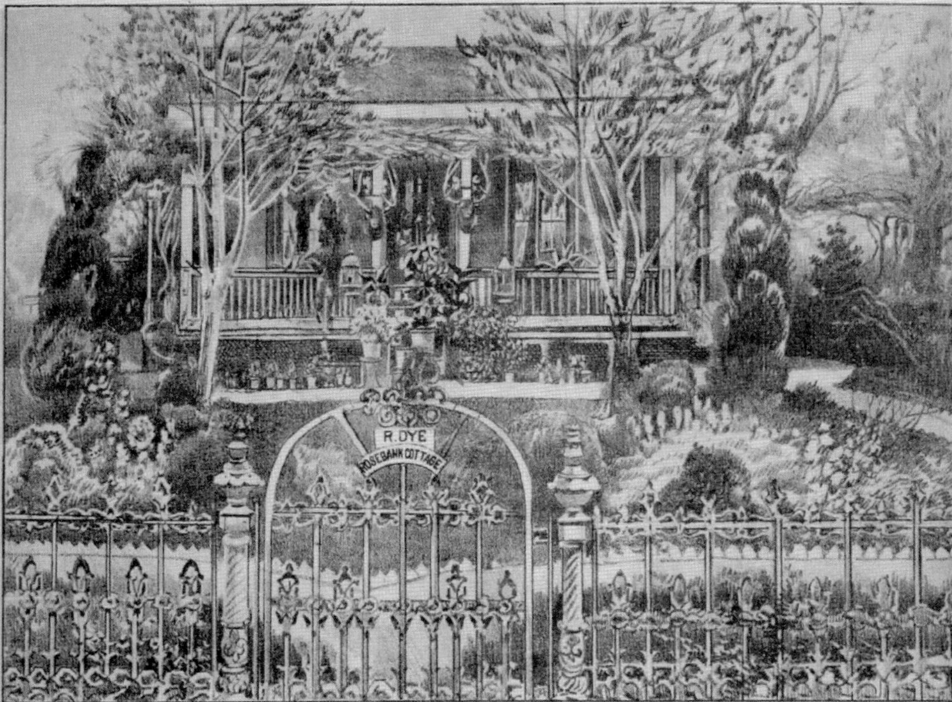

SPRING VIEW.

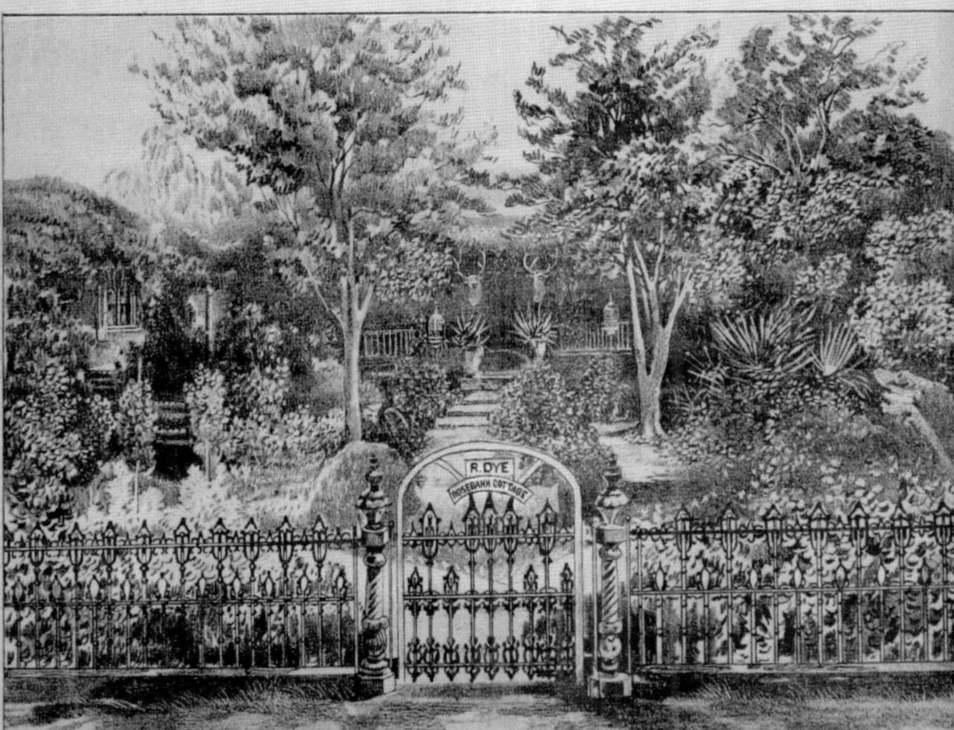

SUMMER VIEW.

RESIDENCE OF ROBERT DYE.

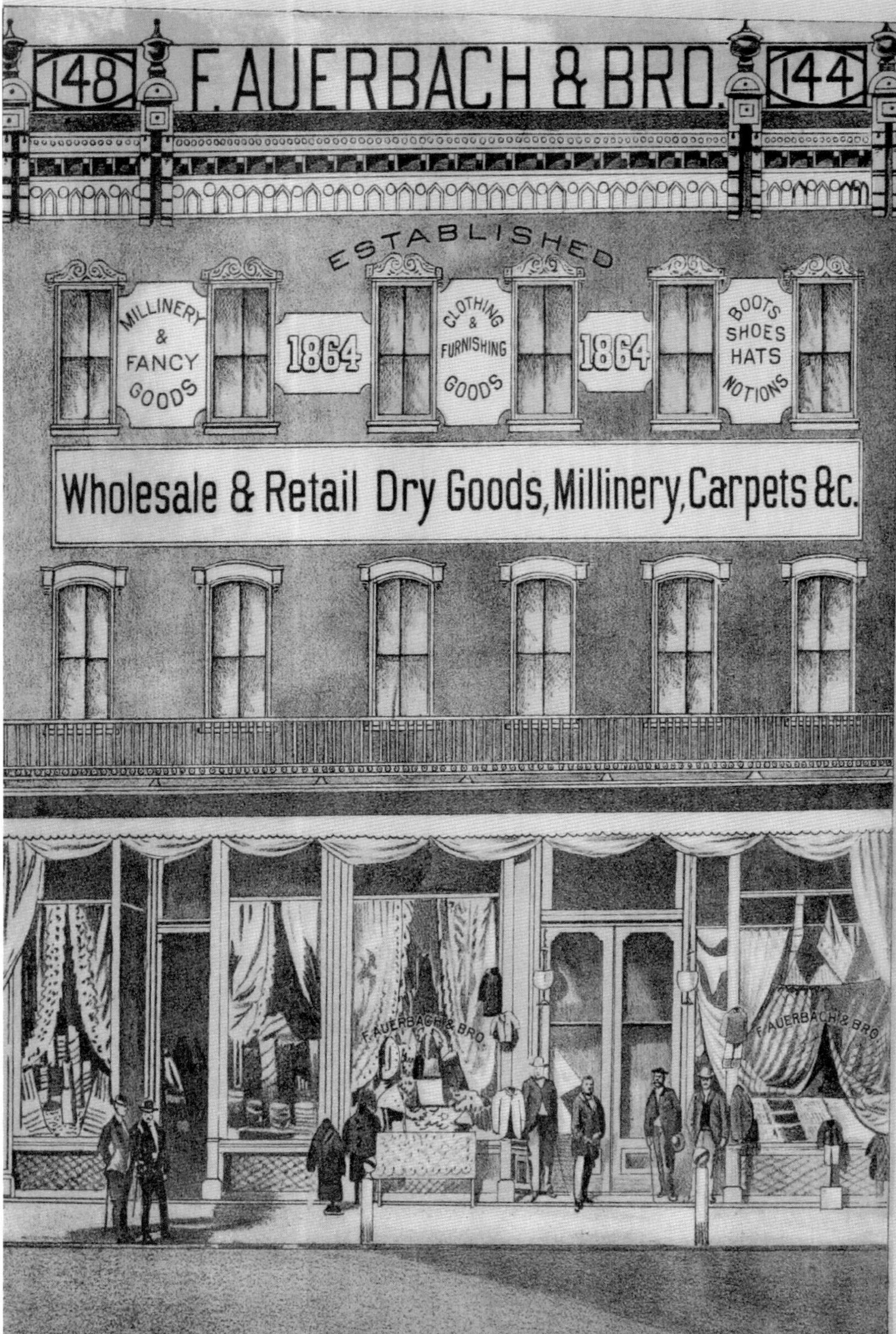

F. AUERBACH & BRO.'S BLOCK.

DESERET NEWS CO.,

—Printers and Publishers of the—

DESERET NEWS

Official Organ of the Church of Jesus Christ of Latter-Day Saints, and OLDEST and MOST RELIABLE Paper in the Rocky Mountain Regions.

SUBSCRIPTION PRICES:

Daily, $10.00. Semi-Weekly, $3.00. Weekly, 2.50 per Year.

Exclusive Publishers of Standard Church Works.

GENERAL BOOK AND JOB PRINTERS

Having the Best Facilities for Work in this Line of any House in the Territories.

OWNERS OF THE

DESERET PAPER MILL,

And Manufacturers of Book, News and Wrapping Papers of all Grades.

OFFICE: Corner South Temple and Main Streets, Salt Lake City, Utah.

ORGANIZED A. D. 1850.

Manhattan Life Insurance Co.

NEW YORK.

CASH ASSETS, January 1, 1887, - $11,310,058.00.

BUSINESS RULES.

PREMIUMS. The lowest safe rates.
POLICY. As little restricted in terms as possible.
NON-FORFEITURE. Secured in the Policy under the law of New York.
SURRENDER VALUES fixed when the Policy is issued. See printed tables.
DIVIDENDS made annually, commencing with the second year.
MANAGEMENT steady, reliable, business-like.
INVESTMENTS. Best security sought, rather than the largest interest.
PRINCIPAL OBJECT. To secure a provision for ourself or for the family.

BENEFICENT RESULTS.

FAMILIES BENEFITED. Nearly 7,000.
CLAIMS PAID. Over $14,000,000.
RETURNED to Policy-holders over $8,000,000 of surplus premiums in Dividends.

FINANCIAL RESULTS.

ASSETS, $11,310,058.00.
SURPLUS, $2,205,106, by New York rule.

If you want Insurance take our Low Premium Non-participating Policy.
If you want Insurance and Dividends combined, take our Mutual Policy.
If you want something for your Old Age take an Endowment Policy.

S. W. DARKE & CO., Agents,
SALT LAKE CITY.

ROWLAND HALL,

A Boarding School for Girls.

A PLEASANT Home, with superior accommodations in the Domestic Department.

A Thorough-Graduating Course, embracing Mathematics, Latin, Natural Sciences, History and English Literature. Careful attention given to Pupils taking Special Studies.

Accomplished Teachers and Professors for Music, Painting and the Modern Languages. Apply to

Rev. G. D. B. MILLER,
SALT LAKE CITY.

GEO. SAVILLE,

AT NO. 21 E. SECOND SOUTH ST.,

Keeps on hand the Best Assortment of

Men's Boots and Shoes

In Salt Lake City. All His Own Make.

LOOK AT THIS:

Men's Calf and Kip Boots, - from $5.00 upwards, all Full Stock.
Men's Calf and Kip Shoes, - - from $3.00 upwards, all Full Stock.

Particular Attention given to Custom Work, and Repairing Promptly Attended to. All Work guaranteed First-class and with Despatch. IN BUSINESS SIXTEEN YEARS.

Remember the Place, No. 21 E. Second South St.

THOMAS W. JENNINGS

Importer, Jobber and Retail Dealer in

Clothing, Hats, Caps, Boots, Shoes

And GENTS' FURNISHING GOODS.

TRUNKS. VALISES.

53 W. First South Street,

SALT LAKE CITY.

JOSEPH W. TAYLOR,

UTAH'S LEADING

Undertaker & Embalmer

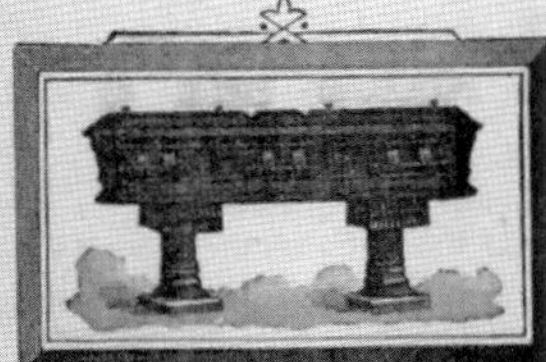

I carry the Finest and Most Complete Line of Coffins and Caskets and Undertaker's Goods in Utah at the lowest prices wholesale and retail.

Office and Warerooms never closed.

TELEPHONE 351.

23 W. Temple St., South.

BARNES & DAVIS,

Is the Best House in Utah for Families to Buy

ALL KINDS OF SUPPLIES.

—Fresh Arrivals Daily of SEASONABLE MERCHANDISE in—

Dry Goods, Groceries, Hardware, Boots & Shoes, Agricultural Implements,

Etc., of the Best Quality, at the Lowest Prices.

Columbia : Bicycles

AND TRICYCLES.

Best Machines in the World!

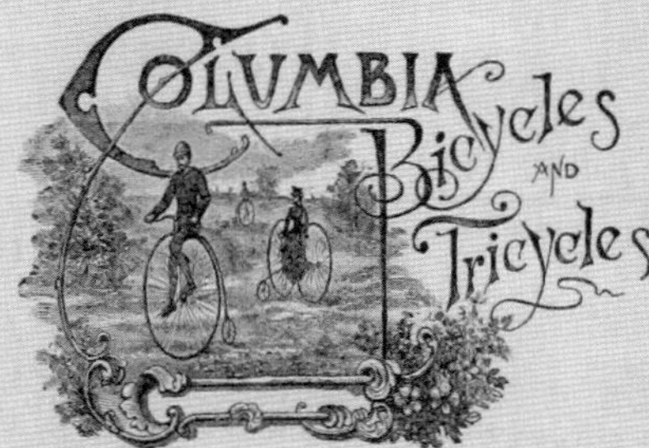

AGENTS FOR

Demorest Paper Patterns, Atlas High Explosive Powder, Orange Sporting and Blasting Powder.

We buy all kinds of Produce in Exchange

BARNES & DAVIS, 128 Main St., Salt Lake City.

GEO. H. KNOWLDEN,

Real Estate, Loan and Insurance Agent,

NO. 21 E. SECOND SOUTH STREET.

Negotiates Loans and Invests Money Carefully for Non-residents. Has a Large List of Properties for Sale in both City and County. Searches Titles to Real Estate.

STRANGERS MADE WELCOME.——.·. .·.——CALL AND SEE GEORGE.

SPENCER HOUSE,

No. 252 First East Street, between Second and Third South,

SALT LAKE CITY, UTAH.

This Hotel is located in Post Office Block, surrounded by the largest and most beautiful Grounds, Lawns and Shades of any Hotel in the City, and is a most popular resort for Tourists and Transients who desire

A Comfortable and Quiet Home at Moderate Rates.

Beautiful Shaded Playground for Children. The Proprietor of this House has been a resident of Utah for 40 years, and is therefore well qualified to give information, introductions, etc. No Runners employed. Have your Baggage checked on the Cars for the Spencer House.

C. V. SPENCER, PROP.

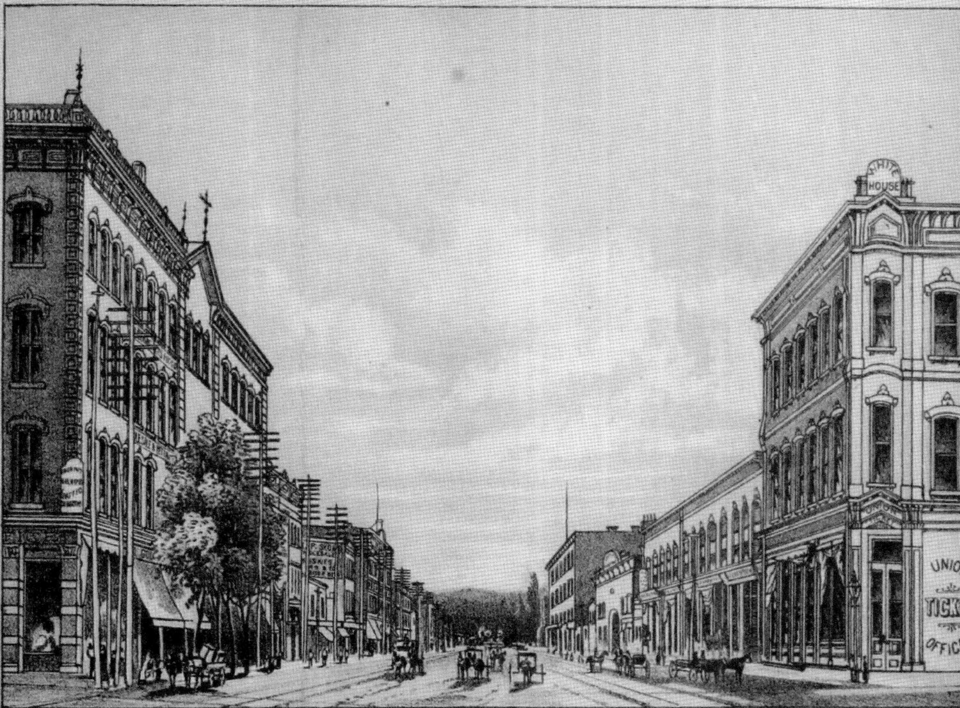

MAIN STREET FROM SECOND SOUTH, LOOKING SOUTH.

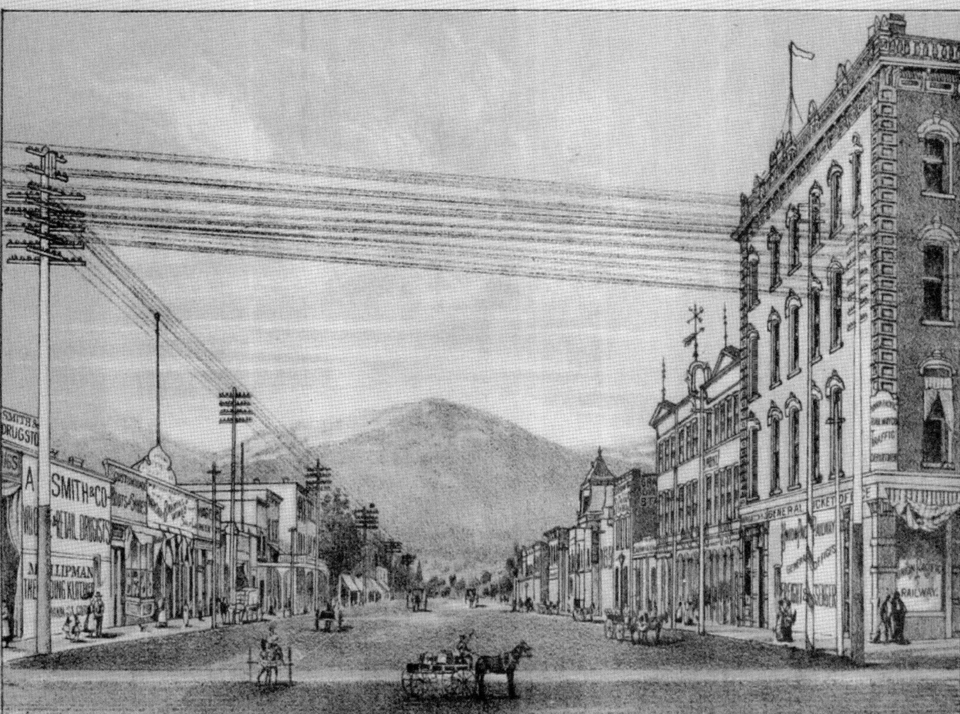

SECOND SOUTH STREET FROM MAIN, LOOKING EAST.

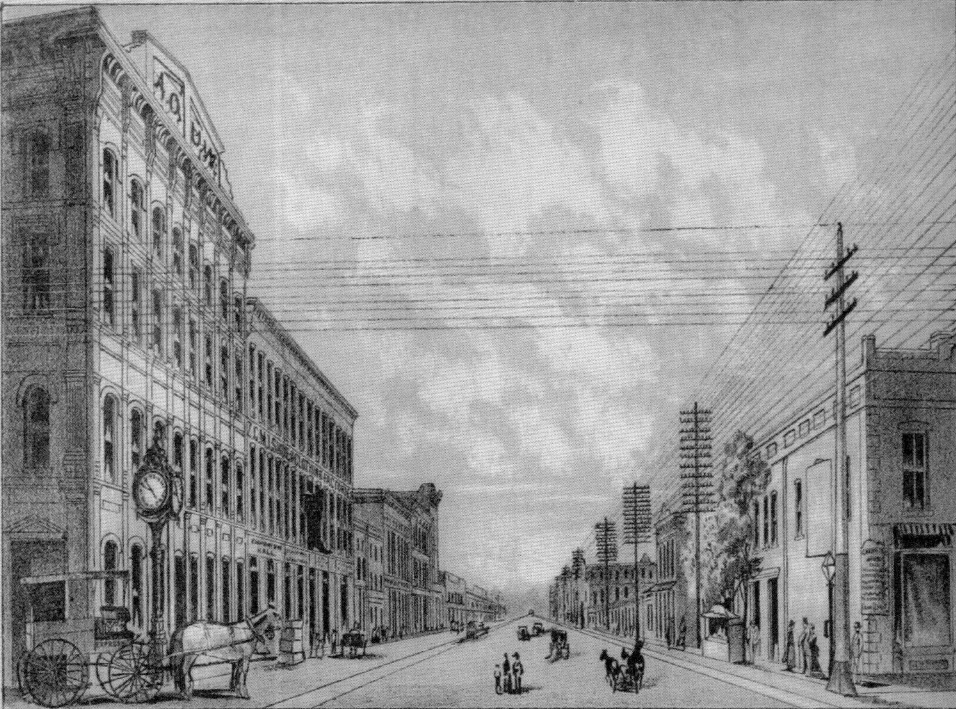

FIRST SOUTH ST. FROM MAIN, LOOKING WEST.

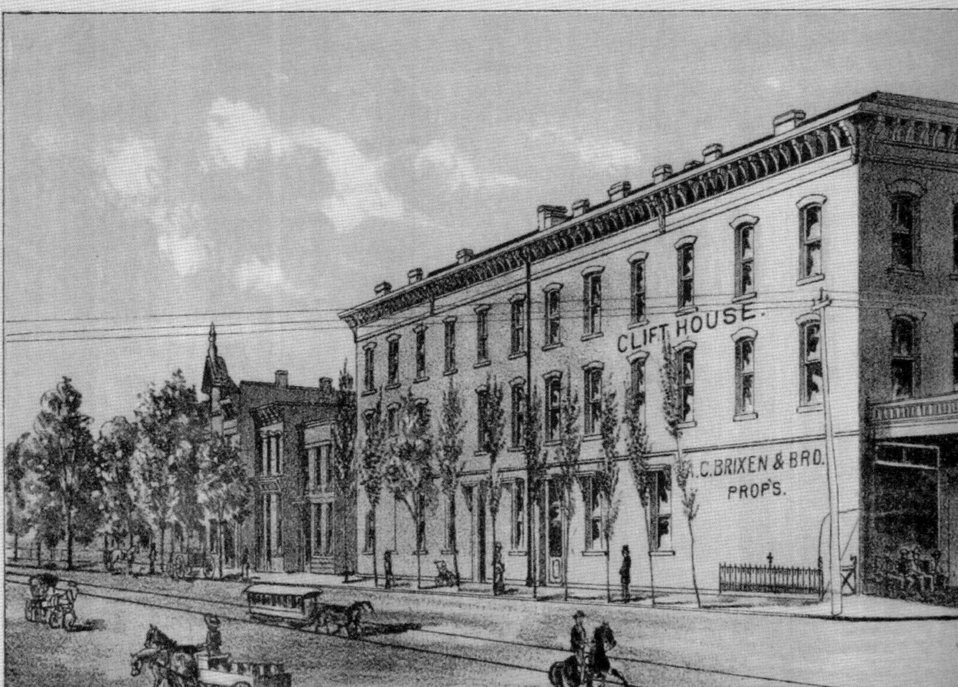

NORTH SIDE THIRD SOUTH ST. FROM MAIN, LOOKING WEST.

, 1852, a Tabernacle, 126 feet long and sixty-four feet de, capable of seating nearly three thousand persons, was ished. The first company of European immigrants, with irty-one wagons, arrived during the year. On the 6th y of April, 1853, the corner stones of the Temple were d, and in August it was decided to build a "Spanish" ll of mud, twelve feet high, six feet at base, around the y, as a protection against the Indians. It was nine miles length, and portions of it remain to this day. The pulation in October of this year was 6,000 souls. In nuary, 1854, a mass meeting was held to memorialize ngress to construct a National Railroad from the Misuri River, *via* the South Pass and Great Salt Lake City, the Pacific Coast. During the Fall of this year, the first migrants from Switzerland, Italy and Australia arrived. 1855 settlers had reached out as far as Salmon River, aho, and the southern part of Utah Territory. During e Summer grasshoppers did serious damage to the crops, stroying nearly everything green in many parts of the rritory. The loss was aggravated by drouth, the comned evils causing a great failure in crops. A large numr of Mormon missionaries left Great Salt Lake City for the astern States and Europe, and the Horticultural Society, d a number of other societies, were organized during this ar. In the early part of 1856 there was a great scarci- of provisions and many domestic animals died of starvion. For months some families knew not the taste of ead—bran and shorts being considered luxuries. Smallx was brought into the valley in July by immigrants om Mississippi. The first fire department was organized October. On account of the early winter, some comnies of immigrants, crossing the plains with hand-carts, ere overtaken in the mountains by snow storms and serely cold weather. Word was brought that they were rishing in the mountains and the people immediately ent to their rescue with men and provisions, but not fore many of the immigrants had died from want and exsure. This winter was excessively severe, snow falling a depth of eight feet in various parts of the valley. he harvest of 1857 was the best Utah had had up to at time. During this fall the "Utah Army" was sent, nder Colonel A. S. Johnston, to settle difficulties which ere reported by Judge Drummond, W. F. Magraw and hers, to have grown up between the Territorial Officers, e Federal Officials and the Government. In March, 1858, e citizens of Great Salt Lake City and the settlements rth of it, agreed to abandon their homes and "go south," ing under the impression that the approaching army as sent to destroy them. By the month of June, Govnor Cumming and the peace commissioners having rived and investigated matters, the difficulties were peacely adjusted, President Buchanan issuing a proclamation pardon. The army passed through Great Salt Lake ity, locating at Camp Floyd, about forty miles southest, and the people returned to their deserted homes and sumed their accustomed labors. In November, 1858, e *Valley Tan* newspaper made its appearance. In 1859, the first number of the *Mountaineer* was published. April 7, 1860, the first pony express from the west arrived, and on the 9th the first from the east; four days from Sacramento and six days from St. Joseph, Mo. In July, 1861, General Johnston with the army, was ordered to the States on account of the breaking out of the Civil War, and the equipments and provisions of the United States army in Utah were disposed of at auction. It was estimated that $4,000,000 worth of goods were sold for $100,000. In October connection was made with the outside world by a telegraph line. In the Spring of 1862, the Theatre, a building 175 feet long, 80 feet wide, and 60 feet from floor to ceiling, seating comfortably 1,700 people—one of the best theatres in the Union—was completed and opened to the public. During the same Spring the Indians in the neighborhood of Fort Bridger, having destroyed the mail stations, coaches and mail bags, and killed the stage drivers, President Lincoln called for a company of Cavalry, and in April, Lot Smith's company of 100 men was mustered into service by Chief Justice Kinney, and left the city to protect the mail route. The expedition was a very hazardous and toilsome one. Colonel P. E. Connor with the California Volunteers, arrived on October 20, and located at Camp Douglas, the present site of Fort Douglas. The immigration this year numbered over 5,000 people, all coming by teams and wagons. Settlers from this city and other places having located in what are termed the southern settlements, raised about 100,000 pounds of cotton this year. In January, 1863, Colonel Connor with some 200 troops, defeated a band of 400 Shoshone Indians in a ravine, near Bear River, in which fourteen soldiers were killed and forty-nine more wounded, and 224 Indians were killed; they also had other engagements with Indians near Cedar Fort, Spanish Fork and Pleasant Grove. The Indians were also quite hostile on the mail route west of Salt Lake. In September a woolen factory on Canyon Creek, in Salt Lake County, was put in operation. In November, Colonel Connor issued a circular giving a permit to the soldiers to prospect for mines, he having evidence that the Territory possessed rich veins of gold, silver and other minerals. The *Daily Vidette* was first issued this month. In July, 1864, the *Daily Telegraph* was published by T. B. H. Stenhouse, and the *Peep o' Day* made its appearance. Speaker Colfax, Governor Bross, accompanied by the City Council and some leading merchants, drove over to Great Salt Lake. During this year, several of the prominent men of the city made an effort to establish a landing on the Colorado River, near the southern border of the Territory, known as Callville, through which it was hoped an easy avenue for the marketing of the products of the Territory would be found, as there was no communication with the outside markets by either railroad or water, at that date. In this year, also, the first mining districts were located, the first mining companies incorporated, and the first smelting furnaces built, they being created about seven miles south of the city. In July, 1867, myriads of grasshoppers appeared and did great damage to the crops, devasting every green field in Salt Lake Valley within twenty-four hours after their appearance. On October 6, the large Tabernacle was completed; this structure is 250 feet long, 150 feet wide, and its immense roof is arched without a pillar; the estimated seating capacity is 10,000. During the next year, the citizens commenced an organized warfare against grasshoppers, whose numbers, voracity and destructiveness were appalling. The Indian troubles were now mostly ended, Colonel Irish and Colonel Head having had many big talks and made treaties with the different bands. This year, Zion's Coöperative Mercantile Institution commenced operations; the institution now occupies a four-story building including basement, having a frontage of ninety-eight feet and a depth of 319 feet, on the Main Street. It has branch houses in Provo, Ogden and Logan, Utah, and at Soda Springs, Idaho. Its stock in trade averages over a million dollars. In May, 1869, a banking concern, which has grown into the present Deseret National Bank, commenced business. The University of Deseret was opened. The first shipment of Utah ore to California was made by Woodhull Brothers from Little Cottonwood to T. H. Selby of San Francisco. In October, a mass meeting was held with a view of again appealing to Congress to have Utah admitted as a State. The *Utah Magazine*, which had been published since January, 1868, under the editorial charge of E. L. T. Harrison, merged into the *Mormon Tribune*, from which has grown the *Daily Tribune*, now published here, one of the largest daily papers between Chicago and San Francisco. On January 10, 1870, the last rail of the Utah Central Railroad was laid and the last spike driven by Brigham Young in the presence of 15,000 people. This was the inauguration of a new era in the growth and commerce of the city. Hitherto, all importations had to be freighted a thousand miles by ox or mule teams and all the settlers had to tramp this weary road over vast and arid plains and toilsome mountains. Honorable W. H. Hooper made his famous "plea for religious liberty," in behalf of the Mormon people, in the House of Representatives at Washington. The Liberal party was organized and the Female Suffrage Bill was passed. In June, the *Daily Herald* was first issued by E. L. Sloan, W. C. Dunbar and John T. Caine, the former of these gentlemen dying in the year 1874. The paper has been under the editorial care of Mr. Byron Groo most of the time since. Mr. W. S. Godbe became somewhat prominent for his efforts with President Grant, in modifying the policy projected by Vice-President Colfax and Governor Shaffer of forcing a rupture with the Mormon leaders. In September, 1871, the corner stone of the Catholic Church, an unimposing brick building in the heart of the city, was laid, the mission being under the care of the Reverend Father Scanlan, now the Bishop of the Diocese of Utah. In November, the corner stone of the Methodist Episcopal Church was laid. It is one of the most commanding buildings, in size and architectural appearance, in the city,—a brick structure of modern style. In 1872, the Salt Lake City Street Railway Company was organized. In the Spring of this year, Thomas Fitch, George Q. Cannon and Frank Fuller left for Washington, as delegates to Congress, to present the claims of the proposed State of Deseret. In September, General Morrow made another treaty of peace with the Indians. In October, a delegation of Ute Indians, accompanied by Doctor Dodge, left for Washington, where they had an interview with President Grant. In November, the Germania Smelting and Refining Works—the first of the kind in Utah—commenced operations. In May, 1874, St. Mark's Cathedral was consecrated. It is a fine structure, built of stone, having a handsome auditorium, with a basement which is used for Sabbath and day schools, and in October the Presbyterian Church was dedicated. In January, 1875, the Utah Western, now the Utah and Nevada Railway, was opened for traffic to Black Rock, a bathing resort on the shores of the Great Salt Lake. In March, the trial of George Reynolds was commenced in the Third District Court, the jury bringing in a verdict of guilty. This was a case agreed upon to test the constitutionality of the law passed by Congress, in 1862, against polygamy. It was, in the month of January, 1879, decided by the United States Supreme Court at Washington, the Court unanimously confirming the constitutionality of the Anti-Polygamy Act. In October, President Grant visited Salt Lake City and held a public reception in the Walker House; before leaving, he honored the late Honorable William Jennings by a personal visit at the Devereux House. In April, 1876, forty tons of powder, in magazines immediately north of the city, exploded, resulting in the loss of four lives and great destruction of property. Dom Pedro, Emperor of Brazil, arrived on a visit, also Earl Dufferin, Governor-General of Canada. In June, a sudden melting of the snow in the mountains caused heavy floods. The *Bikuben*, a newspaper in the Danish language, was published. Brigham Young, the founder of Salt Lake City, and, in fact, of Utah, after an eventful life, died at his residence on the 29th of August, 1877. In September of the same year, the corner stone of the Assembly Hall, the projection of which we might truthfully say was the last public act of Brigham Young's life, was laid. The design is unique and it is one of the attractions of the city, the ceiling being painted with pictures representing events in the Church history and showing paintings of the several Mormon temples. In the month of April, 1879, the first Utah wheat was shipped to Liverpool, San Francisco, by S. W. Sears, and in May, 1880, the corner stone of St. Paul's Chapel were laid, a stone structure, built and owned by the Episcopal Church, its design and surroundings being very attractive. In September, President Hayes and party visited Salt Lake; and in December, the Utah Eastern Railway was constructed from Coalville to Park City, principally by Salt Lake capital. After the death of Brigham Young the Twelve Apostles had controlled the affairs of the dominant church, but in October John Taylor was elected President, with George Q. Cannon and Joseph F. Smith as counsellors. In August,

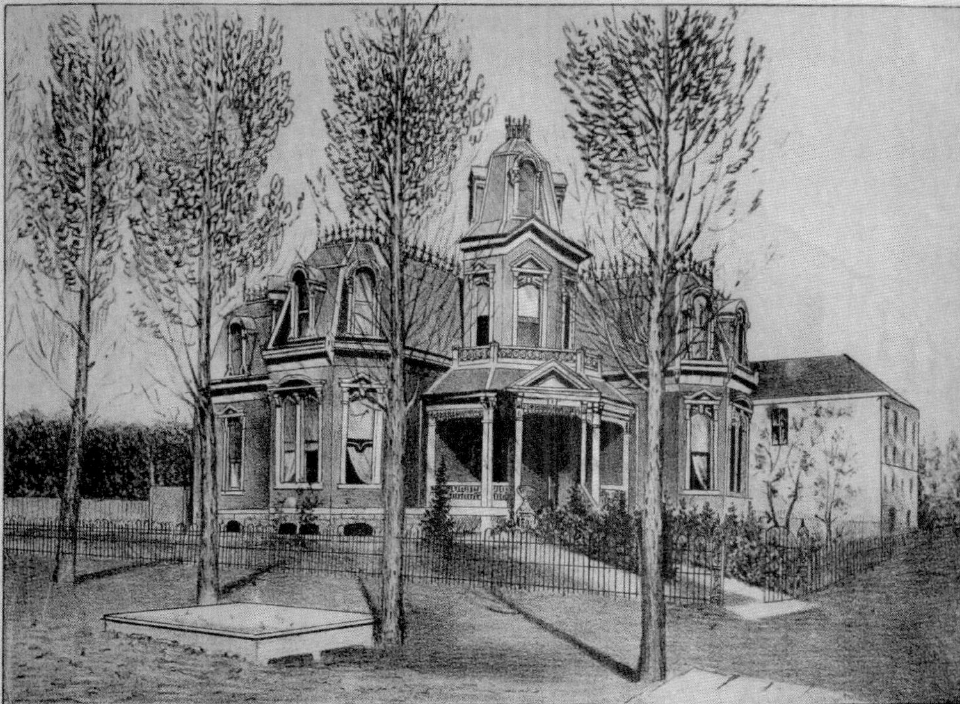

RESIDENCE OF J. R. NICHOLS.

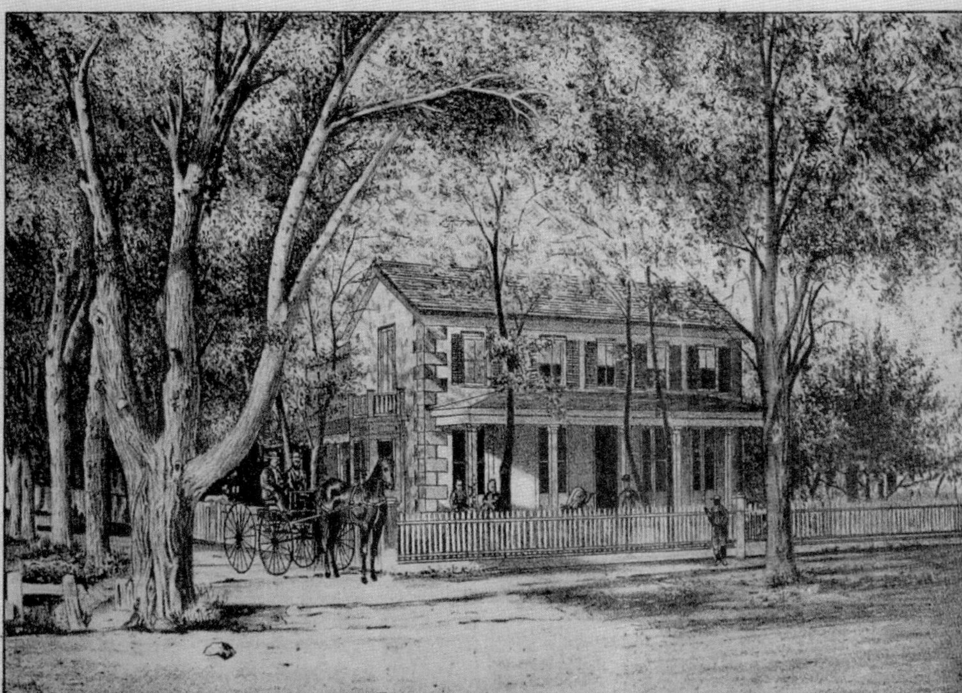

RESIDENCE OF DR. J. M. BENEDICT.

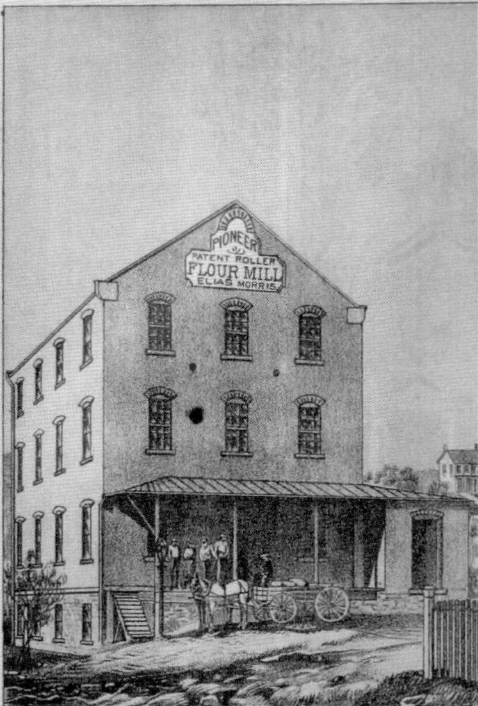

ROLLER FLOUR MILL.

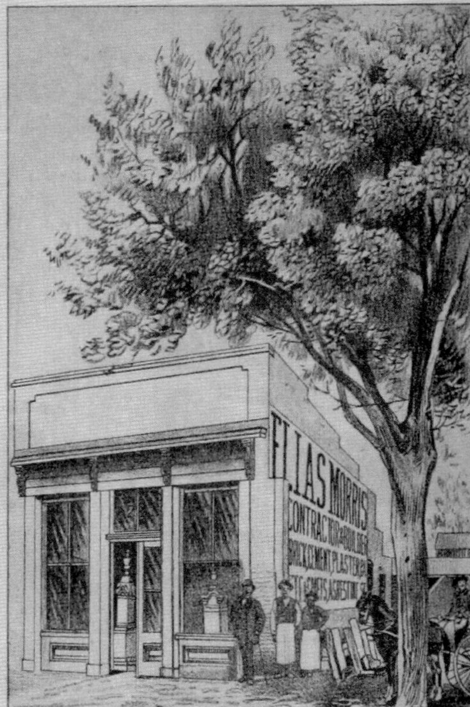

MORRIS' MARBLE WORKS.

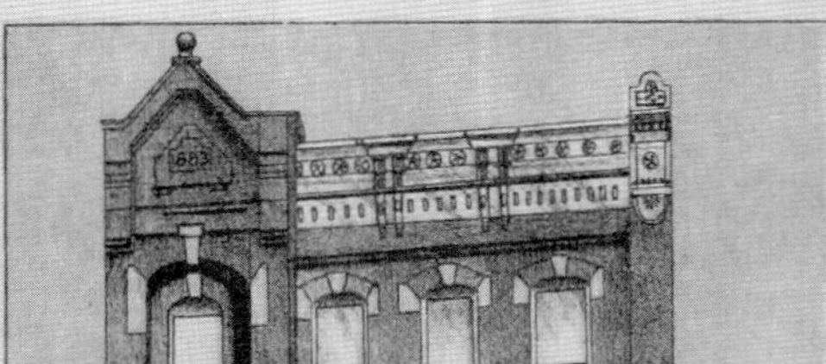

HEESCH & ELLERBECK BUILDING.

DENHALTER'S SODA WORKS.

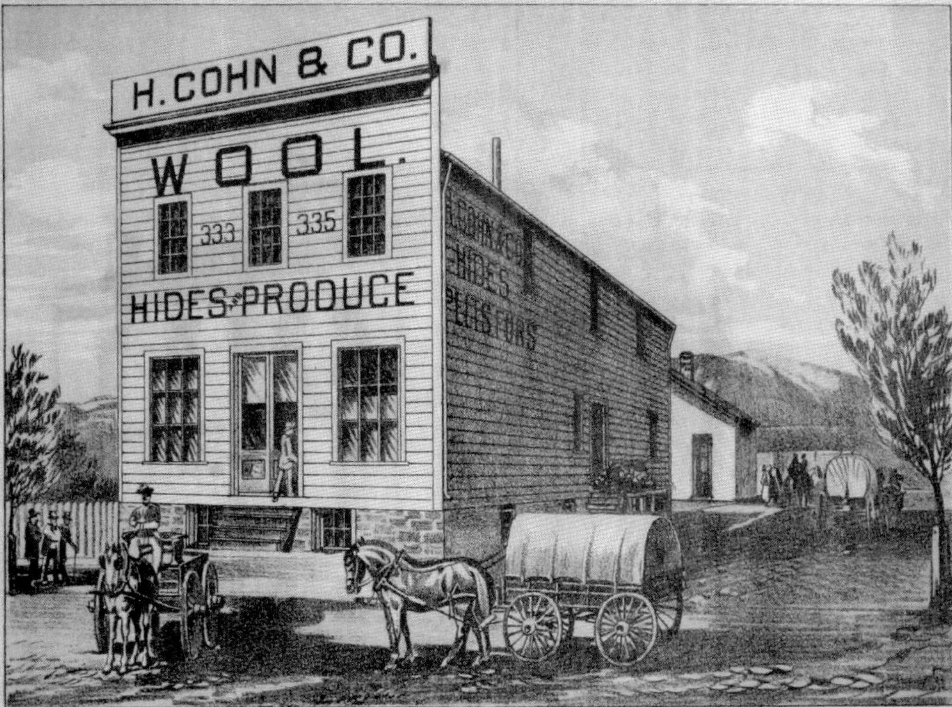

H. COHN & CO.'S WAREHOUSE.

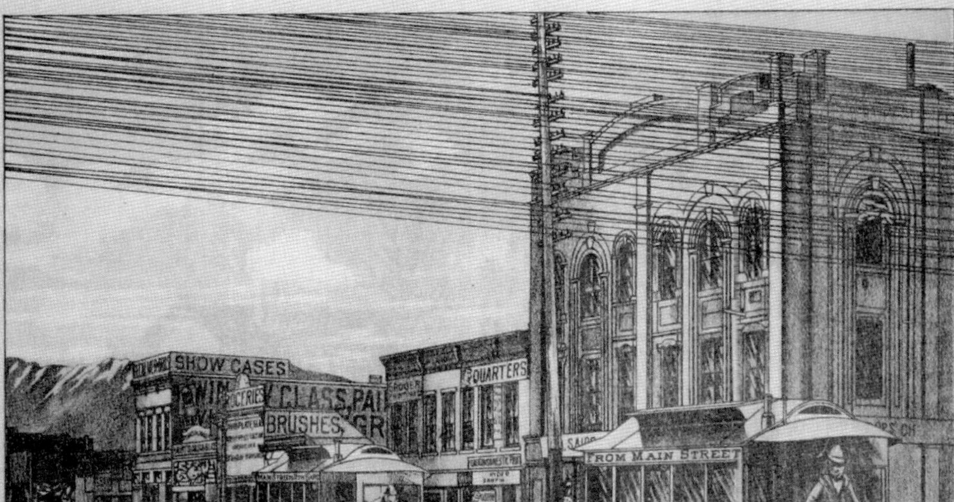

SOUTH SIDE 1st SOUTH STREET, FROM MAIN LOOKING EAST.

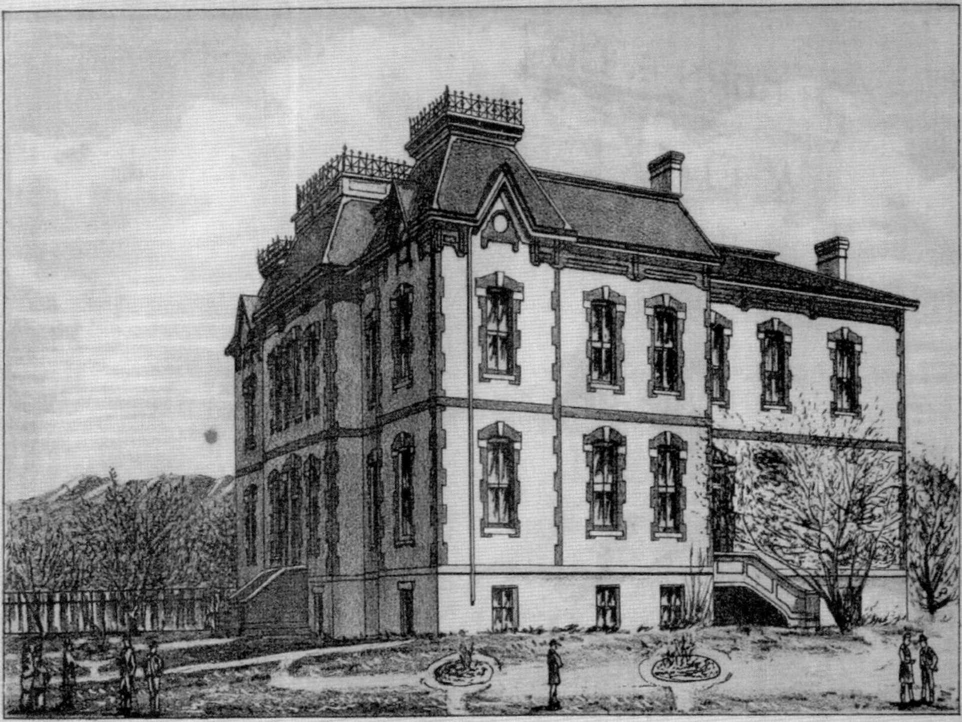

HAMMOND HALL.

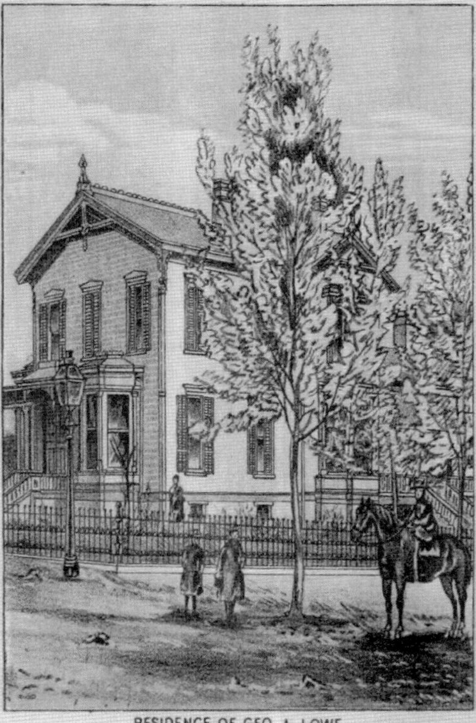

RESIDENCE OF GEO. A. LOWE.

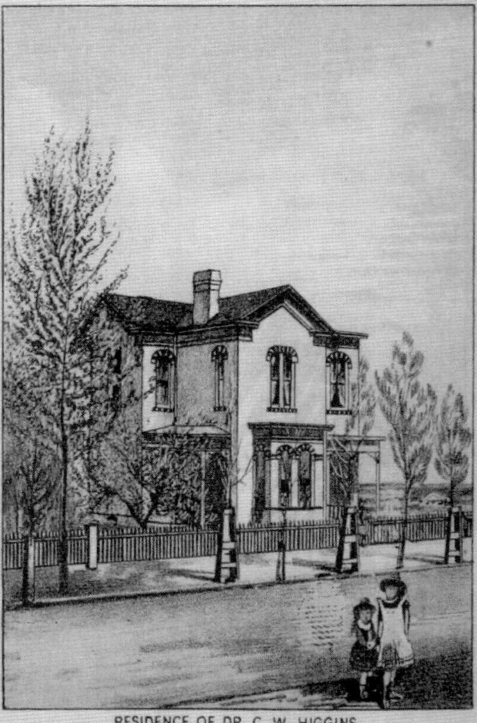

RESIDENCE OF DR. C. W. HIGGINS.

1881, the corner stones of the Walker Opera House were laid. The building was started as the Academy of Music, under the auspices of the McKenzie Temperance Reform Club, but subsequently fell into the hands of the Walker Brothers; it is 165 feet long, 67 feet wide, and 60 feet from floor to ceiling,—a pleasing building on the exterior, with a very tasteful front; the interior is highly ornamented; it cost $130,000. In the fall of 1882, the noted political campaign took place in which Honorable John T. Caine, of the People's Party, and Judge P. T. Van Zile, of the Liberal Party, made a tour of nearly the whole Territory, delivering stump speeches. In June of this year, Liberty Park, previously known as Locust Grove, having been purchased by the City Corporation, was formally opened to the public; the Park contains 120 acres, and is being rapidly improved. March, 1883, saw the Denver and Rio Grande Railway completed between Salt Lake and Denver; giving a new field for our enterprising merchants, and opening another avenue for a business, of which this place gets the larger share. In 1885, the *Democrat* was issued, and the Democracy ran a party ticket for the Territorial election in the fall of the same year. The Union National Bank, the outgrowth of the banking house of Walker Brothers, was organized; it has the largest safe deposit vaults between Chicago and San Francisco.

Salt Lake City lies in the northeastern corner of a splendid valley—a valley bounded on the east by the Wasatch Range, perhaps the most striking and magnificent in the whole Rocky Mountain chain; and on the west, partially by the Oquirrh Range, which terminates on the north by fringing the American Dead Sea, and runs but a limited distance south. From the northern extremity of the Oquirrh Range, Great Salt Lake forms the boundary line until connection is made with another valley still farther north, for the Rocky chain is a succession of grand mountains, gorgeous canyons and fair and lovely valleys. The city rests almost on the base of the Wasatch Range—rather on a gentle slope from it, leaning to the south and southwest. Thus, it enjoys a most desirable exposure in the directions mentioned, and is also protected from harsh northern and eastern winds by the grand and towering background which the Wasatch Range forms. Fringing the western limit of the city, and winding its measured way through a large portion of the valley—like a silver thread as seen from some o'erviewing eminence, until it is lost in the Great Lake, is the Jordan River, a stream that gives beauty and wealth to many parts of the valley through irrigation channels. The city is fed with water from numerous mountain streams, clear and pure. These are divided again and again. Running through the city in every direction, conjoining everywhere, and again separating, forming an infinitude of small water ways along either side of all streets, so that one never loses sight of them, they give an air of freshness, of sweetness and of purity that lends to the surroundings a charm captivating and irresistible. These are useful for irrigation, they are ornamental for giving life to the trees planted at regular distances along their courses, which afford a grateful shade in Summer by their dense foliage, and enrich the air with their perfumes. These streams carry health, wealth and perennial delight to citizen and visitor in their constant flow. Irrigation in the city is materially aided by means of a canal some twenty-one miles long, which taps Utah Lake, a fresh water reservoir in a valley to the south, and brings a large body of water to the city at a time when it is of very great value. The Summer rains are uncertain; they cannot be relied upon for the fostering of agriculture, a difficulty common to all higher altitudes, but which nature has made a blessing here by the vast accumulation of snow in the mountain fastnesses that render irrigation possible, and give an assurance of returns to the farmer which is not enjoyed even in countries where the rainfall is most trustworthy. All that fills the eye with gladness, all that has blessed honest toil in this new beautiful and bountiful land, all that has made homes, waving fields, thriving orchards, growing cities, all that gives to the heart that pure sense of happy rest, the consciousness of ineffable charms produced by untiring toil—all that in this country attracts the stranger, and he who would find a quiet and prosperous home in this region—all, all is due to the season's snows, to the mountain fastnesses where it lies bedded till a Summer's sun gradually dissolves it, till it finds its way to mountain streams which, pouring into the valleys, are led by a thousand arteries (the result of honest toil) over the thirsty land, till they bless and gladden it as they do the eyes and the hearts of all who behold its results. Coupled with human exertion and the intellect and skill of man, it is the savior, the maker of all that is best in this goodly land. The site of Salt Lake City is one of great natural beauty, growing and building in a valley of unsurpassed productiveness. The soil, containing an abundance of the most precious elements of fertility, is rich and deep and rests on a substratum of clay. Surrounding all are the eternal mountains, lifting their huge heads into the azure bosom, their summits crowned even in midsummer, with snows as eternal as themselves. Seen in the Fall of the year, when the rugged mountain steeps are purple, yellow and crimson, when they burn with the scarlet of frostbitten leaves and vegetation nipped by the early frosts, when up from the midst of embowering trees rises the smoke of quiet and peaceful settlements that follow the mountain contour, when the green of meadow and the rich golden hue of ripening harvests, like a mantle of gold and silver, shimmer beneath the rays of an unclouded sky, then indeed come thoughts or memories of the splendors of Alpine regions, compared with which even these scenes do not pale nor fear comparison. The city stretches along the sloping plateau for a distance of about three miles east and west and two miles north and south. The southern and western parts—and they are the larger—are laid off into blocks of ten acres each, with streets 132 feet wide, running at right angles. The north-eastern part is divided into blocks of five acres each, with streets eighty feet wide. Encircling the business portion of the town are the residences of citizens, surrounded by gardens, embowered in orchards and magnificent shade trees, and traversed by the living streams of water which render the atmosphere pure, one is led to view the Home of the Saints as the Garden of the Gods. Each street presents the appearance of a long avenue of poplar, locust, box elder, catalpa and other ornamental shade trees, often hiding with their foliage the outlines of some cottage, or the more pretentious and imposing architecture of a mansion. The accompanying views of Salt Lake City give an idea of its general appearance. On the east, at the foot of the Wasatch Mountains, lies Fort Douglas, two miles from the city, one of the most solidly constructed and well kept and beautiful forts of the Union. On the west are the depots of the Utah Central, Utah and Nevada, and Denver and Rio Grande Railroads. On the north are City Creek and the far famed Hot and Warm Sulphur Springs. The Great Salt Lake is visible from the city, and across it are frequently seen the most remarkable sunsets, unrivalled in any part of the world. Though showing well the extent and general character of the town, they do but faint justice, as far as the business blocks and residences are concerned. The various causes that have combined to render this a place of commercial importance, are the facts that it is a trade centre, the metropolis of the Rocky Mountain region, that it is fed by the great trans-continental roads—the Union Pacific, Central Pacific, Denver and Rio Grande Railroads and their connections; its University, Seminaries and High Schools, its Hospitals, Smelters, and the surrounding country with its never failing agricultural products. There is no general market, but in its place can be found, at a convenient distance from almost any point, a bountiful supply of the products of the Territory, and of other regions, and at prices so fair that strike the new comer with amazement. Salt Lake merchants are heavy exporters of cereals, tubers and other products to the eastern and western States, and even as far as the British Isles. Clean Utah wheat and barley hold first-rank in the Chicago market, and Utah potatoes have no equal for size, quality and flavor combined. Within thirty-six miles, on the east side, lies Park City with its famous Ontario, Daly, Crescent, and other extensive silver mines. The wonderful Ontario, is without an equal on the globe. Its officers are: L. T. Haggin, president; Wm. Willis, vice-president; and J. B. Haggin, treasurer, all of San Francisco; R. C. Chambers, superintendent, Salt Lake City. The mine was located in 1872, the present company having been organized in 1876. In round figures the cost of the building, foundations and Cornish pump, amount to $500,000; the value of improvements, with tunnels, $2,675,000; output to March, 1887, $18,000,000; amount of dividends paid to March, 1887, 130 in number, $8,050,000. On the west, are the lead and silver mines at Bingham, Tintic and Stockton, some of the Bingham mines having turned out as much as a hundred and fifty thousand tons of ore. On the south, are the Cottonwood mines within a few miles, and the Horn Silver and other mines at Frisco and Silver Reef. Sandy, twelve miles south, is the Swansea of Utah, where are located several smelting and refining works, to which are brought the ores from the mines in Utah, Idaho and Nevada. Utah now ranks third of the large precious metal producing States and Territories of the Union. Wells, Fargo & Company's statement of the mineral product of Utah, for the year 1886, places the mint valuation at $10,365,044.67. Perhaps the most important—though by no means the most accessible or desirable—iron ore deposits are in Iron County, which, when reached by railroad—now only a few miles distant—will certainly develop a Pittsburg in the western part of the continent. Professor Newberry says of these vast iron fields:—"The deposits of iron ore near Iron City and Iron Springs, in southwestern Utah, are probably not excelled, in intrinsic value, by any in the world. The ore is magnetite and hematite, and occurs in a belt fifteen or twenty miles long and three or four miles wide, along which there are frequent out-crops, each of which shows a length and breadth of several hundred feet of compact, massive ore, of the richest quality. There are certainly no other such deposits of iron ore west of the Mississippi, and, should it be found practicable to use Utah coal for the manufacture of pig and bar iron and steel from these ore beds, it would be difficult to overestimate the influence they would have on the industries of the Pacific Coast." In Juab County, developments in iron deposits exhibit the most gratifying and astonishing results, while Tintic has for years furnished large quantities of iron ore. A company is now organized for the operation of these mines, and so far the results are most gratifying. In an insignificant blast, with crude facilities, 65 per cent. of iron was reduced from the ore. It seems only a question of time when from these mines will be supplied largely the furnaces at Pueblo, Colorado. Besides these are large iron resources in Weber County, which are now being investigated with a view to their utilization. In fact, the iron resources are absolutely boundless. The coal fields of Utah are remarkable for their vastness. The main supply, of the Salt Lake market, is furnished from the Valley of the Weber, although the Pleasant Valley and Sanpete beds are formidable competitors. In Pleasant Valley, the deposits are of that magnitude that the railroad cars are backed into the mines and there loaded with an excellent bituminous coal. The coal fields of this Territory, in conjunction with the Union Pacific mines in Wyoming, on the eastern border of Utah, supply Montana, Nevada, Idaho, Wyoming, Colorado and Nebraska, and yet the development of the coal resources are at present only in their incipiency. In the year 1886, the Pleasant Valley coal beds supplied 72,000 tons of coal; the Weber Valley mines, 46,200 tons; and the Union Pacific mines, 738,986 tons. It is claimed, that with proper ovens, a fairly good coke can be made from the Pleasant Valley and Sanpete coals. Within easy reach by railroad, are also rich and immense deposits of antimony, sulphurs, salts, copper, sandstone, limestone,

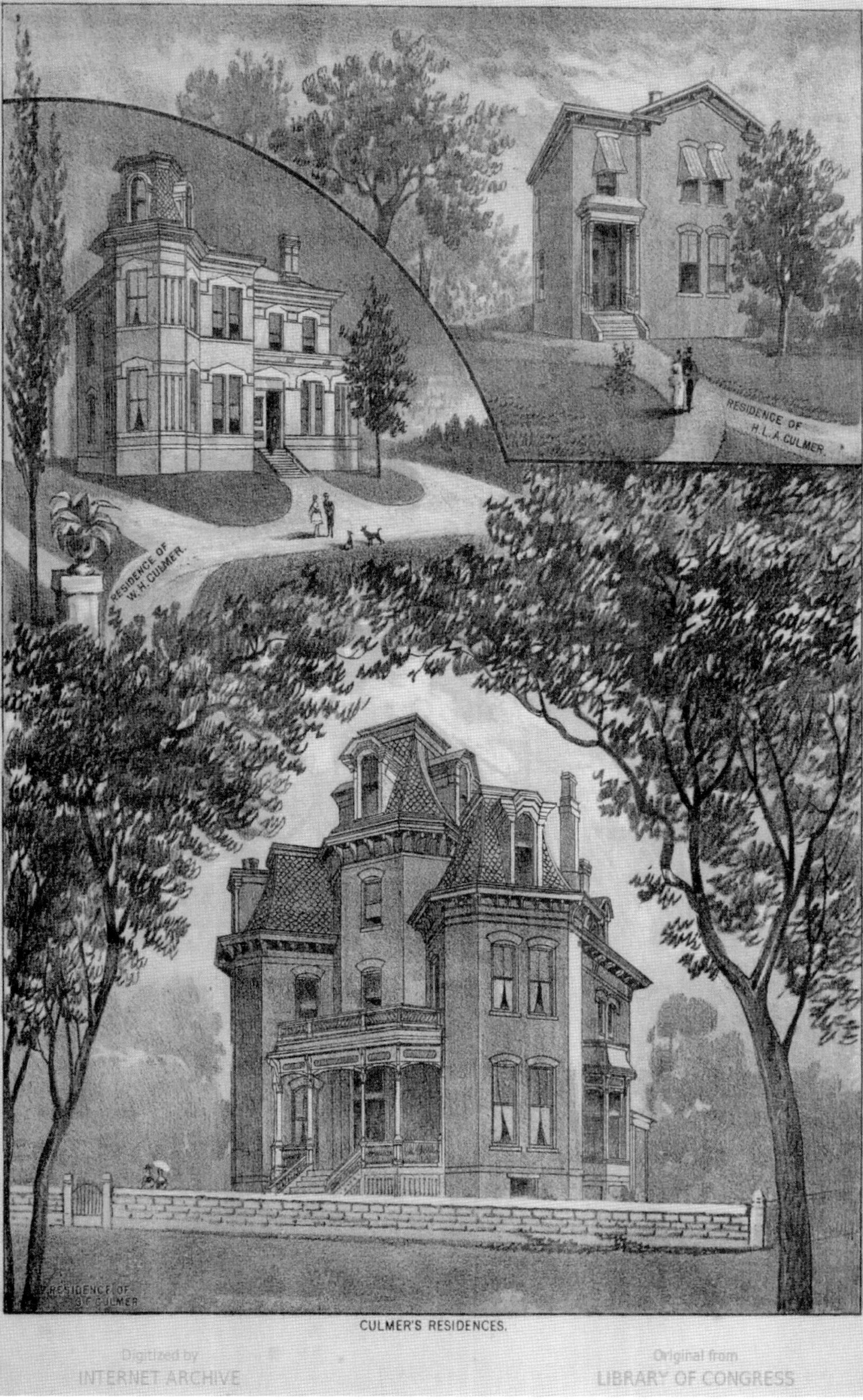

CULMER'S RESIDENCES.

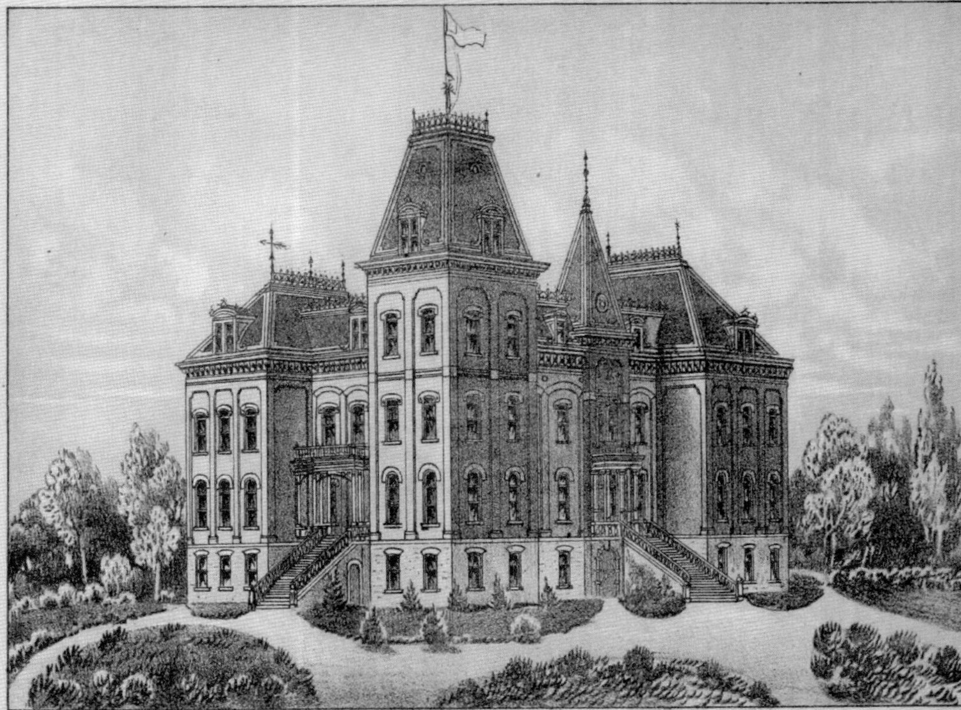

DESERET UNIVERSITY.

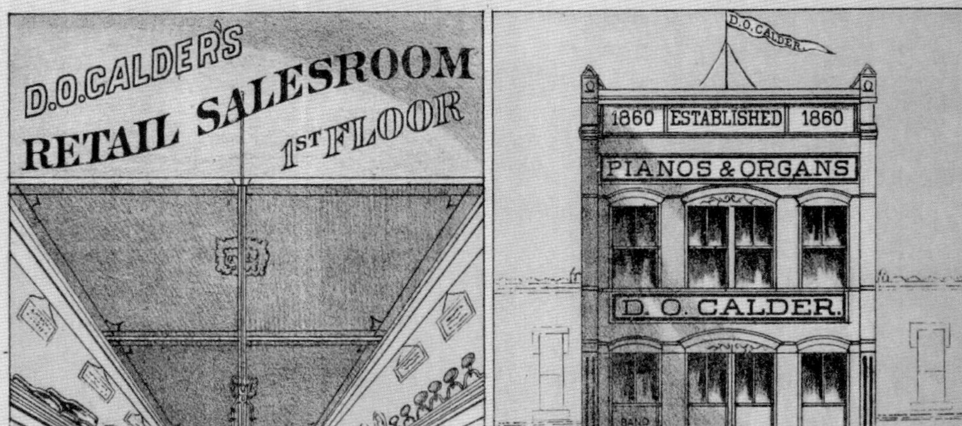

CALDER'S MUSIC PALACE.

ESTABLISHED 1870

THE

SALT LAKE HERALD,

THE PEOPLE'S PAPER

DAILY, SUNDAY, WEEKLY AND SEMI-WEEKLY.

THE HERALD CO. (Incorporated), Props.

Subscription Prices, payable in Advance:

Daily, $10; Sunday, $2; Semi-Weekly, $3; Weekly, $2.

Address all Communications Direct to

THE HERALD CO.,

Salt Lake City, Utah.

A GREAT NOVELTY,

HOME KNIT

ORIENTAL SMYRNA RUG

A Novel, Elegant and Useful Pastime for Ladies.

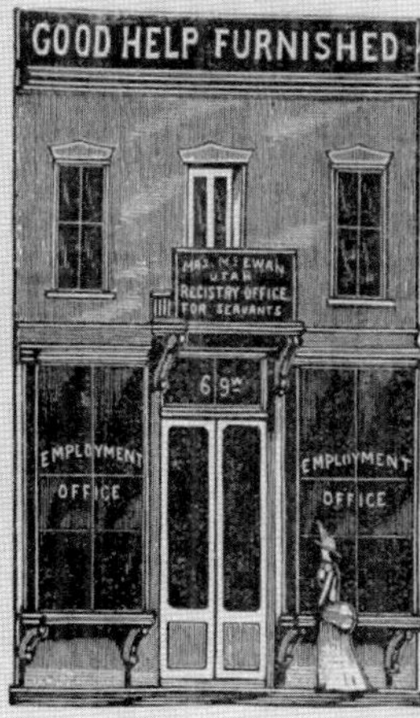

Smyrna Boxes,

Containing Specimen of Work Materials for Trial Strip and Instructions.

ORIENTAL (SMYRNA) WOOL,
SMYRNA COTTON,
SMY NA DESIGN BOOKS,
SMYRNA DESIGNS,

COLOR CARDS
SMYRNA STAFFS,
SMYRNA KNITTING PINS.
Etc.

The above Goods are obtainable from

MRS. I. McEWAN, Sole Agent for Utah,

53 W. First South Street, - Salt Lake City, Utah.

P. O Box 551 | Orders by Mail Promptly Attended to.

LEWIS P. KELSEY,

(Successor to ELI B. KELSEY)

Real Estate and Loan Agency,

OFFICE: No. 25 and 27 E. First South Street,

Four Doors East of Deseret National Bank.

A General Real Estate Business Transacted strictly on a Commission Basis.

COLLECTION DEPARTMENT.

Houses Rented, Rents Collected, Money Loaned on Approved Real Estate Security, and the Collection of Interest a Specialty.

Established in 1877. LEWIS P. KELSEY.

HOUSES AND LOTS
In all Parts of the City.
FOR SALE
FARMS AND FARMING LAND
In all Parts of the County

T. E. HARPER,

—DEALER IN—

Groceries, Provisions, Vegetables, Poultry, Fish & Game.

Goods Delivered Promptly. **Lunches for Tourists and Parties to the Lake a Specialty.**

Telephone 54. **52 E. FIRST S H ST., SALT LAKE CITY.**

MUD CREEK MINE.

M. D. FOLEY,
H. JOHNSON,
W. H. REMINGTON.

REMINGTON, JOHNSON & CO.,

(SUCCESSORS TO WALKER BROS.)

WHOLESALE GROCERS

18 and 20 West, Second South Street,

P. O. Box 245. —SALT LAKE CITY, UTAH.

AGENTS FOR UTAH FOR: Safety Nitro Powder Co., Utah Powder Co., J. W. Dimmit & Co., D. S. Erb & Co., El Modelo Cigar Co., Julius Ellinger & Co., Allen & Ginter, The J. B. Pace Tobacco Co., Colorado Soap Co., and Proprietors of the La Reina Vuelta Cigar Factory in Key West.

We are the ONLY EXCLUSIVELY WHOLESALE GROCERY HOUSE in Salt Lake City. Carry one of the Largest Stocks of Staple and Fancy Groceries in the West, and supply the Trade in Arizona, Colorado, Nevada, Wyoming, Montana, Idaho and Oregon.

New Fire Proof Brick Warehouse, 60x100 feet, immediately in rear of Stores.

1864. ESTABLISHED 1864.

JOHN READING,

SEEDSMAN AND FLORIST.

Greenhouses:
CORNER SECOND EAST
AND
SECOND SOUTH STREETS.

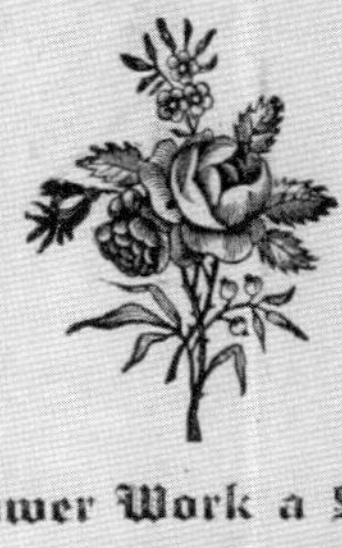

Greenhouses:
CORNER SECOND EAST
AND
SECOND SOUTH STREETS.

Cut Flower Work a Specialty

Weddings, Parties, Receptions, Funerals, etc., Furnished with Floral Decorations and Designs on Short Notice. Particular Attention Paid to Shipping Cut Flowers and Designs to Distant Points. A Fine and Complete Assortment of Greenhouse and Bedding Plants, especially adapted to this climate.

LANDSCAPE GARDENING.

P. O. Box 358.
Telephone 73.

SALT LAKE CITY.

Henry F. Clark,

29 E. First South Street.

THE TAILOR.

SALT LAKE CITY, UTAH.

VALLEY-TAN REMEDIES.

UTAH'S FAVORITE FAMILY MEDICINES!
SOLD AT ALL STORES.

JOHNSON'S
ESSENCE OF LIFE
FOR SUMMER COMPLAINTS.

AGENTS WANTED. C. E. Johnson. SALT LAKE CITY, UTAH.

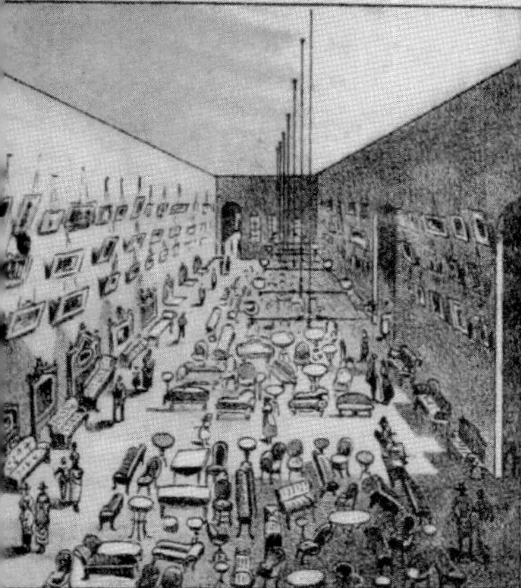

PARLOR FURNITURE, SECOND FLOOR.

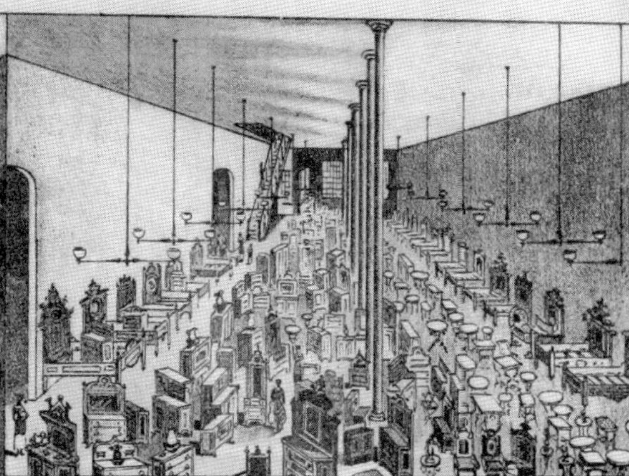

CHAMBER FURNITURE, SECOND FLOOR.

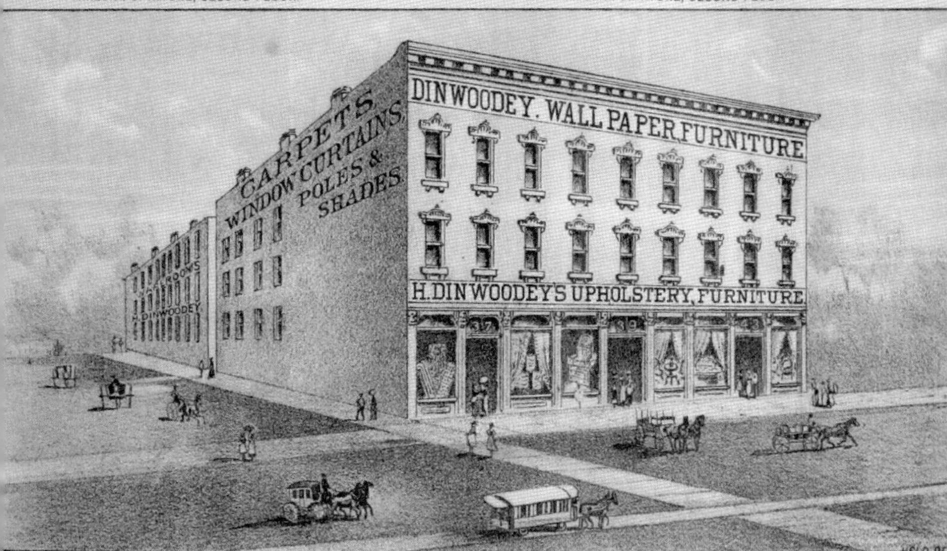

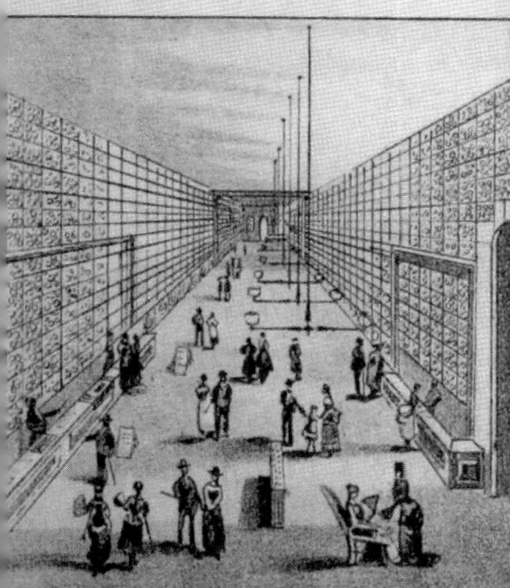

WALL PAPER AND CARPETS, FIRST FLOOR.

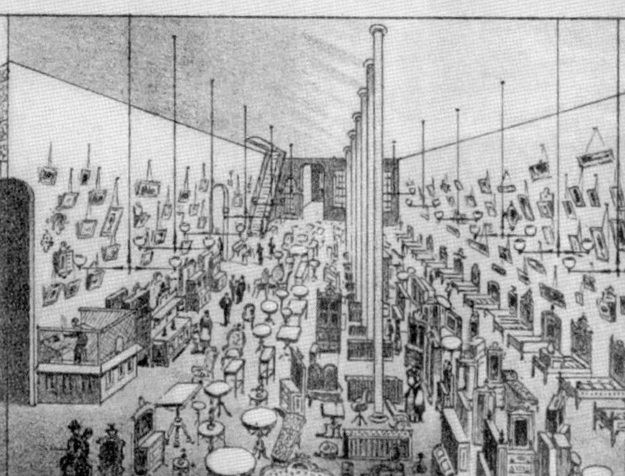

FURNITURE, FIRST FLOOR.

H. DINWOODEY.

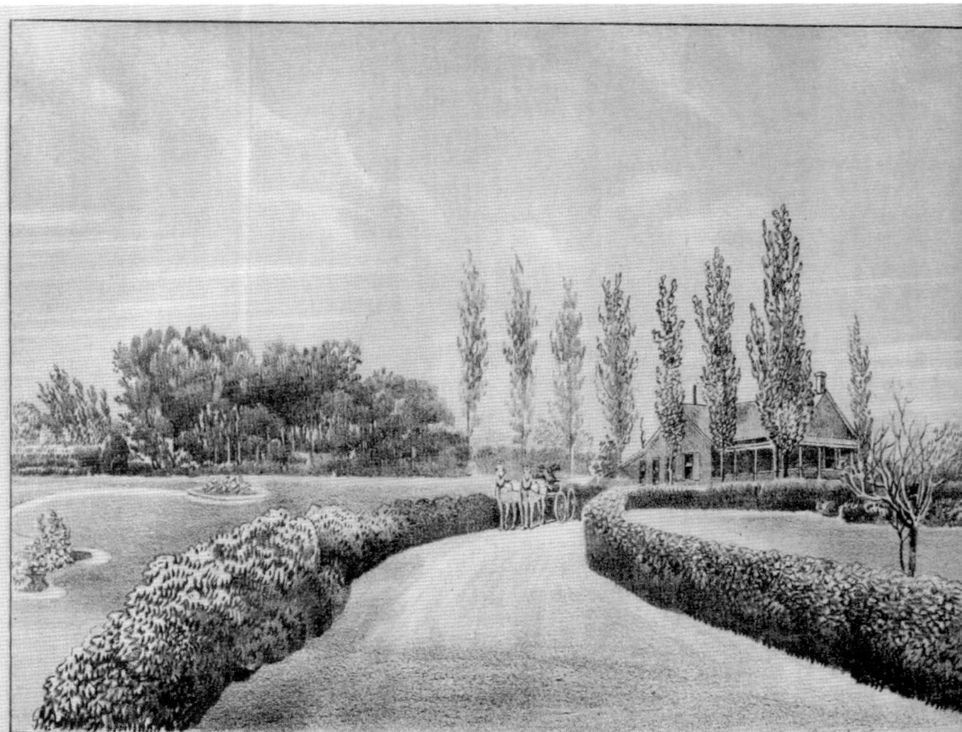

RESIDENCE OF J. T. GILMER.

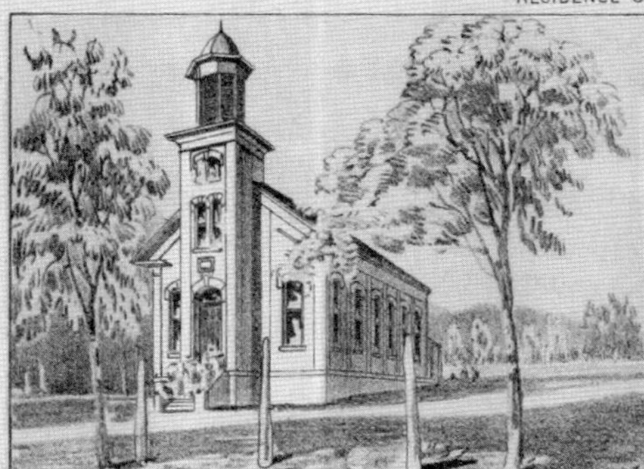

20th. WARD MEETING HOUSE.

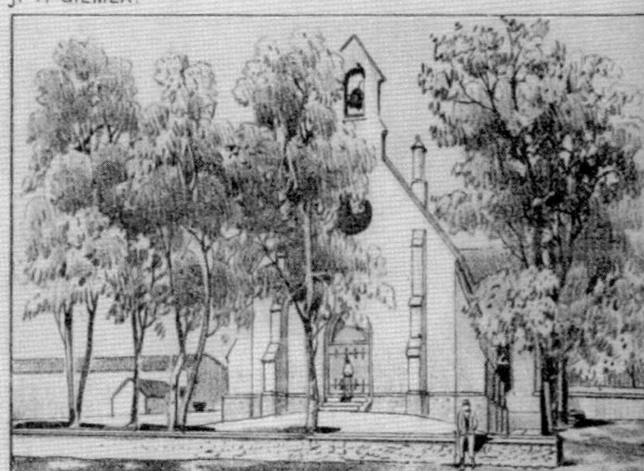

ST. MARK'S CATHEDRAL.

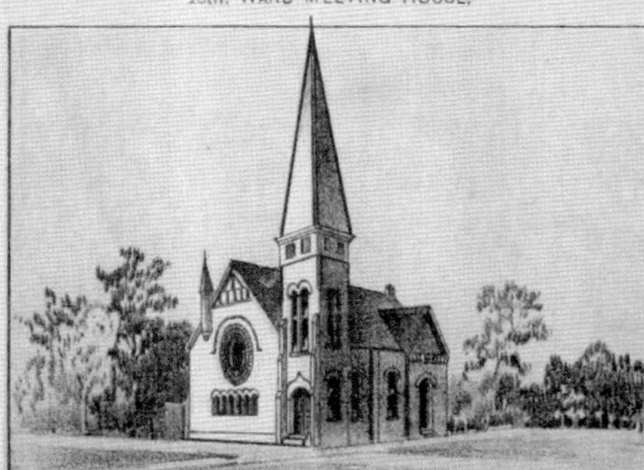

FIRST BAPTIST CHURCH

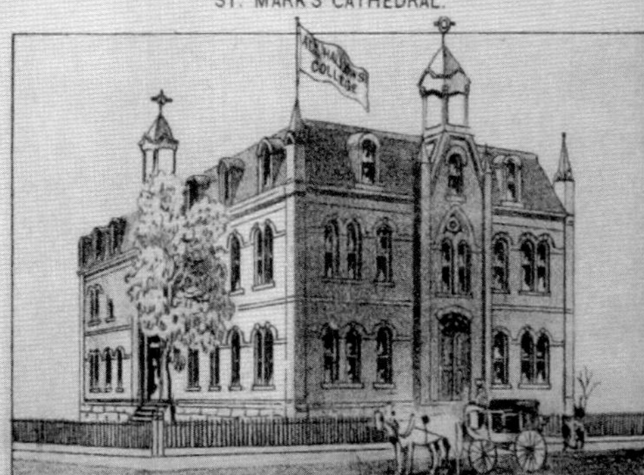

ALL HALLOWS COLLEGE.

marble, slate, brick clays, potters' clays and firestone. The luscious fruits, the plump grain, with the sheep and stock industries, form some of our principal sources of wealth, the importance of which can no more be measured than a few years ago it could be predicted. There is here a foundation of prosperity and greatness which will grow as the population and years increase. The climate and soil are singularly adapted to fruit growing, trees being vigorous growers and generous bearers, while small fruits do remarkably well. The following table will give an approximate idea of the yield:

Barley	averages	32	bushels	to the acre.
Corn	"	27	"	"
Oats	"	36	"	"
Wheat	"	28	"	"
Pears	"	75	"	"
Peaches	"	120	"	"
Plums	"	165	"	"
Apricots	"	145	"	"
Cherries	"	75	"	"
Grapes	"	6260	pounds	"

This remarkable city, having a population of nearly thirty-five thousand, has many fine residences, set back in smooth lawns, fringed by parterres of flowers, shaded by umbrageous foliage and bearing about them the marks and indications of wealthy owners. Street-car lines diverge from Main Street through the town to all points of the compass. The immense quantity of shade and fruit trees growing in the city, give it, in the Spring, the appearance of a flower garden—the trees being then all in blossom, the pure, sparkling water flowing down the streets in rich abundance, a sight is formed that cannot be surpassed anywhere. The wide, level streets, lined on each side with rows of shade trees, form elegant drives in this city of magnificent distances, and towards evening of any fine day the streets are crowded with the fine turnouts. The Utah Driving Park Association, in their Spring and Fall races, attract the best blooded stock from Montana, California and Colorado. As good steppers can be found on our streets as anywhere in the Union. The Summers are warm and dry, the Winters generally mild and open. The average fall of snow is light in the valleys and heavy in the mountains. "The climate is agreeable and salubrious, the air dry, elastic, transparent and bracing, and, on the whole, is not unlike that of northwestern Texas and New Mexico, and is agreeable except for a month or so in Winter; and then the temperature seldom falls to zero, or snow to a greater depth than a foot, and it soon melts away, although it sometimes affords a few days' sleighing. The Spring opens in March, the atmosphere becomes clear as a dew-drop, deciduous trees burst into leafy bloom, and the green of the valleys pursues the retiring snow-line up the mountain slopes. The Summer is pleasant in its onset, accompanied by fragrant airs and full streams. Springs of sweet water, fed largely from the surface, bubble forth everywhere. But, as the season advances the heat increases, the winds become laden with dust, the storms are mainly dry, the springs fail or become brackish from concentration of their mineral salts, the streams run low, and vegetation parches unless artificially watered. Still, from the rapid radiation at the earth's surface, the nights are agreeably cool and give strength to bear the heat of the days. In October, the air clears up again as in Spring, and the landscape softens with the rich colors of the dying vegetation, which reaches up the mountain sides to their summits in places, but on them the gorgeous picture is soon overlaid by the first snows of approaching winter. The Fall is delightful and generally lingers to the end of the year." The mean Summer temperature is about seventy-four degrees at two o'clock, p. m., and in the evening but fifty-seven degrees. Those who have to swelter through many nights in a season, with the thermometer between eighty and ninety degrees, would appreciate this difference. The mean temperature, in Winter, is about thirty degrees, the denizens of Salt Lake often enjoying a warm sun while reading of the biting cold and piercing blizzards of a lower altitude. Plowing is frequently done during the Winter months of December and February. Salt Lake City is well supplied with hotels—large, roomy, furnished with the latest improved elevators, electric lights and bells, fine billiard halls, and a table at which nothing in the way of eatables is lacking. The prices have a range that suit the circumstances of every person. There are published in Salt Lake City: the *Deseret News*, (daily, semi-weekly and weekly); the *Herald*, (daily, semi-weekly and weekly); the *Tribune*, (daily and weekly); the *Democrat*, (daily and weekly); the *Bikuben* and the *Svenska Harolden*, (weekly); the *Juvenile Instructor* and the *Woman's Exponent*, (semi-monthly); the *Contributor*, *Rocky Mountain Christian Advocate*, *Parry's Literary Magazine*, *Z. C. M. I. Advocate*, the *Historical Record* and the *Grocer*, (all monthly). The Fraternal and Benevolent Societies are well represented, comprising lodges of the Masonic Order, Odd Fellows, Knights of Pythias, Ancient Order United Workmen, Temple of Honor, Foresters, Brotherhoods of Locomotive Engineers and Locomotive Firemen, and Grand Army of the Republic, the first mentioned having a magnificent library, with the Odd Fellows following close in its wake. The water supply is furnished by a stream flowing from City Creek Canyon, and by one from Emigration Canyon, also by several flowing artesian wells in the southern and western parts. The Water Works are of the gravity system—settling and filtering tanks or reservoirs, for the main part of the city, being placed half a mile up the City Creek Canyon, in the natural bed of the stream, the height of the location of the tanks giving an average pressure of seventy pounds to the inch. The theoretical discharge is 1,560 gallons per minute. Other tanks or reservoirs are placed further up the creek, supplying the elevated portions of the city on the north bench; all being fed by the natural flow of the mountain stream, and thus rendering the lifting process unnecessary. The Water Works System is owned by the City Corporation, and comprises sixteen and a quarter miles of mains with one hundred and fifty-one fire hydrants. The Fire Department consists of a chief engineer, two assistant engineers, secretary, six foremen of companies, four engine companies, hook and ladder company, and two independent companies, with a membership of 145. The Department has 4,000 feet of hose. Salt Lake City has been peculiarly fortunate in the absence of destructive fires and the Department has had but little to do compared with other cities of equal importance. The large size of the blocks, and the wide streets, render a sweeping conflagration almost an impossibility. The insurance rates are low, owing to immunity from extensive fires. The annual rate of taxation, is: Municipal tax, five mills; County, six mills; Territorial, three mills; Special School tax, three mills; making a total of twelve mills on the dollar. The bonded debt of the city is so trifling, that it is hardly worth mentioning. Main Street and First and Second South Streets are lighted by electricity, both by the Brush and incandescent lights. The Gas Works, in which the City Corporation owns a large interest, has several miles of main pipes laid, which are being steadily extended. The business portion of the city is covered with a net work of telephone lines, while telegraphic communication is had with all parts of the Territory and the world. The most prominent building in the city is the Temple, which is one hundred and eighty-six feet and six inches long, and ninety-nine feet in width. It was commenced April 6, 1853, the foundation is sixteen feet in thickness, and the walls, up to the square, nine feet nine inches; there will be three towers at each end of the the building, the centre ones rising to a hight of two hundred feet, and its total cost when completed is estimated at $10,000,000. It is constructed of speckled granite rock, brought from the mouth of Little Cottonwood Canyon, some twenty miles south-east of the city, and when completed promises to be one of the most magnificent buildings in the country. The large Tabernacle on the same block and to the west of the Temple, is elliptical in shape, two hundred and fifty feet long, one hundred and fifty feet wide and seventy feet in height from the floor to the ceiling. The interior of the building presents the appearance of an oval arch without any centre support, being the largest self-supporting arch in America, with the exception of that of the Central Depot of New York. The building has a seating capacity of 10,000 persons. It has twenty doors nine feet wide. It contains a grand organ, one of the largest and best toned in the world. The Salt Lake Assembly Hall is of Gothic architecture, and is one hundred and twenty feet long, sixty-eight feet wide, and is one hundred and thirty feet to top of tower rising from centre of building. This hall will accommodate 3,000 people. In this building is another fine organ, which like that in the Tabernacle, was built entirely by Utah artizans. The Council House, forty-five feet square and two stories high, was one of the most substantial and pretentious public buildings erected during the early days of the Territory. Here the first Legislative Assemblies convened, and it has been used for many important purposes since then. Some three years ago the building was nearly destroyed by fire, nothing but the bare walls now remain. The *Deseret News* office and tithing stores were until recently church buildings. In the former are printed the church papers and books; in the latter is received and paid out the tithes and donations of the Mormons. On the same block is the Lion House, the Beehive House and the Eagle Gate, all old landmarks of Utah, and in close proximity is the Gardo House, the residence of the President of the Church. The City Hall, a red sandstone building of two stories high, which was erected at a cost of $70,000, contains the offices of the Municipal Government. The Territorial Legislative Assembly holds its sessions in this building. The Deseret University building, the Catholic Hospital, St. Mary's School, Hammond Hall, All Hallows College, are all imposing edifices, attractive in design and built to stay. The County Court House, in the southwesaern part of the city, is a two story adobe structure, containing the County Offices, the basement being used as a County Jail. Plans are now making for a new County Jail which is to be constructed on the most approved methods. The Federal Court holds its sessions in the Wasatch Block, originally designed as a hotel. The Theatre and the Opera House are both fine large structures with ample stage room and appurtenances to accommodate even the largest theatrical companies that cross the continent. Salt Lake is recognized as a good show town, all the large and best companies make it a point to stop here. Lately the Opera House has not been used for theatrical purposes. The Museum building, though delapidated, contains an attractive and rare collection of curiosities and unique specimens, collected from every part of the world, and Utah in particular. The Indian relics form a prominent feature. Its cabinets are well filled, for it receives material aid from Mormon missionaries who gather curiosities for it when traveling abroad. Much can there be found relating to the history of this Territory from its first settlement to the present time. Zion's Co-operative Mercantile Institution building, the Jennings' Block, Walker House, Deseret National Bank building, the D. O. Calder and Dinwoodey Blocks, the Hooper & Eldredge Block, Palace Hotel, Cullen's New Hotel, White House, Union Block, Wasatch Building, Masonic Hall, Clift House, St. James Hotel, Hill & Symons Block, Denhalter Block, Commerce Block and Ryman Block, Ellerbeck and Madsen Blocks, Metropolitan Hotel, Walker Bros. Block, Auerbach Block, Keyser's Building, Herald Building, and G. M. Scott & Co.'s Warehouse, all give evidence of the confidence our moneyed men have in the stability of the city and its growth. Fort Douglas, located two miles east of the town, is one of the most tastefully laid-out and cleanly-kept military posts in the Union. The officer's quarters and barracks are all built with rock and brick. The Sunday concerts by the Fort band during the Summer months are a source of attraction to the citizens, and the lovely drive is very generally

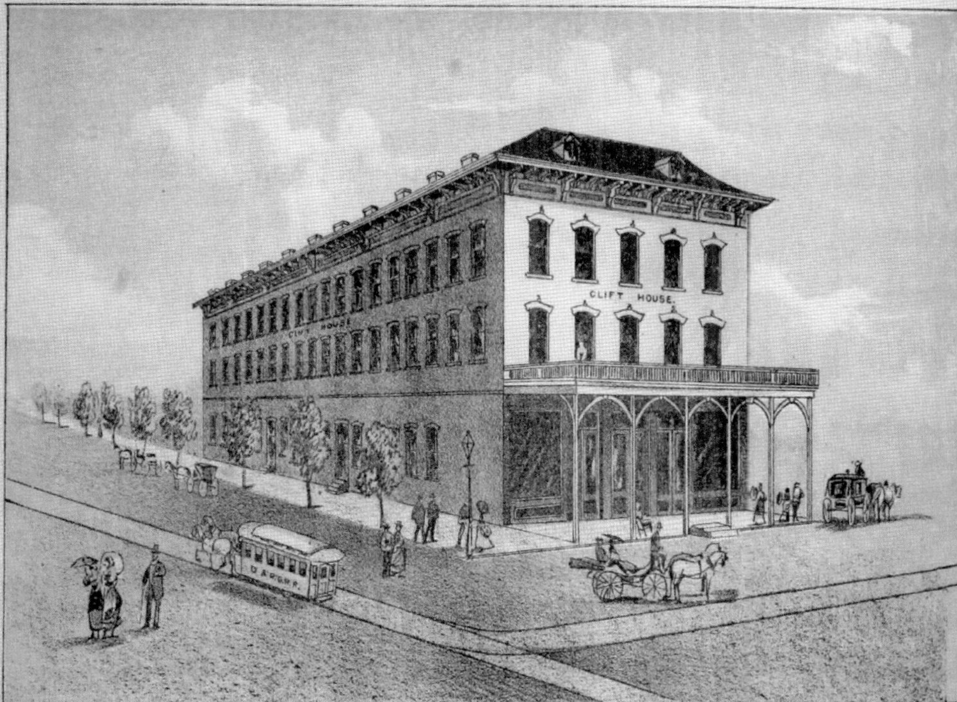

CLIFT HOUSE, A. C. BRIXEN & BRO., PROPRIETORS.

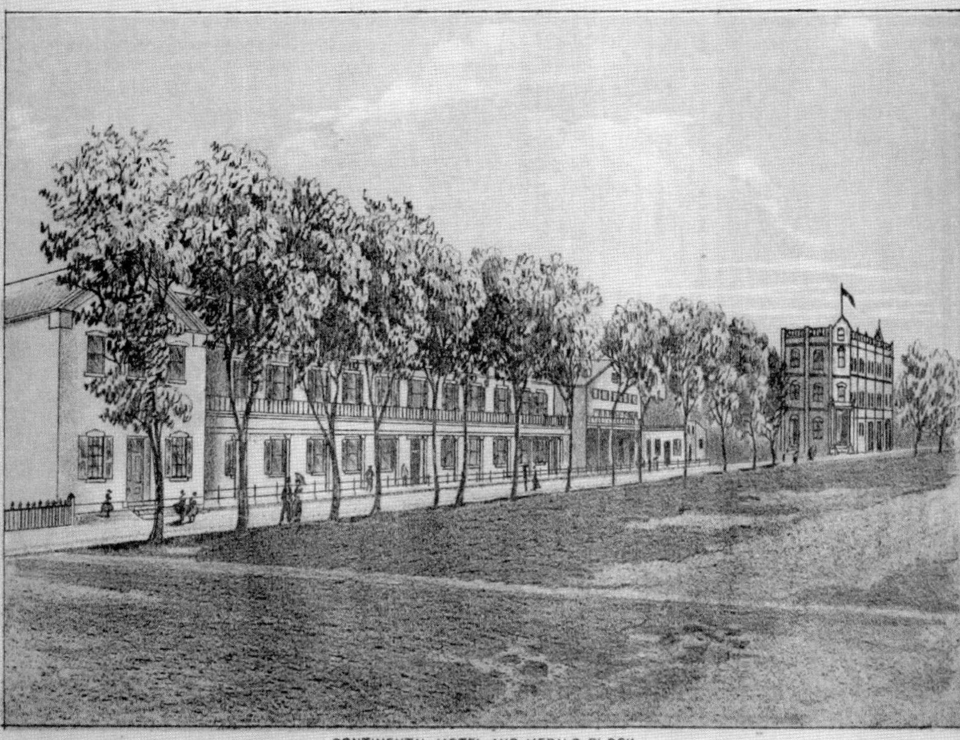
CONTINENTAL HOTEL AND HERALD BLOCK.

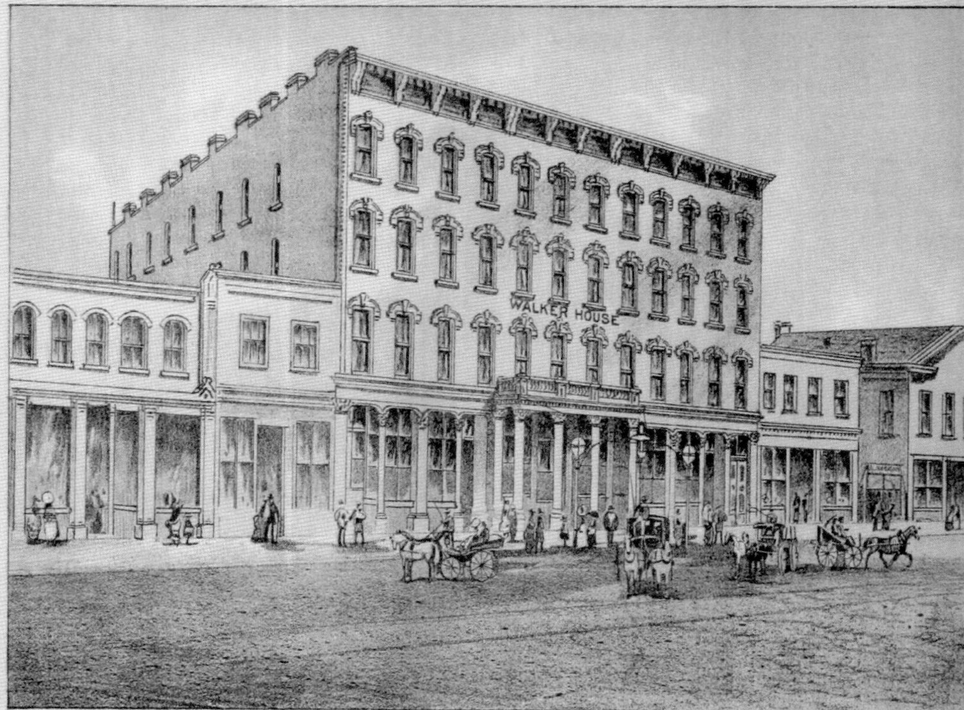

WALKER HOUSE HOTEL, G. S. ERB, Prop.

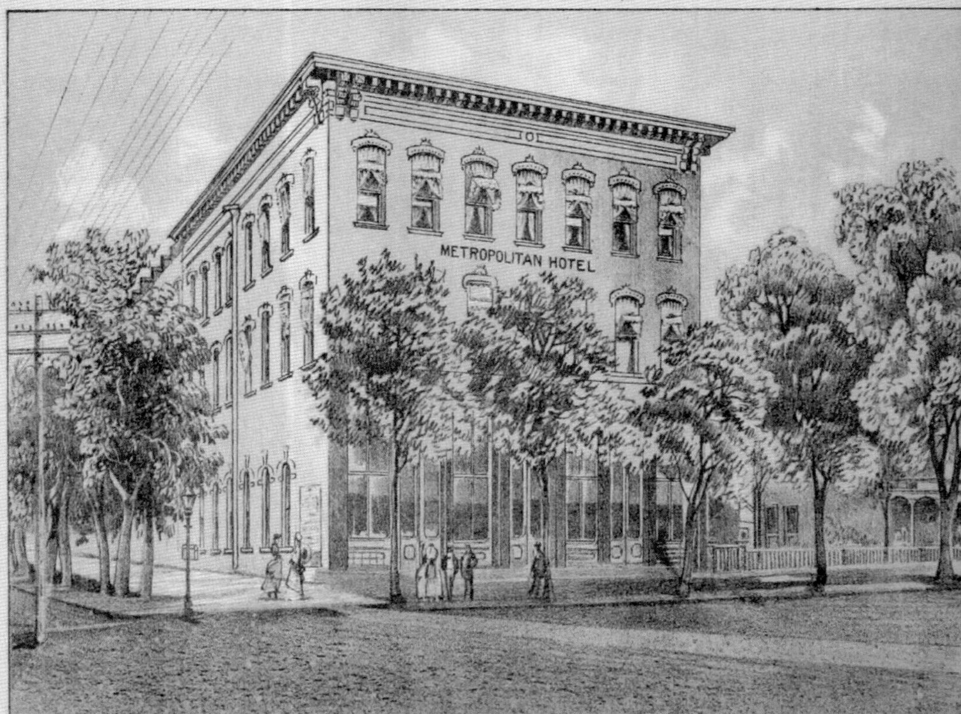

METROPOLITAN HOTEL, G. S. ERB, Prop.

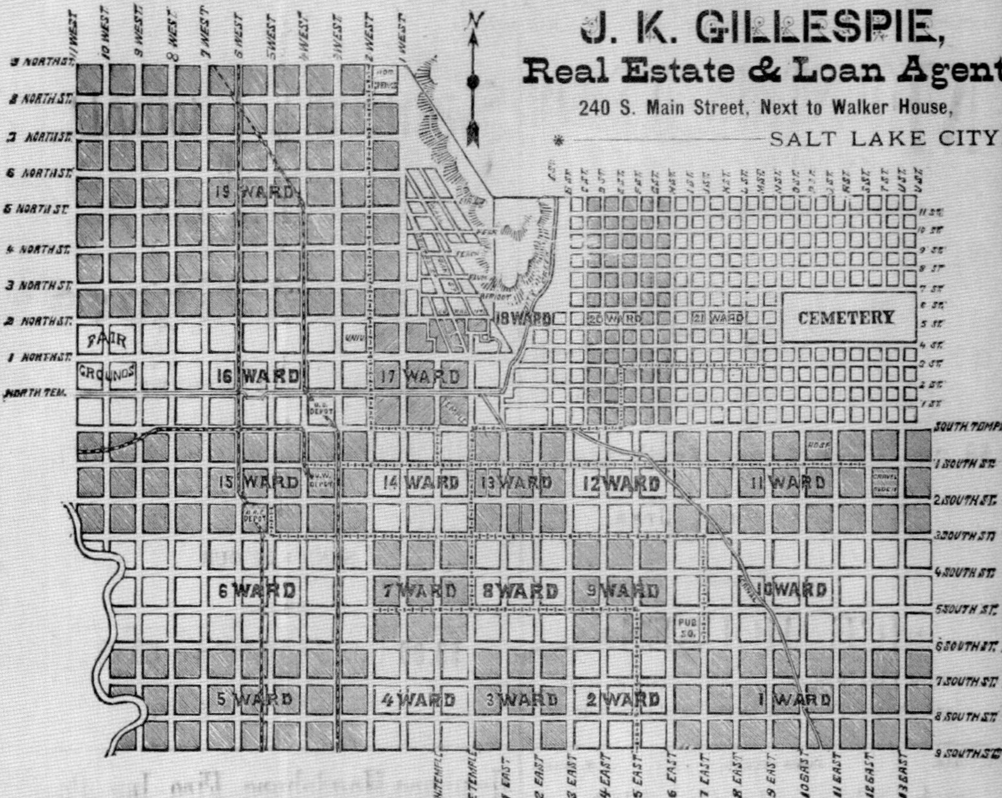
N
11 WEST
10 WEST
9 WEST
8 WEST
7 WEST
6 WEST
5 WEST
4 WEST
3 WEST
2 WEST
1 WEST
9 NORTH ST.
8 NORTH ST.
7 NORTH ST.
6 NORTH ST.
5 NORTH ST.
4 NORTH ST.
3 NORTH ST.
2 NORTH ST.
1 NORTH ST.
NORTH TEM.
FAIR GROUNDS
19 WARD
18 WARD
20 WARD
21 WARD
CEMETERY
16 WARD
17 WARD
15 WARD
14 WARD
13 WARD
12 WARD
11 WARD
6 WARD
7 WARD
8 WARD
9 WARD
10 WARD
PUB. SQ.
5 WARD
4 WARD
3 WARD
2 WARD
1 WARD
SOUTH TEMPLE
1 SOUTH ST.
2 SOUTH ST.
3 SOUTH ST.
4 SOUTH ST.
5 SOUTH ST.
6 SOUTH ST.
7 SOUTH ST.
8 SOUTH ST.
9 SOUTH ST.
W. TEMPLE
E. TEMPLE
1 EAST
2 EAST
3 EAST
4 EAST
5 EAST
6 EAST
7 EAST
8 EAST
9 EAST
10 EAST
11 EAST
12 EAST
13 EAST

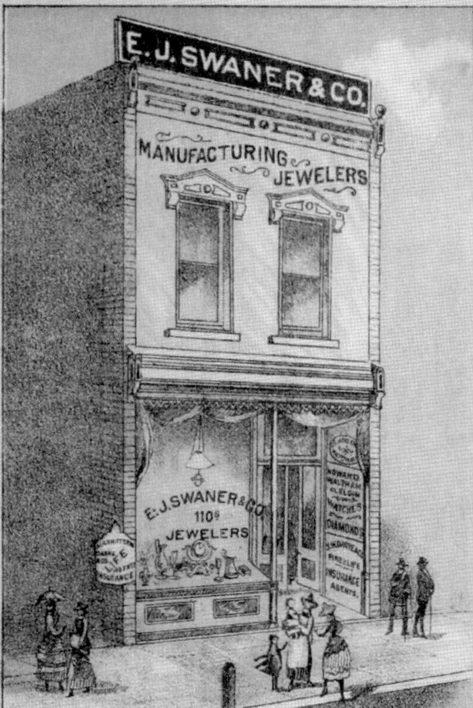

E. J. SWANER & CO.

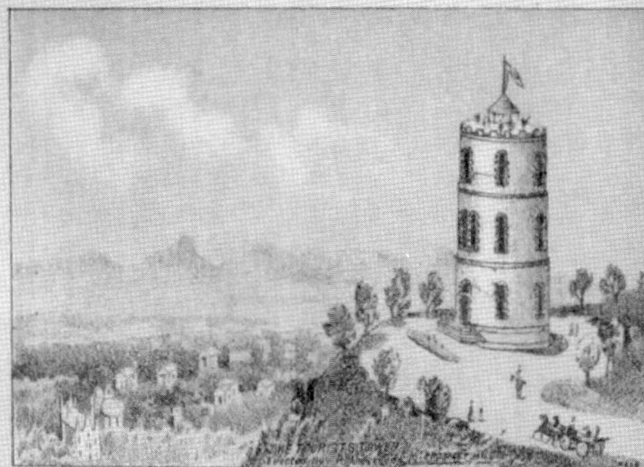

PROSPECT HILL.

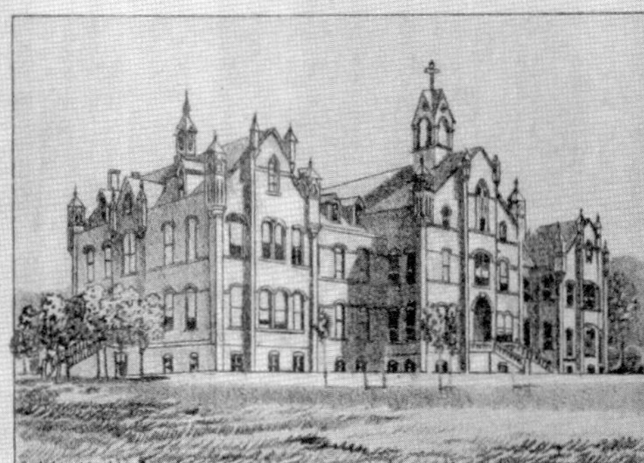

CATHOLIC HOSPITAL.

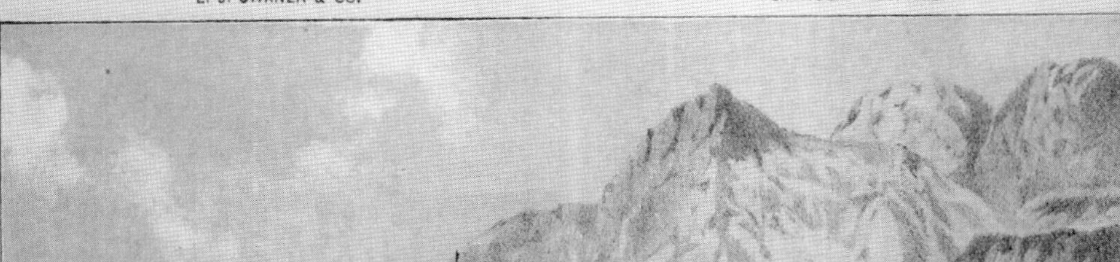

WAGENER'S CALIFORNIA BREWERY.

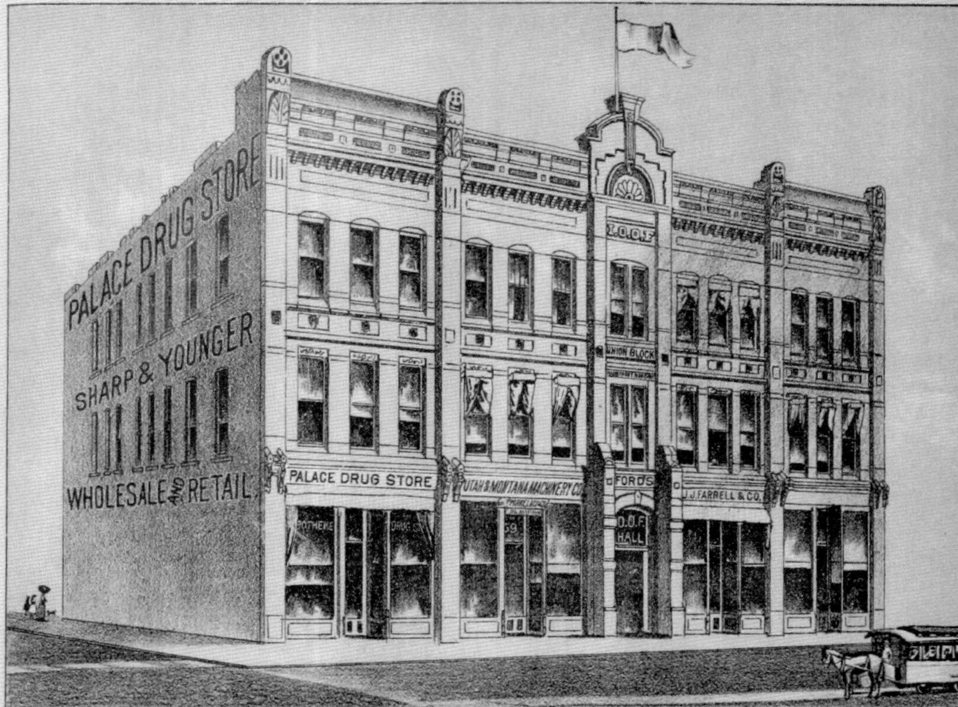

UNION BLOCK.

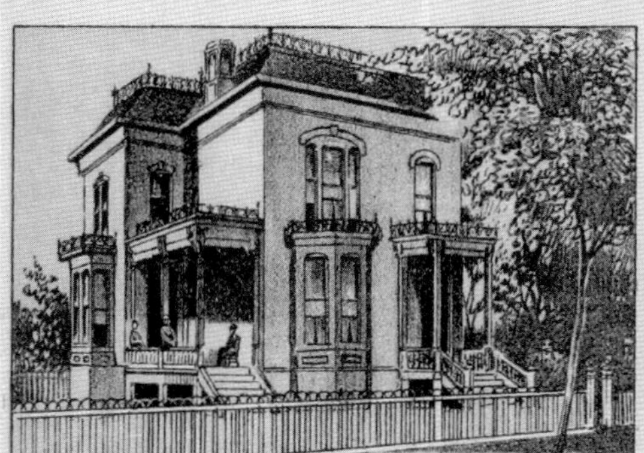

RESIDENCE OF S. F. FENTON.

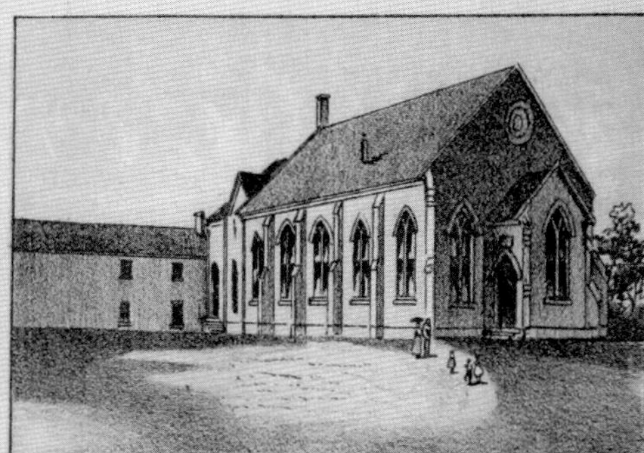

FIFTEENTH WARD ASSEMBLY HALL.

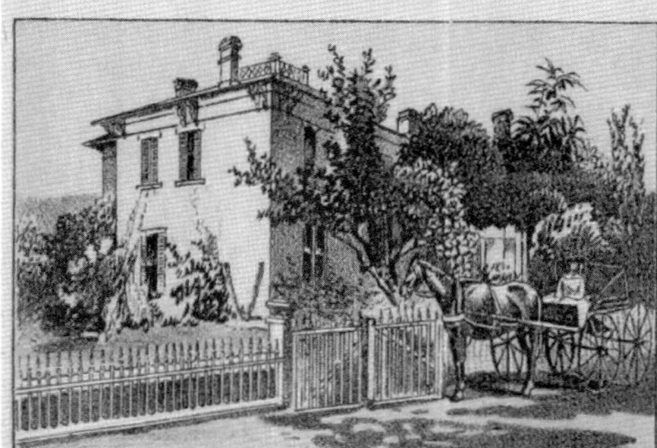

RESIDENCE OF REV. G. D. B. MILLER.

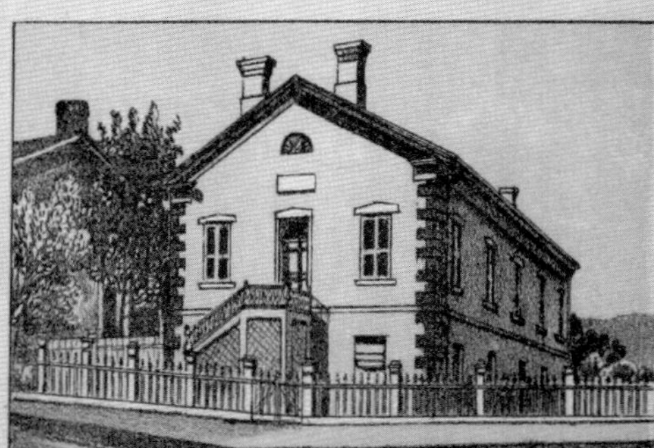

SOCIAL HALL.

patronized. But above all, the Great Salt Lake is the attraction for tourists. Its length is about eighty-five miles, by fifty miles wide, with an average depth of twenty feet, and is reported to nowhere exceed sixty feet. The islands in the Lake are nine in number—one of them being twelve miles, another sixteen miles in length. The water of the Lake is so salty that it forms one of the purest and most concentrated brines known in the world. It compares, with other bodies of salt water, about as follows:

	WATER.	SOLIDS.
Atlantic Ocean	96.5	3.5
Mediterranean	96.2	3.8
Dead Sea	76.	24.
Great Salt Lake	86.	14.

And in specific gravity, distilled water being unity:—

Ocean Water	1.026
Dead Sea	1.116
Great Salt Lake	1.107

It is easily approached, by a short ride on the Utah & Nevada Railway, or in a half hour by the Denver & Rio Grande Railway. The exhilarating effects of a bath in its waters are fully appreciated and enjoyed by the residents, as much so as by the tourists; 48,279 people were conveyed, in the Summer of 1886, by the Utah & Nevada Railway and 53,347 by the Denver & Rio Grande Railway. The fare, for the round trip, is but fifty cents; and the accommodations for excursionists, at both places, are remarkable for this inland Territory. On public holidays, the attractions are sometimes as varied as those of Coney Island or Manhattan Beach. Bath houses and fresh water baths are supplied for the use of bathers, and the surf is frequently as enlivening as that on the shores of the Atlantic or Pacific Oceans. Although it is termed the Dead Sea of America the waves often make it appear quite "lively." The Lake has no outlet. The mountain streams, converging within a radius of nearly 200 miles, north and south, and forming rivers, all empty into this Lake. The mountain soil is deeply impregnated with salts and minerals, and the water caused by the melting snow, running through it becomes laden with them in solution. These salts are thus carried to the streams, thence into the rivers and by them into the Lake, where they remain forever. The Lake does not evince any perceptible rise or fall, save following unusually severe Winters or exceedingly mild ones; and it is relieved from overflowing the accustomed bounds only by evaporation. By this process the salts remain in the Lake, and thus, year by year, though imperceptibly, the saline density of the Lake increases. The result is that the Lake is one of the greatest and most inexhaustible salt producers in the world, and it is freely taken advantage of. Not only is salt made for local purposes, but it has been largely exported, especially to the North, where it is used in the mines as a lixivator. One experience is always sufficient to make bathers careful to keep the water out of their mouths and nostrils, for its strength is such as to make strangulation an easy possibility. Its buoyancy is almost incredible. In some places it is impossible to sink. On its waters ride the old Garfield, and the little steamers—the Susie Riter and the Whirlwind. During the months of July, August and September, the water is enjoyably tepid. The following is an analysis of the water of the Lake, made by Doctor Smart, of the United States Army, in 1877. He found an imperial gallon to contain nearly twenty-four and a half ounces of saline matter, amounting to nearly fourteen per cent:—

Common Salt	11.735
Carbonate of Lime	.016
Sulphate of Lime	.073
Epsom Salts	1.123
Chloride of Magnesia	.843
Percentage of Solids	13.790
Water	86.210
	100.000

One hundred grains of the dry, solid matter, contained:—

Common Salt	85.089
Carbonate of Lime	.117
Sulphate of Lime	.531
Epsom Salts	8.145
Chloride of Magnesia	6.118
	100.000

Beck's Hot Springs baths have achieved a wide notoriety for their curative properties. Here are supplied public or private plunge baths, with hotel accommodations, for the requirements of invalids desiring to test the full properties of these famous sulphur springs. The temperature of the water is 128°. They are distant about three miles north of the city, and are easily reached either by the railroads, or by excursion wagons which run hourly to the springs. The Warm Sulphur Springs, within easy reach by street cars, are worthy of note; they are owned by the City Corporation and are considered efficacious in the cure of rheumatic, skin and kindred diseases. The water is conveyed in pipes to plunge and tub baths, which are freely patronized by Salt Lake residents as well as by all visitors. Although there are several manufacturing interests represented in the city, it is apparent to those who look into the matter thoroughly that the one great drawback to the material and rapid advancement of Salt Lake City is the want of manufactories. Millions of dollars are sent from here annually for articles that can be made as cheaply and better at home. Take, for instance, the one item of boots and shoes, the quantity imported, if made here, would support a large number of laborers, besides keeping the money in the community, instead of sending it away to support commonwealths in a great degree foreign to us. There is absolutely no excuse for not manufacturing them all here, as the experience of Zion's Co-operative Mercantile Institution in their shoe factory has demonstrated. Hides are exported, (freight paid on the outward trip,) converted into

Commercial Insurance Co.

OF CALIFORNIA.

OFFICE: No. 439 California St., San Francisco

SAFE DEPOSIT BUILDING

Fire and Marine.

COMMERCIAL INSURANCE COMPANY CALIFORNIA

CAPITAL PAID IN FULL, - *$200,000.00*
Assets, January 1st, 1887, - - *446,611.09*
Losses Paid since Company was organized, *$1,581,849.51*

JOHN H. WISE,	CHAS. A. LATON,	A. R. GUNNISON,
President.	Secretary.	Gen. Agt. and Adjuster.

S. W. DARKE & CO., Agts.,
Salt Lake City.

Sporting Goods AND Specialty House

EVANS & SPENCER,

SALT LAKE CITY.

GUNS, AMMUNITION, REVOLVERS, FISHING TACKLE, BASE BALL GOODS, BICYCLES, TRICYCLES, VELOCIPEDES AND BICYCLE ACCESSORIES.

Tents in Stock and Made to Order.
Guns, Tents and Bicycles for Rent.

AGENTS FOR GRAND RAPIDS PORTABLE HOUSES,
(Adopted by the Lake Park Resort Co.)

Agents for Caligraph Writing Machine.

IMPORTERS AND JOBBERS OF FINE CUTLERY.

General Repairing & Locksmithing Done.

Salt Lake Academy

(INCORPORATED 1878.)

L. E. HOLDEN,	EDWARD BENNER,
President.	Principal.

FOUR PREPARATORY SCHOOLS

IN SALT LAKE.

THE ACADEMY is under the patronage of the New West Education Commission.

HAMMOND HALL, with grounds costing over thirty thousand dollars, beautifully located, unequalled in heating, light and ventilation.

The Academy has a well-selected Library, excellent Cabinets, valuable Physical Apparatus and Charts; also a large and choice collection of Stuffed Birds.

The Students of the Academy carry on a flourishing Reading Room.

The Academy has a full corps of highly-educated and experienced instructors.

Courses of Academic study, three years; classical and scientific, four years; English, three years. These courses are severe, and adapted to the needs of young men and women who are ambitious and well. In respect of health and mental energy, this institution invites comparison.

A NEW DEPARTMENT of Manual Training shortly to be organized. Large additions are now being made to the resources of the Institution for this purpose. Announcements later.

EDWARD BENNER,
Principal.

ELBRIDGE TUFT'S

RESIDENCE,

118 E. Third South St.,

Salt Lake City.

Centrally Located—Two Blocks from Post Office.

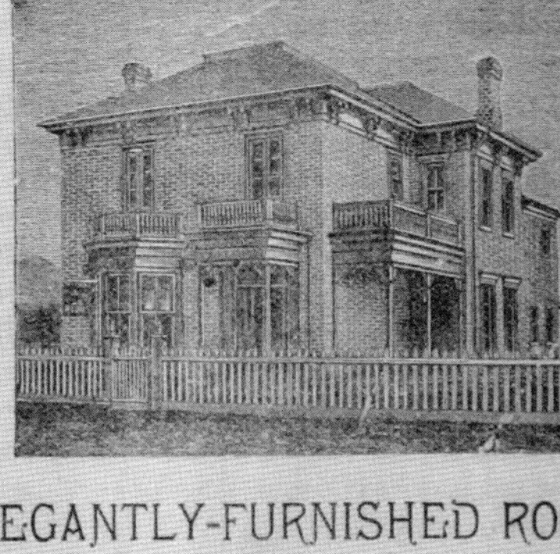

Accommodations First-class. Plenty of Shade.

ELEGANTLY-FURNISHED ROOMS

Either Single or En Suite, With or Without Board,

AT MODERATE PRICES.

A FINE ARTESIAN WELL ON THE PREMISES

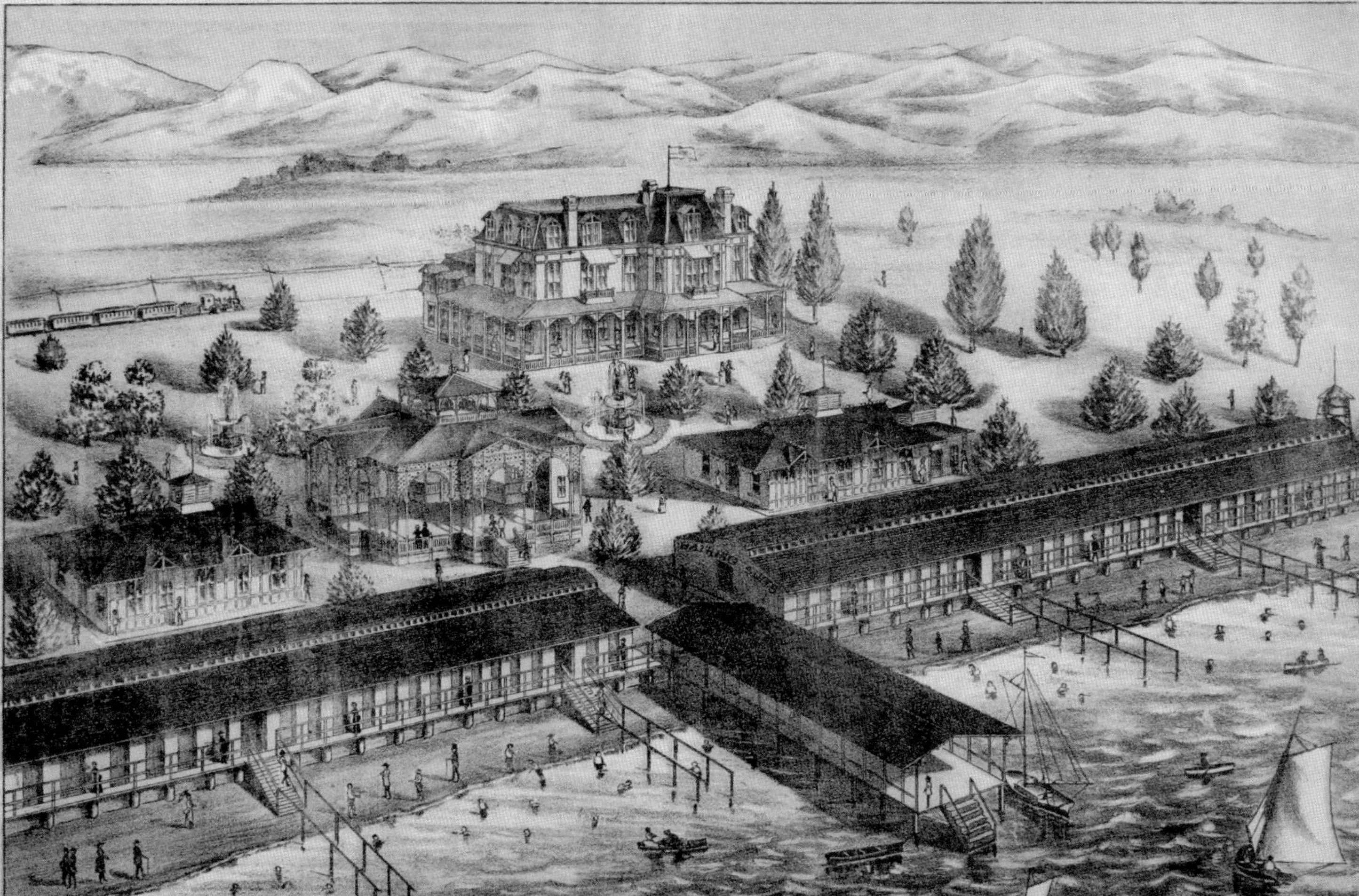

Aug. Gast Bank-Note & Litho. Co., St. Louis & N. Y.

LAKE PARK BATHING RESORT, GREAT SALT LAKE.

DENVER & RIO GRANDE WESTERN RAILWAY.

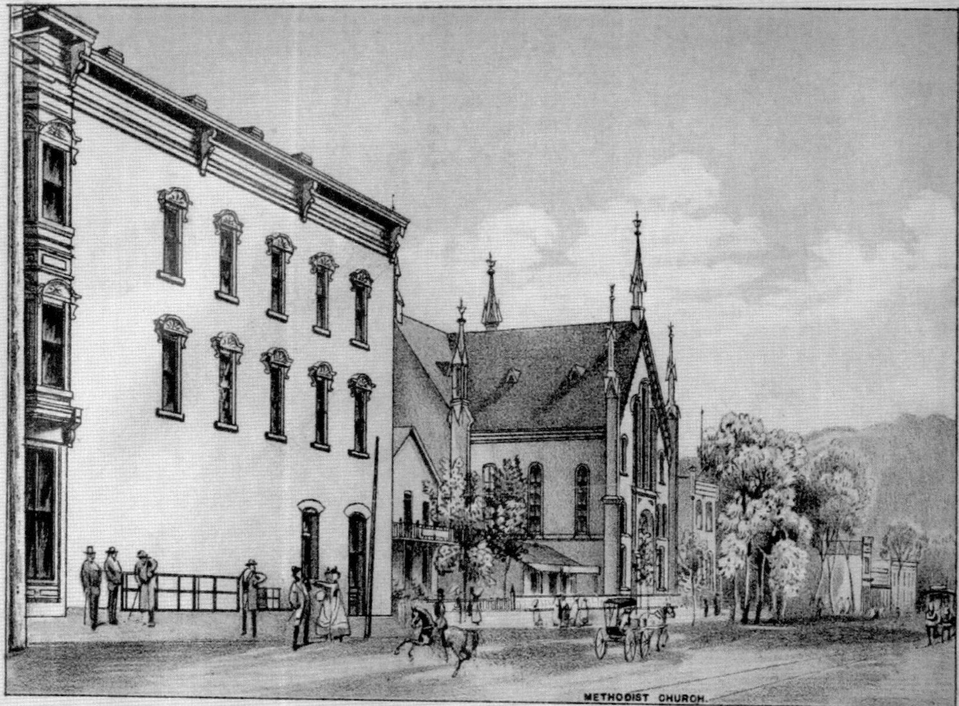

THIRD SOUTH STREET, FROM MAIN LOOKING EAST.

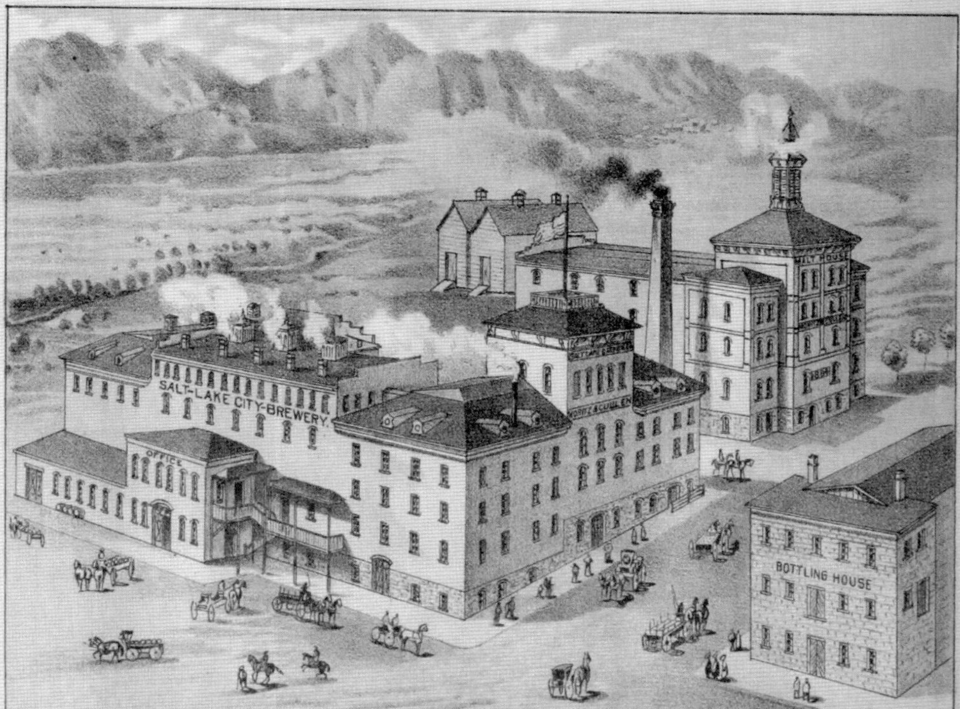

SALT LAKE CITY BREWERY.

boots and shoes, and freight again paid on their inward trip; so also with the larger portion of harness used here. So, likewise, with our clothing and blankets. The Provo Woolen Mills and the Deseret Woolen Mills have proven the practicability of converting some grades of our home-raised wool into goods and material equal to, if not better than, any imported. The list of practicable necessities which might be manufactured or supplied by our home markets, could cover nearly all the staple imports, viz: butter, candles, pickles, nails, crockery ware, cement, paints, white lead and lead pipe, and many other things, the material for the production of which is always with us. We call the attention of our capitalists to this important matter, as it will prove a material saving in time and expense, giving employment to quite a number of people and bringing a large sum of money into circulation. We have almost equally good water power as the New England States manufacturing districts, within a very few miles of this city; a new market and one that grows steadily year by year. Salt Lake City, has, within it the Deseret University—the State school—governed by a Chancellor and Board of Regents, first organized in 1850, and incorporated by the Legislature, having but a nominal existence until 1869. At that time, D. O. Calder, now deceased, having been placed in charge of the institution, its true value was demonstrated, and subsequently Dr. J. R. Park has worked so energetically that it has taken a place in the front rank of our educational institutions. A normal class is sustained there by appropriation of the Legislature, to which each county is entitled to send a proportionate number of students for tuition, free of charge, with the design of preparing competent teachers for the district or public schools throughout the Territory. There is a department of the Deseret University for deaf mutes—for the training of these unfortunates and teaching them the elementary branches of a common school education. There are in the city twenty-one public or District Schools. These are partly free, a portion of the tuition fee being paid by a Territorial school tax of three mills on the dollar, apportioned *pro rata* according to the school population in each district. The teachers are supplied principally from the normal class of the Deseret University. Utah, being a Territory, has no benefit of the revenue derivable from school lands. Mission work by denominational churches has been done, and the result is a general healthy showing, comparing favorably with many of the older States, the percentage of illiteracy being the same as that of Massachusetts, according to the educational statistics given in the census of 1880. St. Mark's school was established in 1867, under the auspices of the Protestant Episcopal Church, by the Revs. George W. Foote and Thos. W. Haskins. It is organized on the plan of the public schools of the East, and has eleven grades with twelve teachers, furnishing the usual course of study of the common English branches, with mathematics, Latin and Greek, natural sciences, history and English literature in the high school department. Rowland Hall, a boarding school for girls, was opened in 1881, and grew out of a select parish school of St. Mark's Church, which was begun in 1871. Its purpose is to furnish a pleasant home with superior educational advantages both in the studies of a thorough academic course, and in music, painting and the modern languages. The Rev. G. D. B. Miller is the present head master of both schools, and the bishop of the diocese is responsible for their well-being. The Collegiate Institute, under the ægis of the Presbyterian Church, was founded by Prof. Coyner in 1875, now enrolling 305 students, prepares boys for the best Eastern colleges, and gives girls the average Eastern seminary education. It is so crowded that a new building is being planned. Professor Millspaugh, the successful superintendent, is a graduate of the University of Michigan and the Jefferson Medical College, Philadelphia. Hammond Hall (Salt Lake Academy), under the patronage of the New West Education Commission, has cost, with the grounds surrounding, over $30,000; it was organized in 1873, incorporated in 1878, and has a full corps of highly educated and experienced instructors. The academy has a well-selected library, excellent cabinets, and a flourishing reading room. The Commission has also other schools in different parts of the city; in the Tenth Ward is found the one known as the Phillips School. These are free, and many parents avail themselves of free schooling for their children; they are supported in great measure by the Congregational Churches of the United States, and are under earnest Christian teachers. The Commission has been in existence for seven years, and now has twenty-two schools and academies in Utah. New comers will find them equal to Eastern ones. Salt Lake Seminary is an outgrowth of the Methodist Episcopal Church, established in 1870, and is now growing in popular favor. St. Mary's Academy is a Catholic institution, the faculty of which is composed entirely of Sisters of the Holy Cross, and is looked upon as the most successful institution of the kind in the West. St. Joseph's School for boys is operated by the same faculty. All Hallows College, the result of the labors of Reverend Father Scanlan, is under the supervision of Reverend Father Blake. The Swedish Ev. Lutheran Zion's Church, corner of Second South and Fourth East Streets, was organized 1882 and the building erected in the Fall of 1885. Its dimensions are thirty-eight by sixty-six feet and will seat, when fully completed, 600 people. Owing to the fact that a majority of the Scandinavian population formerly belonged to the Lutheran Church, its work here is meeting with encouragement. Reverend J. A. Krantz is its present pastor. The church is also carrying on school work with the intention of having a Graded School at an early date. The Baptist School of Salt Lake was commenced in September, 1883, and completed in the Spring of 1884. It was located on the Church grounds, and cost $1,760. It was totally destroyed, with its contents, on the night of January 5th, 1887, and will probably be rebuilt the present summer. The school is continued in the Lecture Room of the church edifice. The Latter-Day Saints have recently started a denominational school, in the "Social Hall," which has grown remarkably in the short time of its existence, so much so, that another building—the one erected by Brigham Young, in which his large family was formerly educated—has been engaged, and is also used by the committee having the school in charge. The institution is sufficiently provided with funds, by those interested, to insure its permanent financial success. A building is now nearing completion, in the Eighteenth Ward, which is to be used as a Mission or independent school, by the residents of that Ward. Among the important institutions of the city are the hospitals, the use of which is necessitated by the hazardous lives of the workers in the mines and smelters. St. Mark's Hospital was organized in 1872, by the Rev. R. M. Kirby. It was begun in a small rented house; the number of patients treated the first year was 79, the number treated in 1886 was 963. The present building is owned by the association and is entirely paid for. In 1879 the association was incorporated, and since then has greatly increased its usefulness. Nearly 1,000 patients are treated every year, at an expense of $15,000. The money is collected from the miners in the Territory. On the payment of one dollar a month, a miner is assured of medical care, board and lodging until cured, and a decent burial in the case of his death. In 1886, there were but three deaths in nearly a thousand patients. The Rev. C. M. Armstrong is the present superintendent and treasurer. The Holy Cross Hospital was instituted and reared by the Catholics, at a cost of over $50,000. The Sisters have control of all its affairs. The Deseret Hospital, though not as extensive as the foregoing, is doing good work. The First Presbyterian Church, organized in 1871, has been under the pastoral care of Dr. McNiece since 1877. Notwithstanding many removals, its membership is steadily increasing, and its Sunday School has over 220 scholars. Since the recent extensive improvements, the church has an unusually attractive audience room. The Baptist Church was organized in August, 1883, and dedicated in March, 1884. The building cost $13,000, including the land. Rev. L. L. Wood is the present pastor, assisted by two lady missionaries who conduct two mission schools in the city. Mr. Wood is also the editor and proprietor of the *Baptist Mountaineer*, a monthly organ of the Baptist Church. St. Paul's Chapel was begun early in the year 1880, and the building was consecrated March 13th, 1881. Since then, services have been held regularly. In 1882 a parsonage was built, and the building of a schoolhouse is in contemplation, in which the Sunday school will meet and a select school for boys and girls will be opened. The present pastor is the Rev. C. M. Armstrong. The Jewish congregation, presided over by M. C. Phillips, has a neat yet commodious Synagogue, which is also used for school purposes. The Deseret Woolen Mills are located about four miles southeast of the city, and, in 1886, they manufactured into flannels, yarns and linsey sheetings, over 200,000 pounds of wool. The Company also runs a knitting factory, employing about thirty machines in the manufacture of various woolen goods. The Company has money and determination to increase its facilities for manufacture as fast as the demands of the country require it. It has already acquired a flattering mercantile reputation. Messrs. Luke & Sherlock also operate twenty-two knitting machines, and William Pearson eleven machines. The Utah Soap Manufacturing Company produced, in 1886, over 140,000 pounds of laundry and 100,000 pounds of toilet soaps, and have introduced the manufacture of sal soda, having a capacity of 150 barrels per month. During the past year, 150,000 fire brick were turned out, and thirty tons of plaster of Paris made from gypsum from the quarries near Nephi. Elias Morris takes the lead in this specialty. There are three marble works doing a good business in monumental marble and granite work, the value of the labor alone amounting last year to $23,500. The Utah Cracker Factory report the business done by them last year as reaching $60,000. Paper boxes for the manufacturers of shoes, millinery, soap and jewelry were made to the value of $4,500. The product of the silk looms last year aggregated $4,000—the silk being partly home raised. Of the breweries it may be said that last year the Salt Lake City Brewery sold 20,000 barrels of beer; Margetts' Brewery, 770 barrels of ale and beer; Fischer's Brewery, 7,500 barrels; Wagener's California Brewery, 9,150 barrels. In the foundry and machine shops, Davis, Howe & Co. turned out work aggregating $60,000; the Salt Lake City Foundry & Manufacturing Company, $22,000; Silver Iron Works, over $10,000, and the Eagle Foundry $20,000. Zion's Co-operative Mercantile Institution Shoe Factory employs 130 hands, and during past the year manufactured goods to the value of $148,093. Connected with this factory is the manufacture of overalls—the business done aggregating $43,000. The same association also operates a tannery, the product of which was valued at $20,000. Summerhayes & Co. report the value of the product of their tannery at $45,000. The shoe factory of Solomon Bros. & Gold, turned out goods to the value of $60,000. Sam Levy manufactured 350,000 hand-made cigars. Salt Lake Vinegar Company 50,000 gallons of vinegar. There was collected on the Great Salt Lake last Summer, 100,000 tons of salt, a large portion of which was used in the smelters and mills. The Marion Manufacturing Company has started the manufacture of stamped goods in tin, copper and ironware, and arrangements are said to have been made to make tools, screw-dies, taps, etc. The Salt Lake Glass Works, though started only a year ago, runs four pots and nine annealing furnaces constantly in the manfacture of bottles and fruit jars. The product of the eight months prior to December being $29,000. The furniture factories furnish the following amounts as being manufactured here: H. Dinwoodey, $28,245; Sorenson & Carlquist, $10,000; Co-operative Furniture Company, $16,000. The Provo Woolen Mills supplied to the market goods to the value of $180,000, $120,000 worth being sold in this city, and with the facilities of the mills the product could easily have

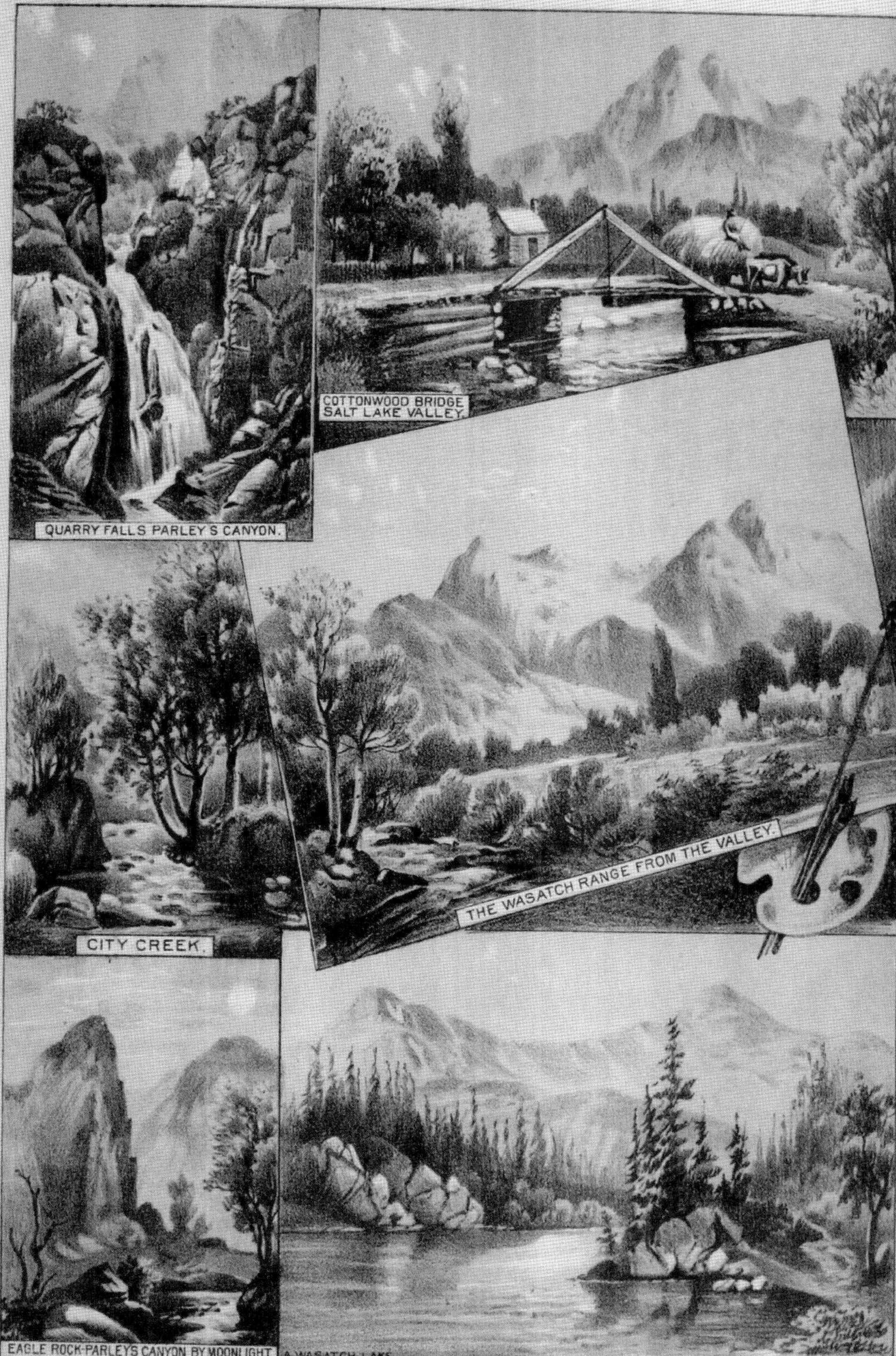

QUARRY FALLS PARLEY'S CANYON.

COTTONWOOD BRIDGE SALT LAKE VALLEY.

CITY CREEK.

THE WASATCH RANGE FROM THE VALLEY.

EAGLE ROCK-PARLEYS CANYON BY MOONLIGHT

A WASATCH LAKE.

From paintings by H.L.A.CULMER.

SCENES NEAR SALT LAKE CITY.

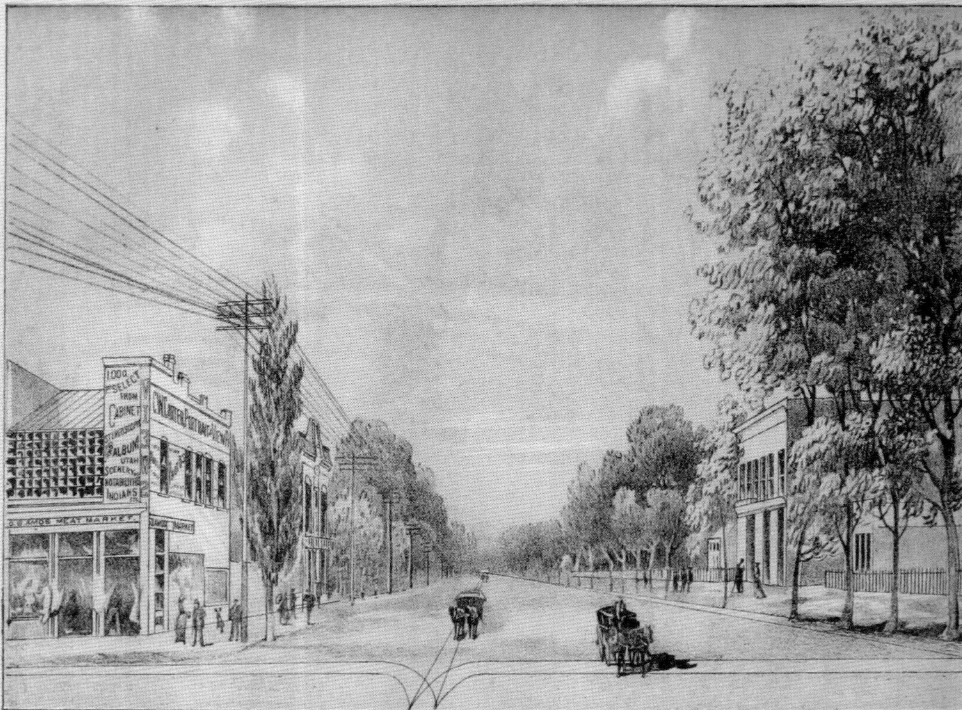

MAIN ST. FROM THIRD SOUTH, LOOKING SOUTH.

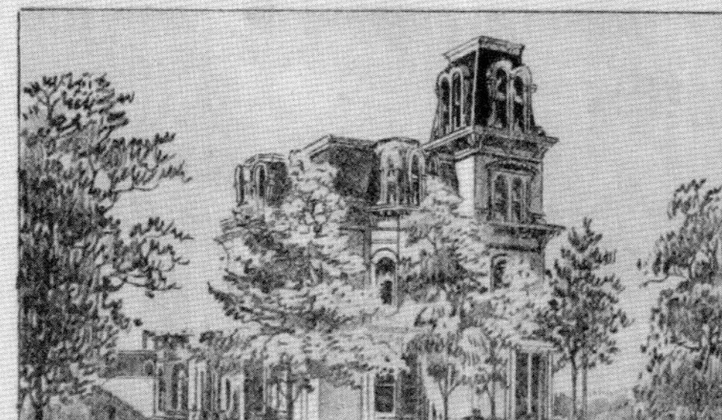

GARDO HOUSE.

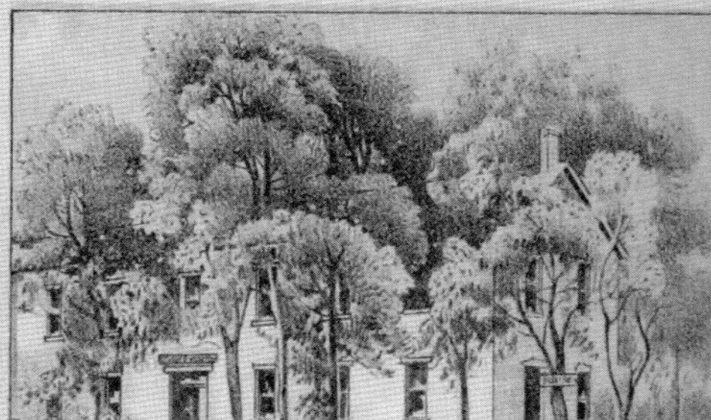

DESERET HOSPITAL.

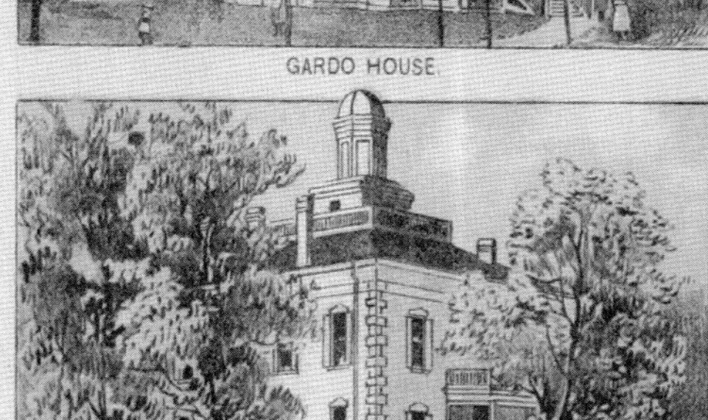

COUNTY COURT HOUSE.

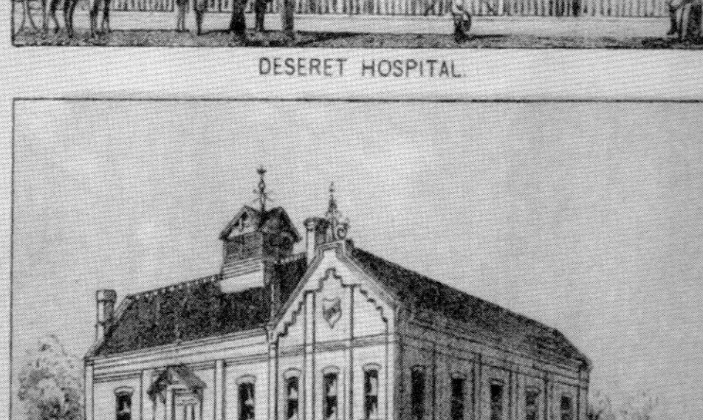

TENTH DISTRICT SCHOOL.

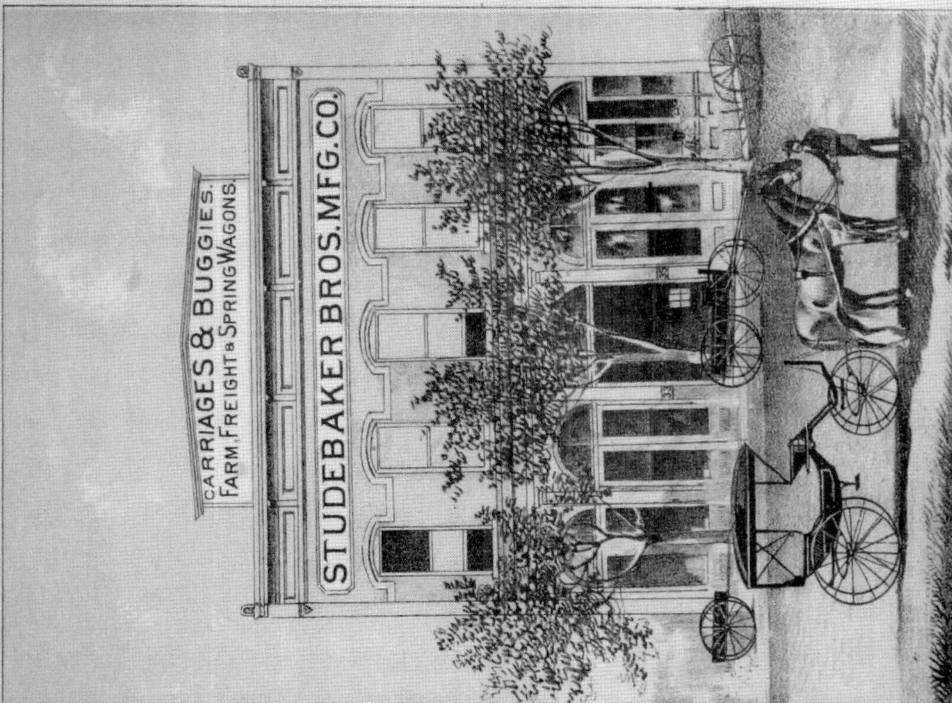

STUDEBAKER BROS. MFG. CO. CARRIAGE AND WAGON REPOSITORY.

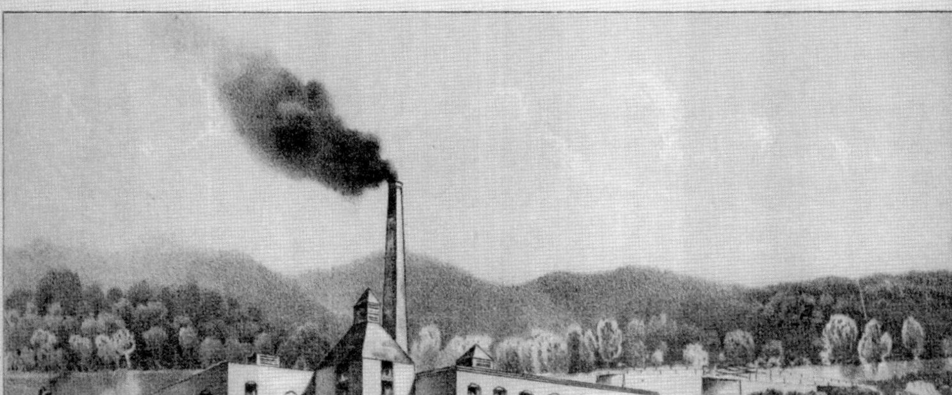

A. FISHER'S BREWERY.

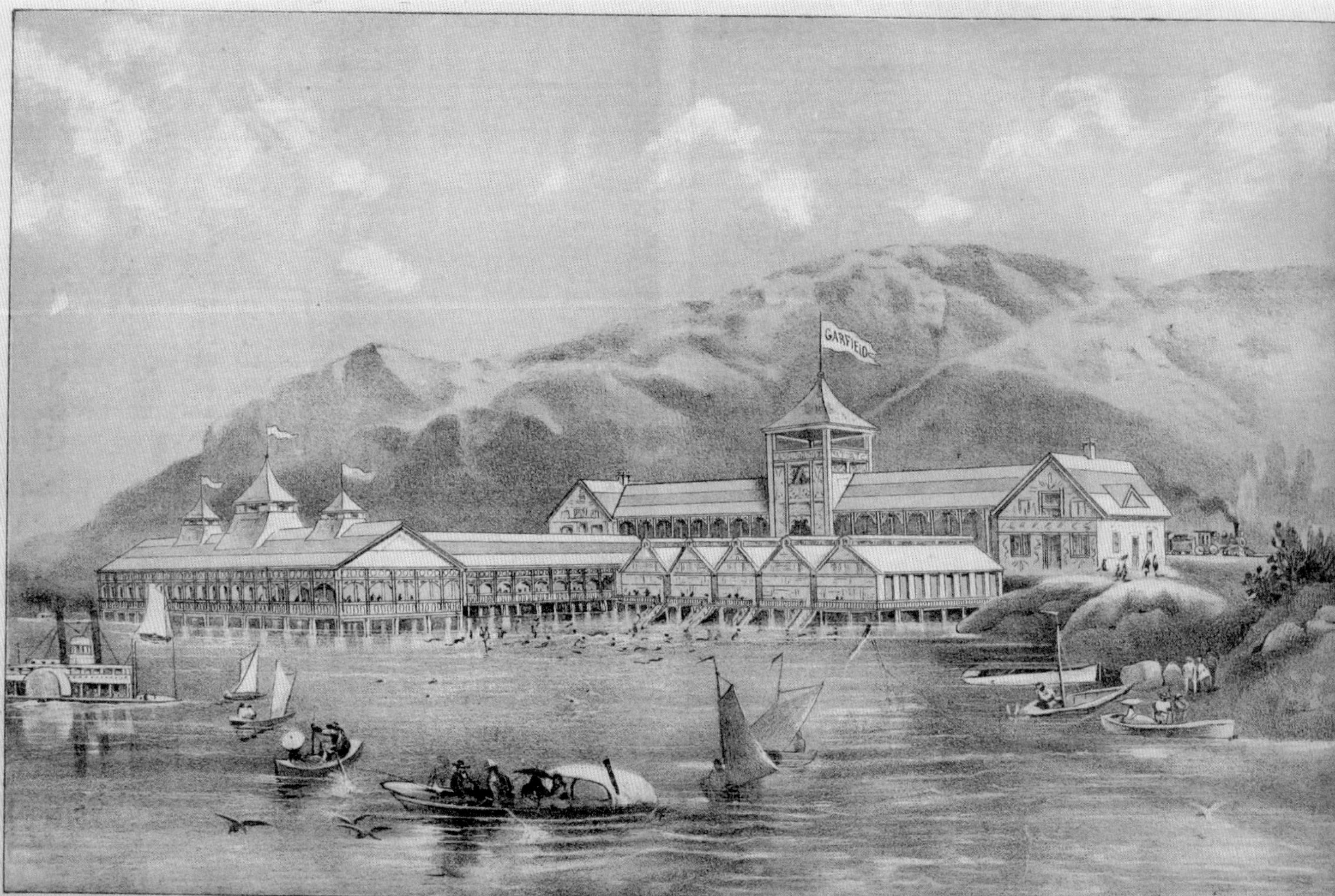

GARFIELD BEACH BATHING RESORT, GREAT SALT LAKE.

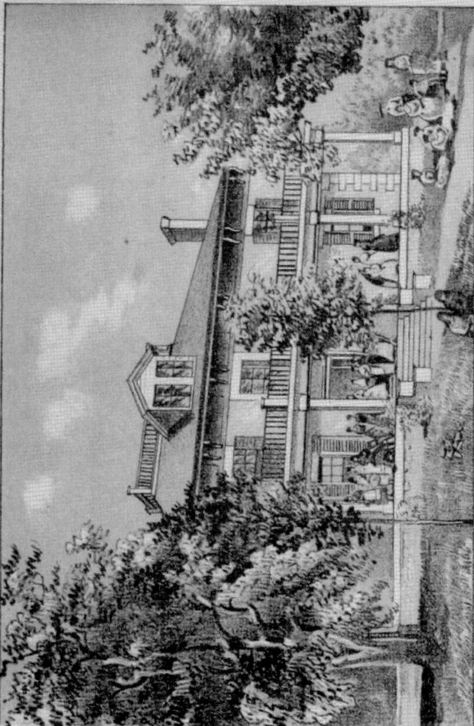

ROWLAND HALL

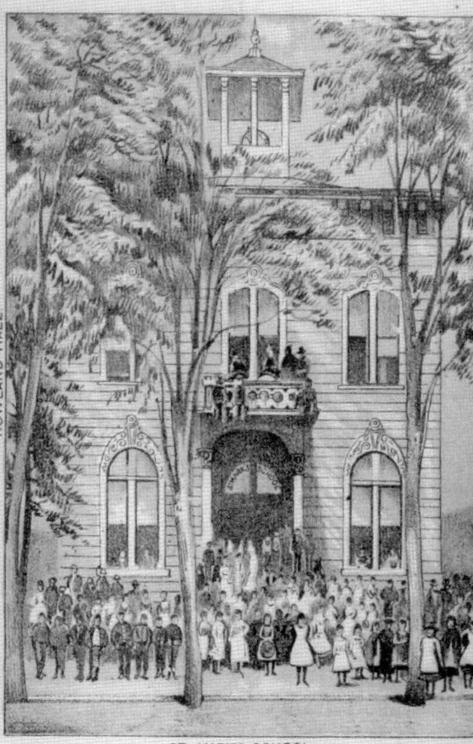

ST. MARK'S SCHOOL.

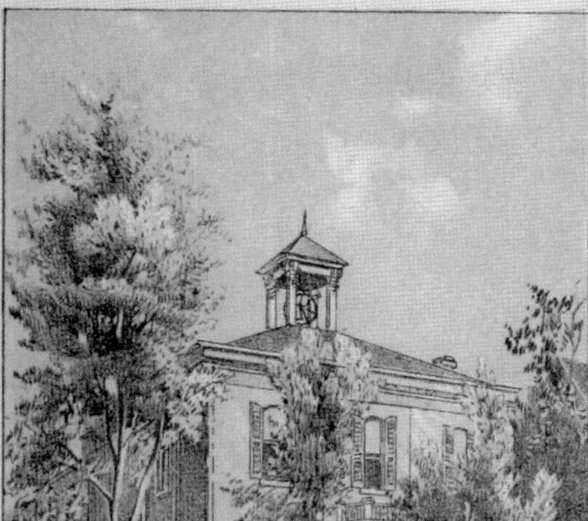

COLLEGIATE INSTITUTE.

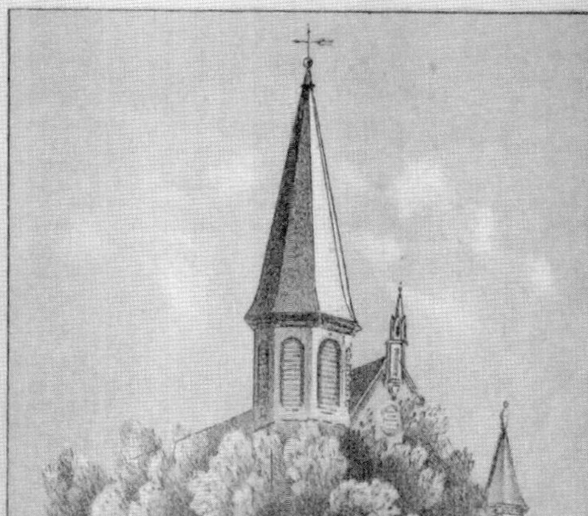

PRESBYTERIAN CHURCH.

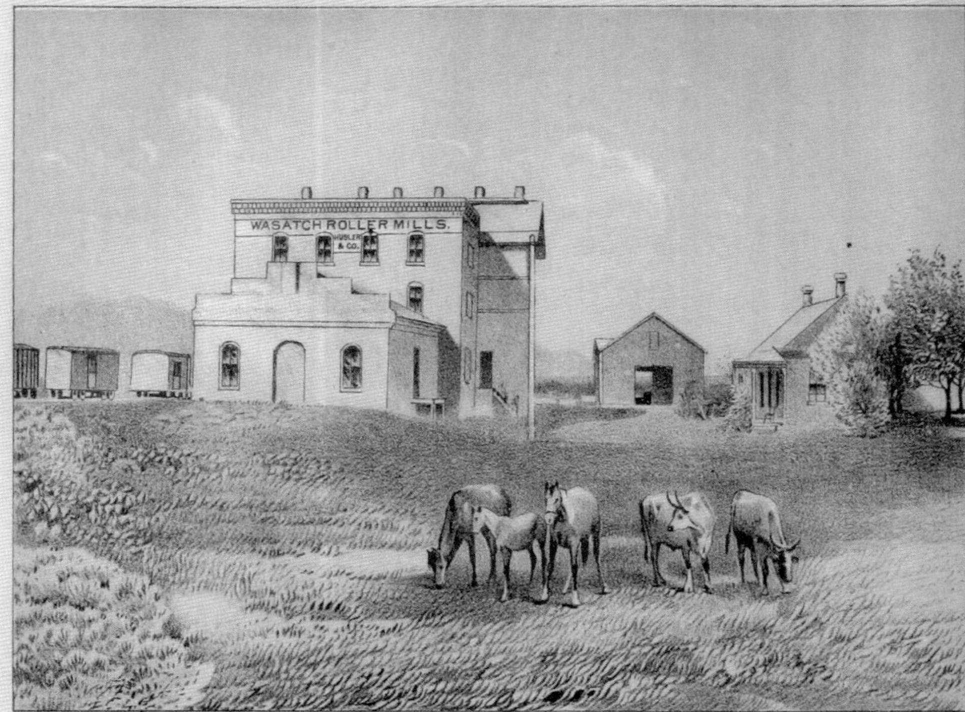

HUSLER & CO.'S FLOUR MILL.

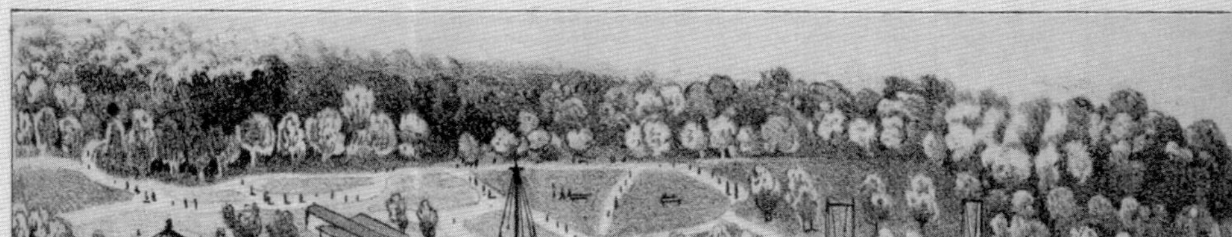

FULLER'S HILL.

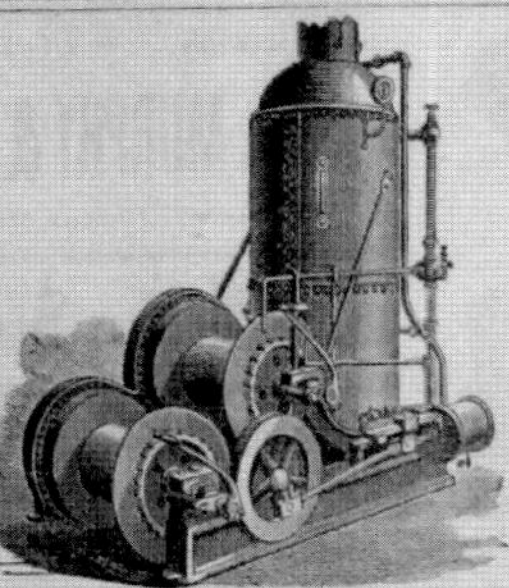

C. P. MASON, *President.* A. M. GRANT, *Superintendent.* T. J. ALMY, *Sec'y and Treas.*

The EAGLE FOUNDRY & MACHINE CO.

Iron ✦ Founders ✦ and ✦ Machinists

FURNACE, MINING, MILLING AND CONCENTRATING MACHINERY.

Wall's Rolls, Iron Fencing & Cresting.

SPECIAL ATTENTION GIVEN TO THE ERECTION OF MACHINERY OF ANY DESCRIPTION.

CORNER WEST TEMPLE AND SECOND SOUTH STREETS.

SALT LAKE CITY.

JOBBING & REPAIRING WORK OF ALL KINDS. P. O. Box 485. Orders from Abroad Solicited. Telephone 314.

The Salt Lake Tribune

DAILY AND WEEKLY,

SALT LAKE CITY.

Most Enterprising and Wide-awake Journal in the Mountain Country.

Larger Circulation than all the other Utah papers combined.

It prints, besides the Regular Telegraphic Report, as much more of Specials.

The best Advertising Medium in the Interior.

The great Non-Mormon Paper.

The Voice of Loyalty and Liberality crying in a Dense Wilderness.

Editorial page unequalled. All Departments unsurpassed.

DAILY, per year, $12. WEEKLY, per year, $3.

ADVERTISING RATES ON APPLICATION.

SUPERB JOB OFFICE.

EMPIRE MEAT MARKET

WHOLESALE AND RETAIL BUTCHER

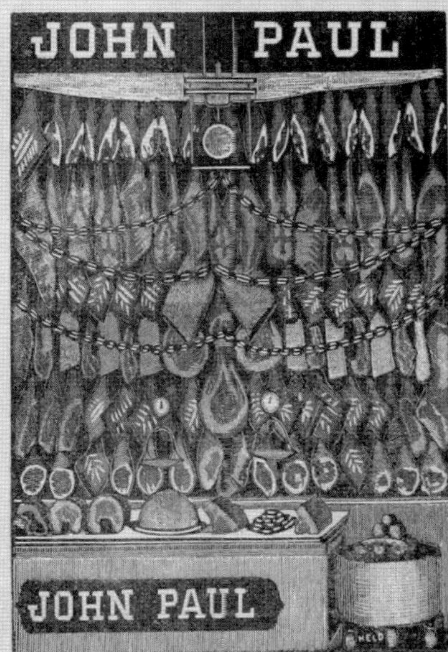

DEALER IN All Kinds of LIVE STOCK

COR. COMMERCIAL AND FIRST SOUTH STREETS,

Telephone 66. SALT LAKE CITY. P. O. Box 1086.

SALT LAKE IRON, LIME & ROCK CO.,

P. O. Box 973. **F. A. PASCOE, Sole Agent.** TELEPHONE 270.

OFFICE AND DEPOT: 108 W. FIRST SOUTH STREET, and 70 S. WEST TEMPLE STREET.

SALT LAKE CITY, UTAH.

Quarry & Kilns, near Brain's Brickyard, just North of Popper's Field.

MAKE NO PURCHASES

—OF—

H. N. GREENE,

THE

Real Estate and Loan Agent

Notary Public & Conveyancer,

At 161 S. MAIN ST. (Under T. R. Jones & Co.'s. Bank),

SALT LAKE CITY, - - UTAH,

Unless you Want Value Received for your Money.

NON-RESIDENT INVESTMENTS A SPECIALTY.

Eastern References given on Application.

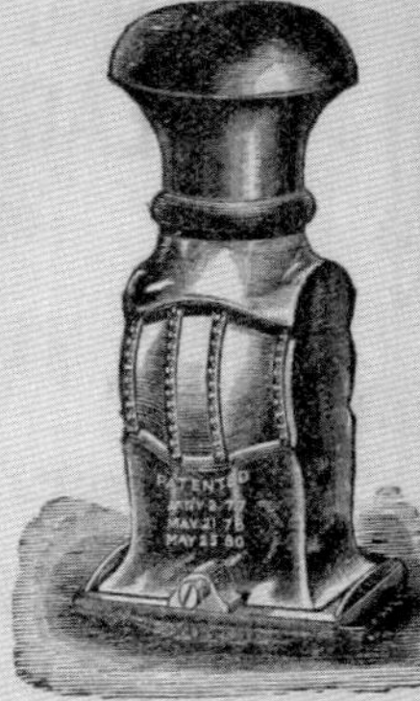

J. C. MURPHY. C. W. CAFFALL.

J. C. MURPHY & CO.

MANUFACTURERS OF

Fine Rubber Stamps

American Pat. Printing Wheels,

SELF-INKING, DATING, POCKET AND PENCIL

—STAMPS.—

ALL THE LATEST NOVELTIES.

218 S. MAIN STREET,

P. O. BOX 456. Salt Lake City.

BLACK OIL CAUSTIC BALSAM.

The Most Wonderful Healing Medicine ever Discovered, for Man and Beast.

EXTERNAL

VETERINARY USE,

FOR

Flesh Wounds,
Burns and Scalds,
Grease Heels,
Harness Galls,
Cracked Teats,
Piles,
Fistulas,
Thrush,
And All Sores that require Healing.

IT HAS NO EQUAL.

No Stable or Household is Complete without it.

It is pronounced by all who have used it to be so much superior to all others that there is no comparison.

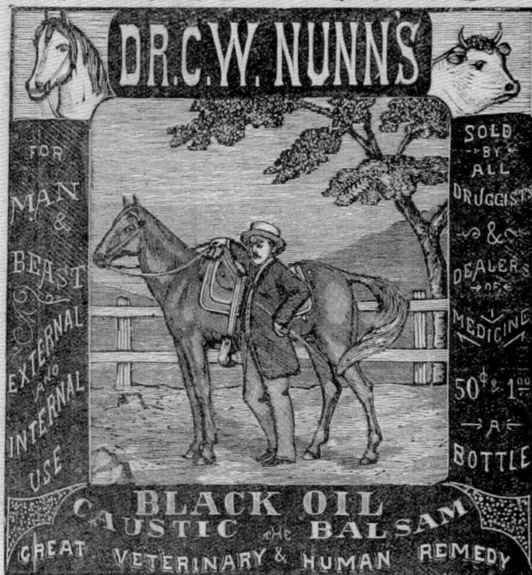

INTERNAL

HUMAN USE,

FOR

Kidney and
Bladder Affections,
Cough,
Croup,
Whooping Cough,
Sore Throats,
Diptheria,
Constipation,
Piles,
And all Pulmonary Affections.

The only Remedy yet found that will cure Bright's Disease.

AGENTS WANTED EVERYWHERE.

Ask your Druggist to Order it for you if he does not have it in Stock.

TELEPHONE NO. 358. ***DR. C. W. NUNN, V. S., Veterinary Pharmacy, 71 W. First South St., Salt Lake City.***

GETTING TO THE FRONT.

JAMES W. EARDLEY

DEALER IN

LUMBER, LATH, PICKETS, SASH, DOORS, BLINDS

MOULDINGS AND OTHER BUILDING MATERIAL.

340 First East St. (State Road), Half Block north of 8th Ward Square,

Telephone 113 **SALT LAKE CITY.**

Salt Lake Vinegar Co.,

J. W. MAXFIELD, - MANAGER.

—Manufacturers of—

PURE MALT & WHITE WINE VINEGAR

157 First East St., between First and Second South,

P. O. Box 657. **SALT LAKE CITY, UTAH.**

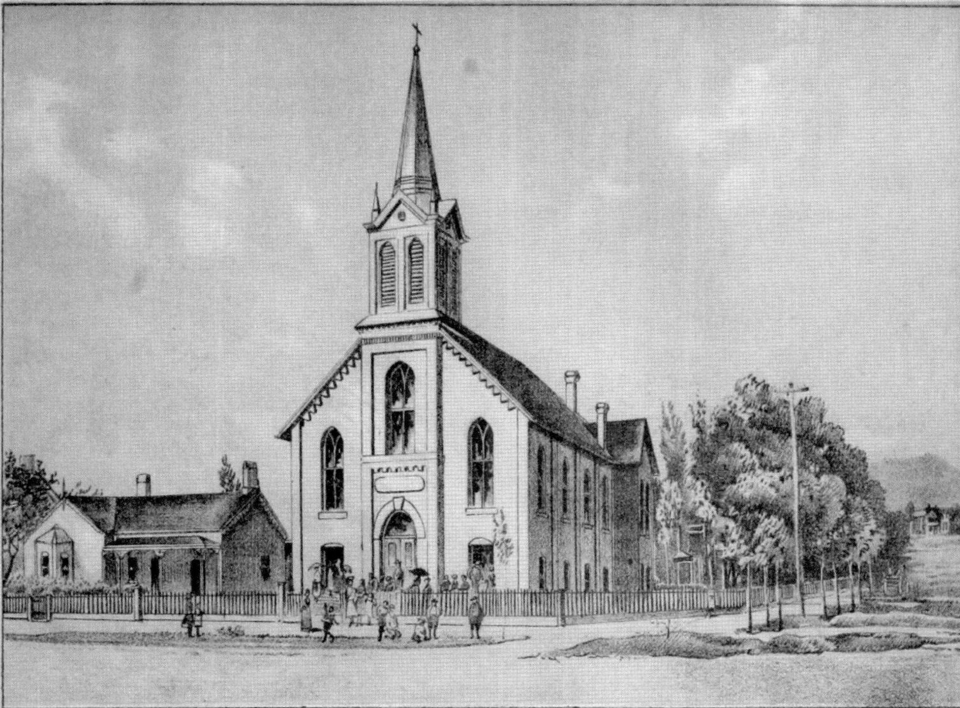

SWEDISH EVANGELICAL LUTHERAN CHURCH.

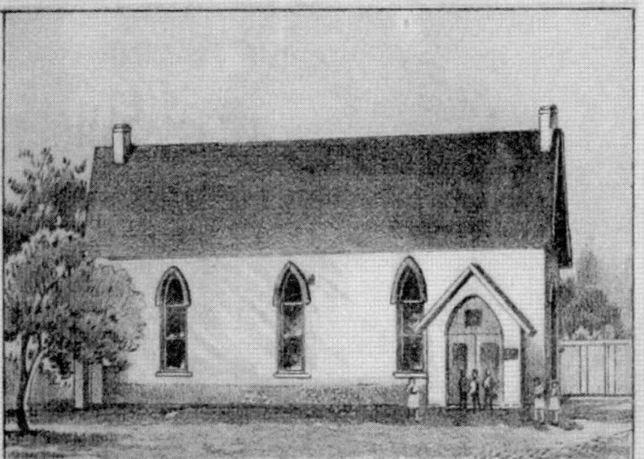

CONGREGATIONAL CHURCH.

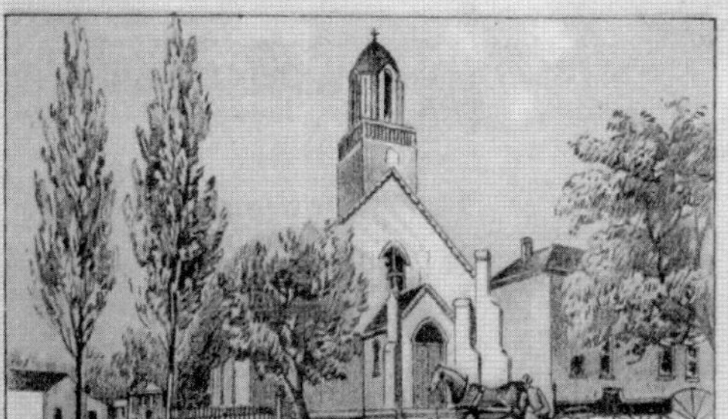

CATHOLIC CHURCH.

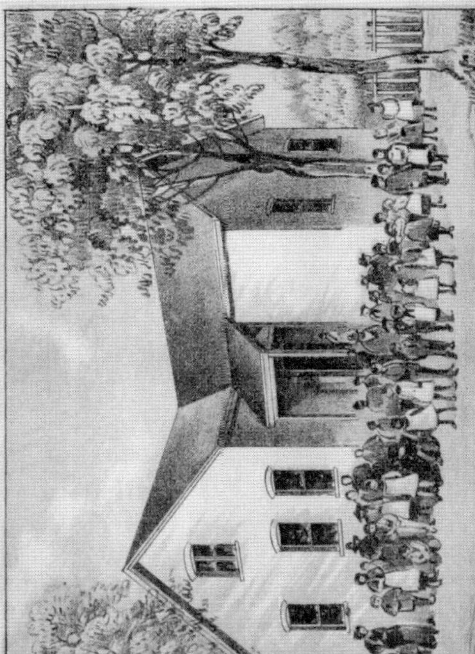

PHILLIP'S SCHOOL, TENTH WARD.

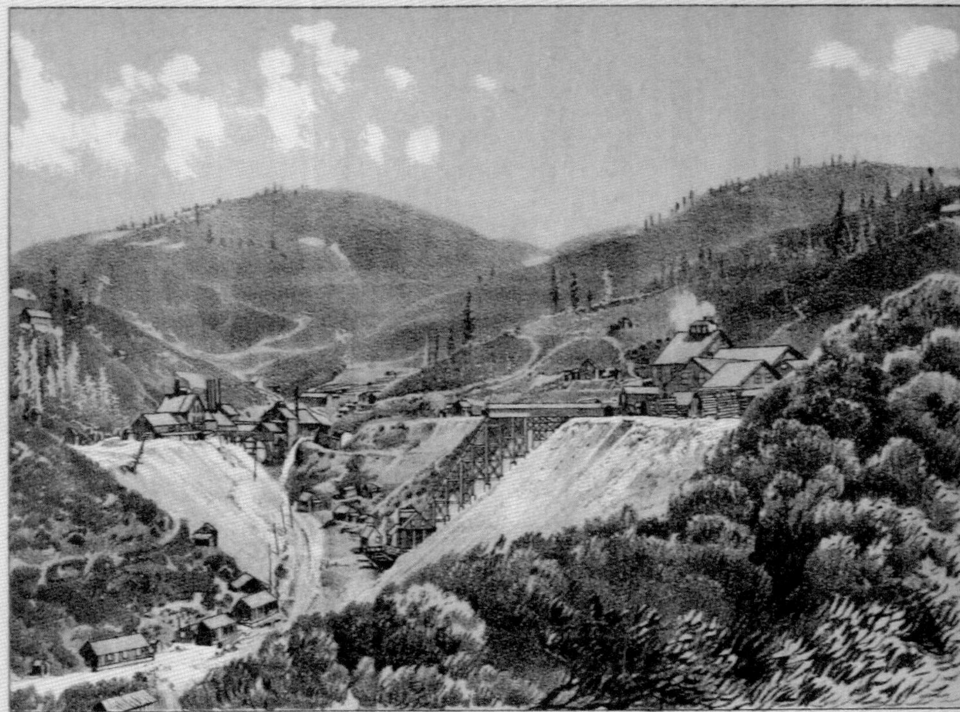

ONTARIO MINE, PARK CITY.

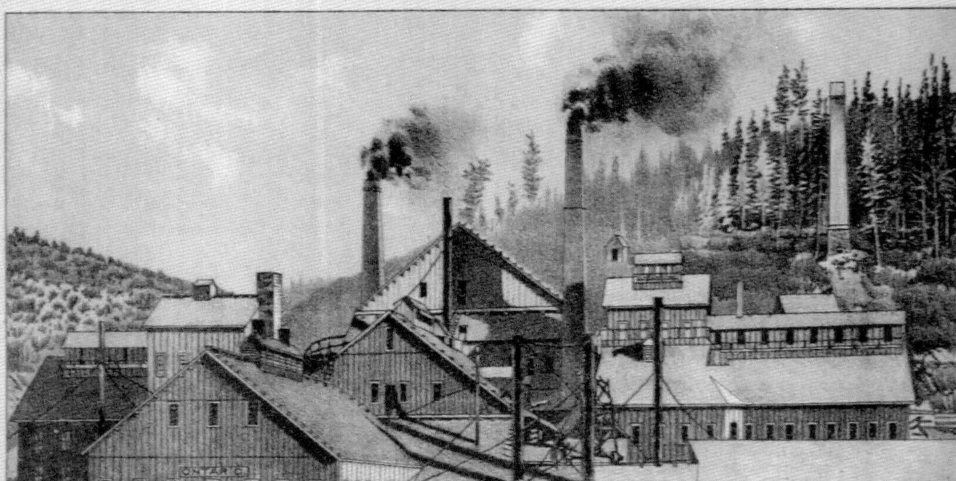

ONTARIO MILL, PARK CITY.

been made to reach double this amount. The company used 400,000 pounds of wool, and shipped 250,000 pounds of the grades not used in this mill to the East. The value of confectionery made was $89,840. Trunks and sample cases valued at $11,000; show-cases, $17,700. Of lime rock there was 30,172 tons quarried for fluxing purposes, fifty cords for building, and 60,000 for making lime. The value of "Valley Tan Remedies," medicines, manufactured by C. E. Johnson, was $4,000. The Deseret Paper Mills manufactured print, wrapping and book papers to the value of $30,000; it is run only part of the time at present. Salt Lake City also boasts of one of the best and largest soda water works in the country, belonging to Denhalter & Sons, who own the finest generator ever sent to the West. The Pioneer Roller Mills consumed 3,600,000 pounds of wheat, and Husler & Co., 10,230,000 pounds. The lumber used during the past year aggregated nearly seven hundred carloads, each car load averaging eleven thousand feet. This amount is in addition to the amount of native lumber used. The manufacture of millinery goods amounted to $35,000; harness and saddles, $150,000. The exports were: Wheat, 12,000,000 pounds; oats, 200 car loads; barley, 500 car loads; lucerne, 1,000 tons; potatoes, 10,000,000 pounds; rye, twenty car loads; sheep pelts, $30,000; hides, $65,000; flint deer hide, 25,000 pounds; buckskin, 10,000 pounds; poultry, $20,000; eggs, $225,000; honey, $16,000; dried fruits, $60,000. The Germania Lead Works has been successful in the manufacture of lead pipe and white lead, made from the ore mined in the neighborhood. Then also, paint is made at Provo, an excellent quality, and a ready market is found here for it. Besides these, there are an infinitude of articles of a domestic nature that are of general manufacture, but regarding which statistics are not available. These include brooms, hats and caps, carpets, yarns, stockings, cements, glue, brushes, willow ware, artificial flowers, strawbraid, coke, brick and adobies, wagons and carriages, crockery and pottery ware, etc. Utah has nearly driven out competition and stopped importation, by the acknowledged excellence of one article produced, viz: the manufacture of cheese. There is scarcely a branch of industry known in the world, which depends upon mineral resource, which can not be inaugurated here with the assurance of the existence of resources that twenty generations will never see indications of being exhausted. It has been said of the Great Salt Lake basin, which forms the larger part of Utah: "The entire basin is a vast laboratory of nature, where all the primitive processes have been carried out, on a scale so vast, as to make man's dominion, at first sight, seem forever impossible." The Salt Lake Chamber of Commerce was organized in April, 1887, for the following purposes, viz: To stimulate and to promote the growth of this Territory; to develop its agricultural, fruit growing and mining interests; its banking and brokerage; its manufactories and arts; its stock and wool-growing, slaughtering and packing interests; its architecture and public improvements; its commercial education; and to organize and provide for a bureau of statistics in relation to manufacturing, mining, commercial, financial and industrial affairs of public interest and value. To correct trade abuses and to secure uniformity in commercial laws and customs; to harmonize and facilitate business intercourse; to arbitrate differences and disputes; to promote equity and to treat with railways in the interest of our commerce; and for representation in all other trade issues. Its officers are: President, W. S. McCornick; First Vice President, George A. Lowe; Second Vice President, Frank W. Jennings; Secretary, Hugh C. Wallace; Treasurer, Thomas R. Jones; Board of Directors—W. H. Remington, George A. Lowe, F. H. Meyers, F. W. Jennings, W. S. McCornick, J. C. Conklin, F. H. Auerbach, E. Kahn, James Glendinning, M. H. Walker, H. L. A. Culmer. The Chamber of Commerce will extend every reasonable aid and give hearty support to the starting of new manufactories and every enterprise which will promote the development of the resources of Utah or the building up of Salt Lake City. Facts, figures and information concerning the resources of the Territory, and the opportunity for investing capital, will be furnished upon application to the Secretary.

The following condensation of a circular issued by the Denver and Rio Grande Railway, in January of the present year, is an interesting and reliable presentation of our agricultural resorces:

Fair Utah wheat ranks in the East with the best No. 2 Red, which is the highest grade that appears in most of the Eastern markets. Our choicest qualities, raised under the most favorable conditions, are a unique product with scarcely an equal in America. A number of points in Colorado, especially Denver, are already buyers of our wheat this year, while some shipments have been made to Kansas City. Enquiries are also being made from California. Utah wheat has a brighter, larger kernel than that of the East, and though no handsomer than that of California, it is firmer and its nutriment more concentrated.

We have known parties who were keeping up work-horses, to pay 25 to 30 per cent. more for Utah oats of ordinary quality than for a fair grade of Eastern. This was a couple of years ago when cut rates of freight permitted the bringing in of Eastern oats. Nothing more conclusive can be said of the real value of our oats than this, which, after all, only represents current opinion among those who have tried both. Utah oats, therefore, command a stiff price and parties looking here for a supply should understand that in return for the comparatively high figure asked, the real feeding power of our grain is proportionately high. Utah oats have ranged in price during recent years from 1¼ to 1⅝ cents per pound on cars.

Usually, our barley is of magnificent appearance and probably fifty car loads of fine quality now remain here awaiting a market. It is of the white club variety for brewing purposes. In 1885, our brewing barley was exported in great quantities to St. Louis, Milwaukee, California and other points, where it invariably graded as fully up to the best Canadian brewing. Utah barley beer is advertised all over the Union, and signifies the highest attainable degree of merit. It is the use of this barley which gives Utah beer so high a standard. Indeed, our white club brewing barley will hold its own anywhere as a strictly fancy product. Besides this grade, Utah has for sale about a million pounds of mixed feed barley.

There are a few cars of rye annually offered here at figures usually ranging over one cent per pound. The quality is superb and the yield fair.

Utah does not pose as a corn country and rarely has any for export. The hot, sultry nights which corn requires are not characteristic of our climate. East of the Wasatch Mountains, however, along the line of the Denver and Rio Grande Western, especially at Green River, it is likely that corn growing will prove a considerable industry.

A special providence seems to have reserved this Territory for the cultivation of lucern, often called Alfalfa, which the farming people of Utah have learned to look upon as one of the greatest blessings that has yet been vouchsafed them. The best crops come from lands that cannot well be plowed because of their rough character. Excellent results have been had by merely clearing off the brush and casting the seed over such ground. It takes longer to get a good start this way, and irrigation is more difficult than if the ground were stirred up, but it thrives better in the end. Lucern will do well even on ground that is too steep for a mowing machine, if only sufficient water can be got on it to give it a start. Its average growth is about three feet, though we have known it to reach over six feet when left for seed. A serious drought may spoil the crop for the time being, but the following year it will come up as good as ever.

Utah is, par excellence, the country for lucern seed and from 300 to 400 tons are exported annually at prices varying from seven to eleven cents per pound.

We raise some Red and White Clover Seed but have little left beyond our own needs for export.

The Utah potato has a reputation for excellence all over America and even in Great Britain. Other climes have tried in vain to match our product but the attempt seems futile. For many years great quantities have been exported from this Territory, and it looks as if we shall continue to do so for all time to come. We have seen a lot of sixteen bushels that went throughout twelve potatoes only to the bushel. The King of the Early, Peerless and Compton's Surprise yield in favored localities about 400 bushels to the acre. With high cultivation, we have even heard of 1,000 bushels being raised to the acre.

Utah has also a fine reputation for carrots, which often yield, of good quality, as much as 1,200 bushels to the acre; also for onions, turnips, parsnips, radishes, etc. Beets thrive astonishingly well, and far-seeing men fortell that one day, the large tracts of low lying but now unwatered lands on the western side of this valley and elsewhere will be under cultivation to the Sugar Beet for the manufacture of sugar.

There is no reason why the cultivation of peanuts should not take its place as one of our foremost root products. It has been clearly demonstrated that our climate and soil are especially favorable to their growth, and every attempt that has been made—which was only on an experimental scale—has born out this idea.

Of green stuffs, we annually export large quantities of cabbage, cauliflower and celery, the latter growing exceptionally fine.

South of Utah Lake and in various other localities are grounds suitable to the growth of flax, which is native to our soil, and would pay well for cultivation.

Hops are also native to Utah, its trailing vines literally overrunning every other kind of foliage in many of our canyons. The picking of wild hops has yielded considerable pin-money to the country people, and Nature could not tell in plainer words that this is pre-eminently a region favorable to their cultivation.

The same causes which give excellence to the grains and vegetables of Utah, also stamp her orchard products with a high caste. Fresh fruits are exported in considerable quantities and, wherever sent, take the highest place and command the readiest sale. In general terms, the superior characteristics are firmness, beauty and, above all, fine flavor. Utah peaches are shipped, wrapped and unwrapped, in boxes of about twenty pounds each and find a ready market in Colorado and Idaho. Our peach trees thrive best on light loam and gravely soil.

The apple is now generally acknowledged to be more free from worms (codling moth) than for some years previous and thousands of boxes have been shipped East and North by parties in Ogden, Salt Lake, Provo, Springville and other places. It is probable that each succeeding year will see our apples freer from worms and that, in a few years, they will have disappeared altogether. By papering the apples and shipping in refrigerator cars they may be safely transported long distances late in the Fall. Green apples are a staple product of the Territory, and notwithstanding the heavy shipments made, the demand last season was not equal to the supply.

There are many fine plums raised in Utah; the growth of plums last season fell much short of our usual quantity and we were far from supplying the demand.

There is a sure demand for more good Utah pears than have yet been produced. There is a lack chiefly of early varieties of which we have few besides the Bartlett. Growers have paid over much attention to Winter pears, which ripen too late to secure favorable sale. They now realize the fact, and it is likely that future years will find a better supply of earlier kinds. The Utah pear is an extremely rich fruit.

In most seasons, Utah has a good crop of apricots for export, and cherries in limited supply, while grapes are in good quantity, but at points favorable for shipping are not

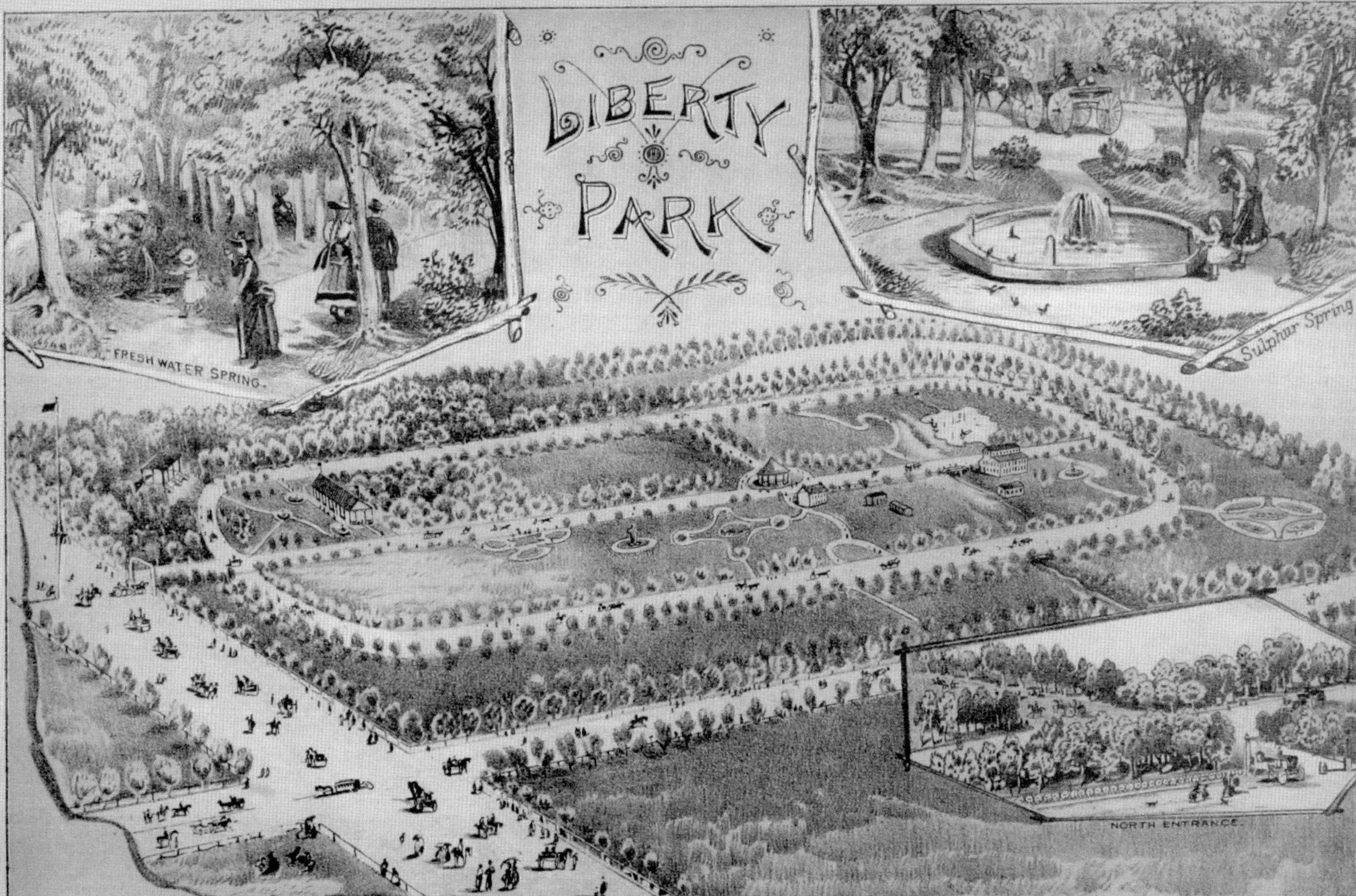

LIBERTY PARK.

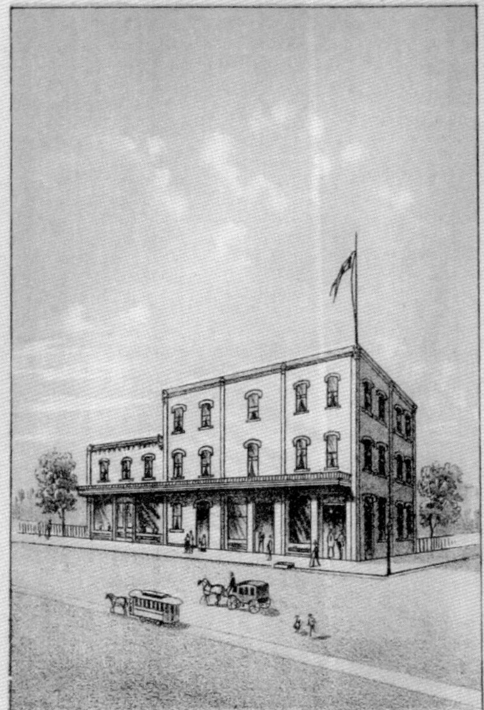

RAILROAD EXCHANGE HOTEL.

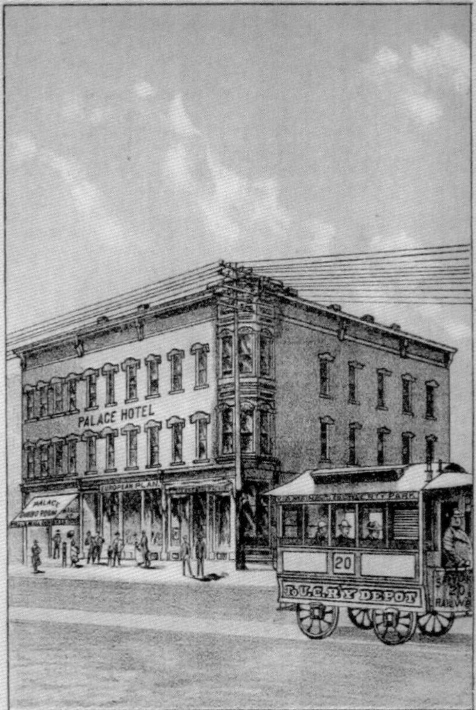

PALACE HOTEL.

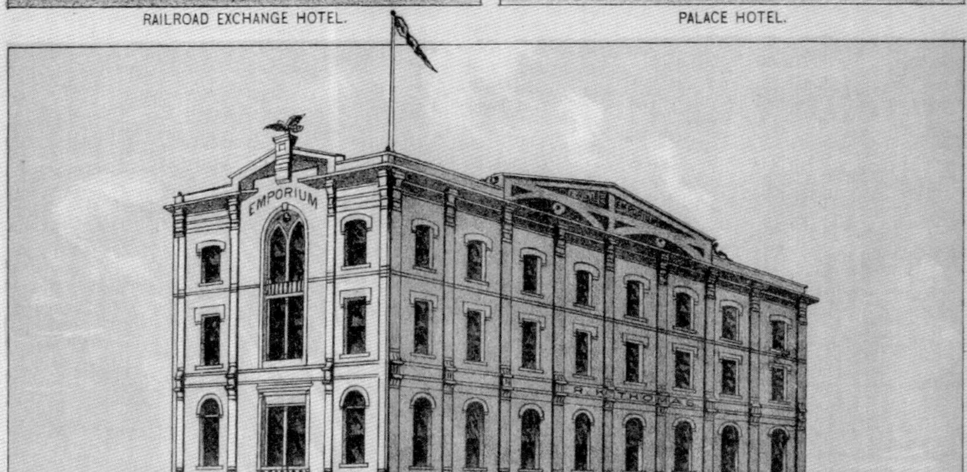

EAGLE EMPORIUM.

P. O. Box 973. **F. A. PASCOE,** Telephone 270.

108 W. First South Street, - Salt Lake City.

Manufacturers' Agent, Art Decorations and Builders' Supplies.

Sole Agents for the Celebrated Willesden (English) Waterproof Roofing, Lincrusta Hangings, Dadoes, Friezes and Mouldings, Encaustic and Fine Art Tiles, Wood Carvings and Mouldings, Picture Frames and Flower Boxes of Lincrusta and Wood Carvings in Gold, Etc.; Magic Window Screens.

Lime, Cement, Fire Brick, Fire Clay, Plaster of Paris, Building Rock, Terra Cotta Enrichments.

CAPS. AGENT FOR THE VULCAN POWDER CO. FUSE.

OFFICE: 218 California Street, San Francisco, Cal.

DWYER'S BOOK STORE,

76 MAIN STREET,

SALT LAKE CITY, UTAH.

The Oldest, Most Reliable and Leading Book and Stationery House in Utah.

Everything that is usually kept in a First-class Book Store can always be found at DWYER'S, at Lowest Wholesale and Retail.

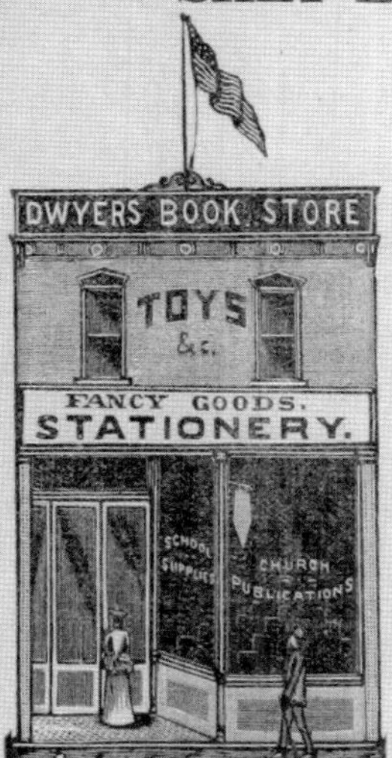

Souvenirs of Utah and Mormon Publications.

EDUCATIONAL : AND : SCHOOL : SUPPLIES

A SPECIALTY.

Orders from out-of-town Promptly Filled.

JOSEPH BAUMGARTEN,

THE

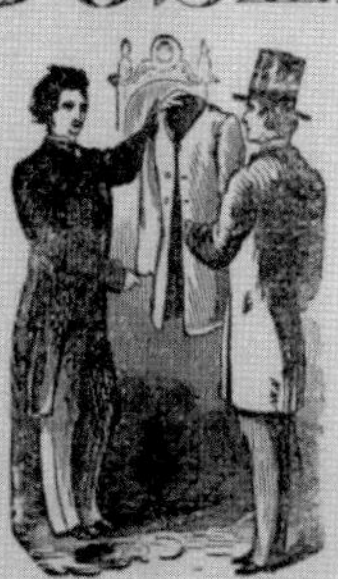

LEADING **TAILOR** FASHIONABLE

French, English and Scotch Cloths are of my Own Importation.

FIRST-CLASS WORK AND PERFECT FIT GUARANTEED.

111 MAIN ST., OPPOSITE EAGLE EMPORIUM

P. O. BOX 356. SALT LAKE CITY.

as handsome as those from California. In Southern Utah they raise beautiful grapes of fine rich flavor, the average yield per acre being 6,260 pounds, according to the latest data. Strawberries and raspberries are both native to Utah, as is the red and black currant. Under cultivation, the yield is very large and of surpassing quality.

Such is the wide reputation which Utah enjoys for the excellence of her dried fruits that they command a fancy price throughout the entire United States. In competition with the best Tennessee they bring in Chicago and other cities from two to four times the price. The cause is, of course, primarily the excellent quality of our fruits with its rich flavor; but we owe to the peculiarity of our climate the ability to sun-dry with such success. A third reason is the singular rapidity with which moisture evaporates in this region, enabling the drying process to take place rapidly in the day-time, while the absence of dew, prevents the back-sets during the night. Fruits dried by artificial processes lose part of their virtues, and it is doubtless whether much of it would be done were other climates as favorable as our own to sun-drying. Thus it is that Utah sun-dried fruits occupy a place by themselves in the markets of America. A fancy article, that has never yet been produced here in anything like the quantity that could be sold, is the Salt Lake peeled peach. There is nothing like it for fine flavor anywhere. It keeps well and commands twice or thrice the figure of the unpeeled. The apricots dried here invariably find a ready market, it being an exceptional year when they are not cleared out before Christmas. The price always ranks high and the fruit is a general favorite.

Sometimes as many as a hundred thousand pounds of plums find their way to this market. Attention is now being turned to the German prune for drying purposes, and these will probably be kept separate. The time is at hand when these will take the place of those imported and, in a few years, exports are sure to follow.

Very few dried pears have, so far, come to market. A very limited supply of nectarines have been brought in and quickly sold at a high price. This fruit is so fine in appearance and so rich in pulpy substance that its drying should be encouraged.

A novel product, which first occasions surprise and then finds great favor wherever introduced, is the dried ground cherry. This fruit is native here and has not been cultivated, to our knowledge. It grows only too freely for the farmers, however, as it spreads with great vigor. When scalded and dried, the fruit is of a beautiful, golden, cleanly sort, making excellent pies, sauce and preserves.

Dull times have apparently passed away, and are being succeeded by a spirit of renewed public confidence in the stability and resources of the city and Territory. Rumors are constantly afloat of railroads from the East and North, organizing and feeling their way hither, and corps of surveyors are scattered over all the surrounding country, seeking for the best routes, with this city as the objective point. Eastern and Western capitalists are investing in our real estate and our mines. Transfers of property in this city run up to $200,000, weekly, and the wise ones predict this as but the commencement of the glorious future which awaits our Garden City, the metropolis of the Rocky Mountain region.

Before leaving our beautiful City we urge upon visitors to take a look at it from the "Tourist's Tower" on Prospect Hill, as from this point can be obtained a satisfying view of the City and its entrancing surroundings, which can be compared with the view of Salt Lake City in 1853, printed with the reading matter in the front portion of this work; also to visit Rosebank Cottage, the pretty home of our townsman, Mr. Robert Dye; both of which places can be taken in on the route of a drive to the Fort.

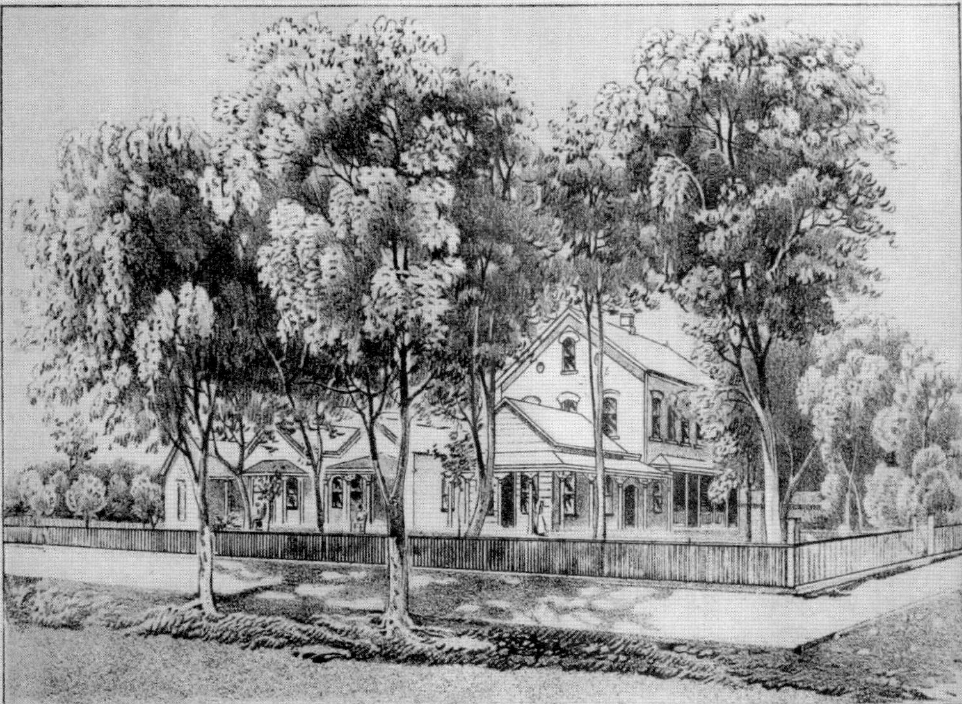

ST. MARK'S HOSPITAL.

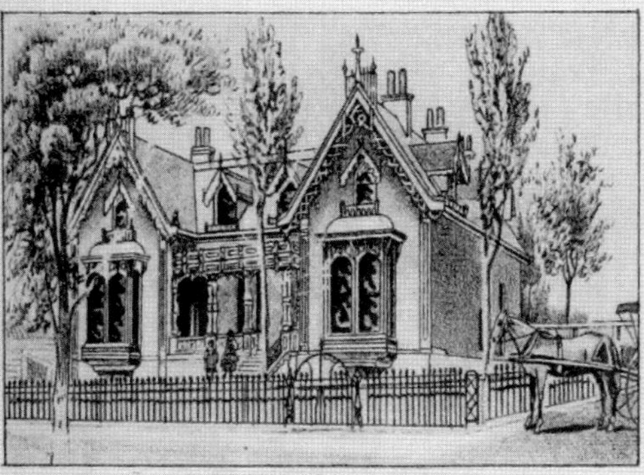

RESIDENCE OF W. S, GODBE.

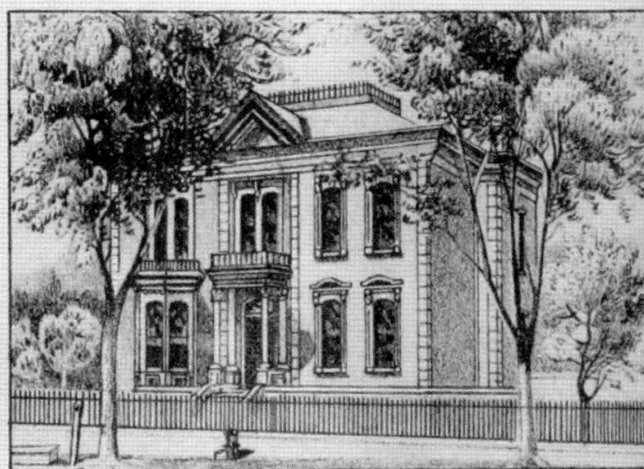

RESIDENCE OF MRS. JULIA A. KIMBALL

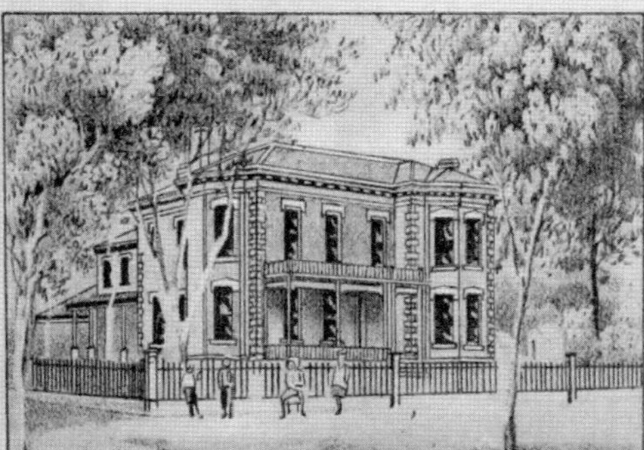

RESIDENCE OF WM. WHITE.

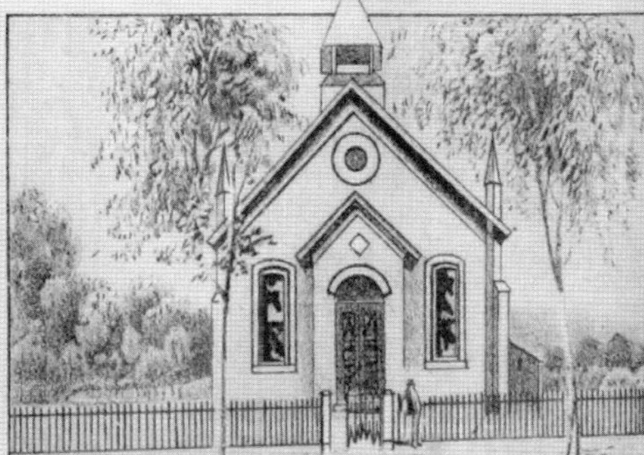

7th DISTRICT SCHOOL.

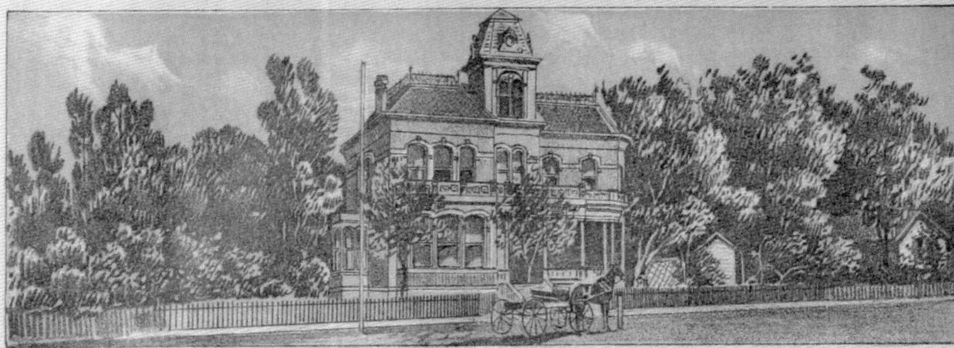

RESIDENCE OF FERD. DICKERT.

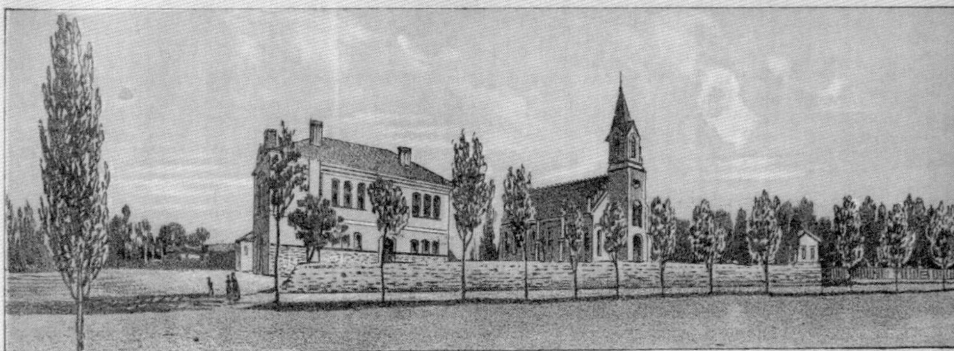

18TH WARD INDEPENDENT SCHOOL AND CHAPEL.

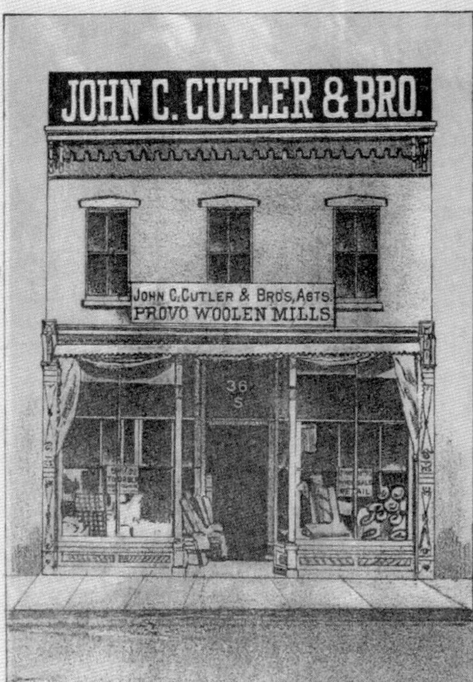

JOHN C. CUTLER & BRO.

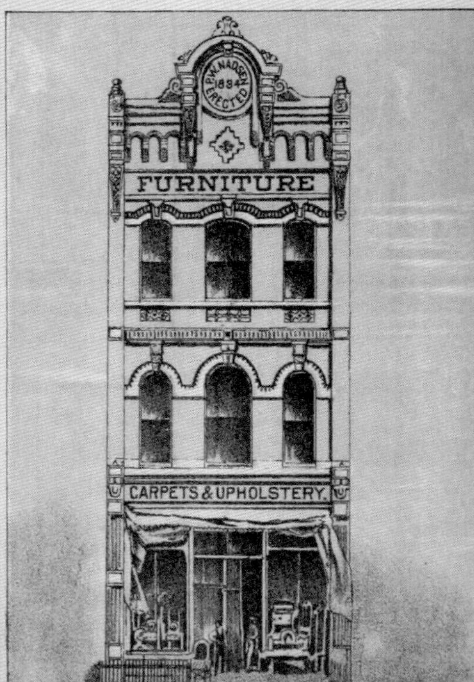

P. W. MADSEN'S STORE.

McCORNICK & CO.,

BANKERS

Salt Lake City, Utah; Hailey and Bellevue, Idaho.

Careful attention given to the Sale of Ores and Bullion. We solicit Consignments, guaranteeing the Highest Market Prices.

COLLECTIONS MADE AT LOWEST RATES.

Execute Orders for the Purchase or Sale of Stocks and Bonds at New York and San Francisco.

We sell Exchange and Telegraphic Transfers on leading Cities of the United States; also furnish Sight Drafts or Remit Funds to London, Dublin, Berlin, Copenhagen, Paris, Stockholm, and all other prominent point in Europe, at Lowest Rates of Exchange.

ACTIVE ACCOUNTS SOLICITED.

PRINCIPAL CORRESPONDENTS:

New York—Importers' and Traders' National Bank, Chemical National Bank, Kountze Brothers.
Chicago—Commercial National Bank.
St. Louis—States Savings Association.
Kansas City—National Bank of Kansas City.
Omaha—Omaha National Bank.
Denver—City National Bank, Denver National Bank.
Evanston, Wyo.—Beckwith & Co.
Helena, Mont.—First National Bank.
Butte, Mont.—First National Bank, Clark & Larabie.
Ogden—Commercial National Bank.
Hailey, Idaho—McCornick & Co.
Bellevue, Idaho—G. A. McCornick & Co.
Elko, Nevada—J. Henderson.
San Francisco—First National Bank, The Crocker Woolworth National Bank.
London, England—Martin & Co.

S. C. DALLAS. W. S. HEDGES.

Dallas & Hedges,

ARCHITECTS AND SUPERINTENDENTS

Deseret National Bank Building,

SALT LAKE CITY, UTAH.

TELEPHONE 359.

Real Estate.

Our List of Properties Can Not be Excelled.

J. M. KNOX & Co.

First Door West of Union Ticket Office,

SALT LAKE CITY.

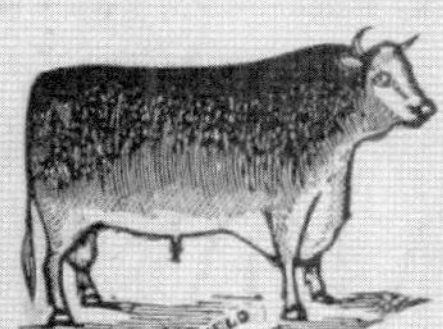

—Breeders of—

Half-breed Polled Angus Cattle

ALSO

Half-breed Hereford Cattle.

SCHOFIELD BROS.,

—Proprietors of—

THE PEOPLE'S MEAT MARKET.

Breeders of Spanish and

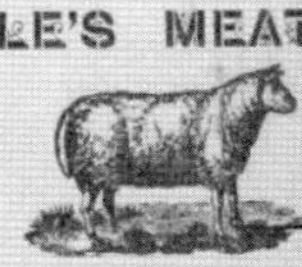

French Merino RAMS.

Wholesale and Retail Dealers in

ALL KINDS OF FRESH MEATS,

Corner Third South and Main Streets,

Telephone No. 169. SALT LAKE CITY.

—Dealers in—

Cattle, Sheep and Horses.

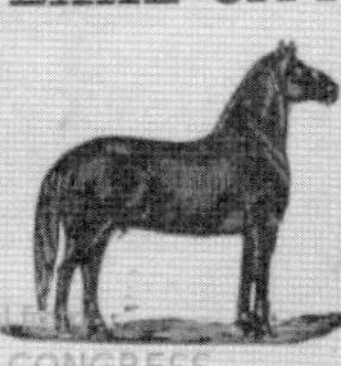

P. O. ADDRESS:

Salt Lake City and Nephi, Utah.

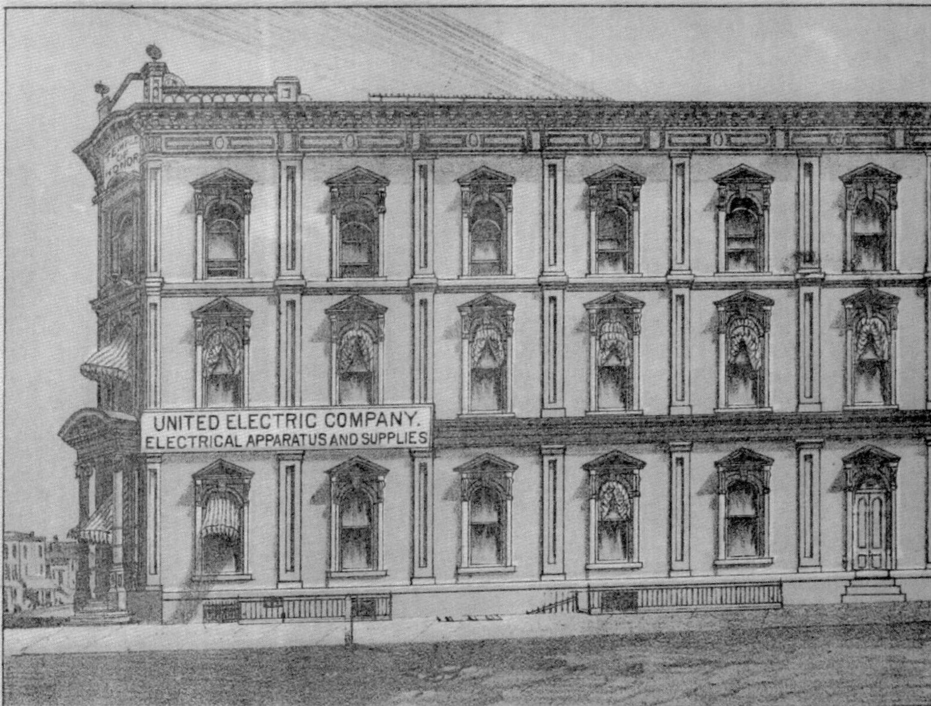

UNITED ELECTRIC CO.

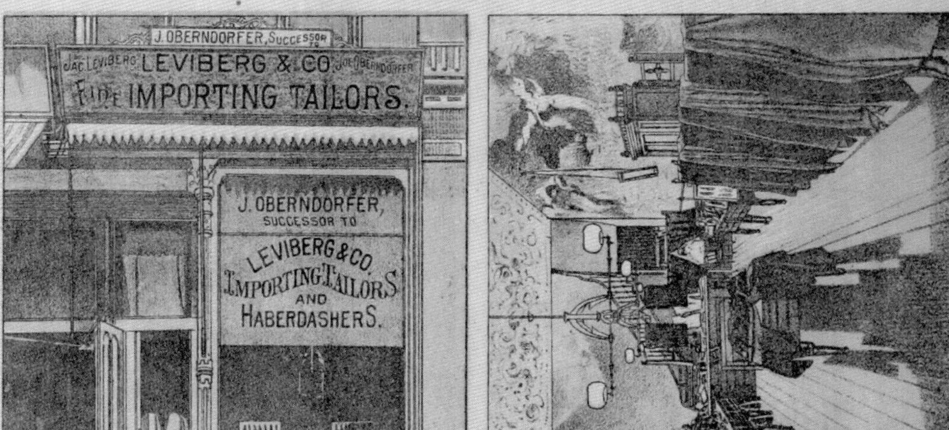

J. OBERNDORFER.

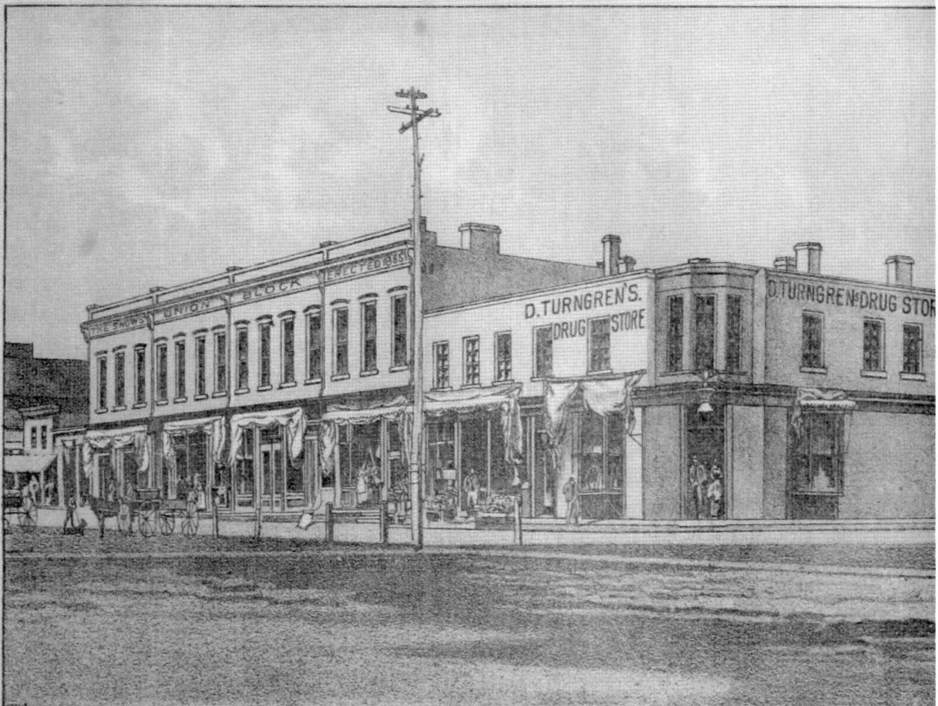

Z. SNOW'S BLOCK.

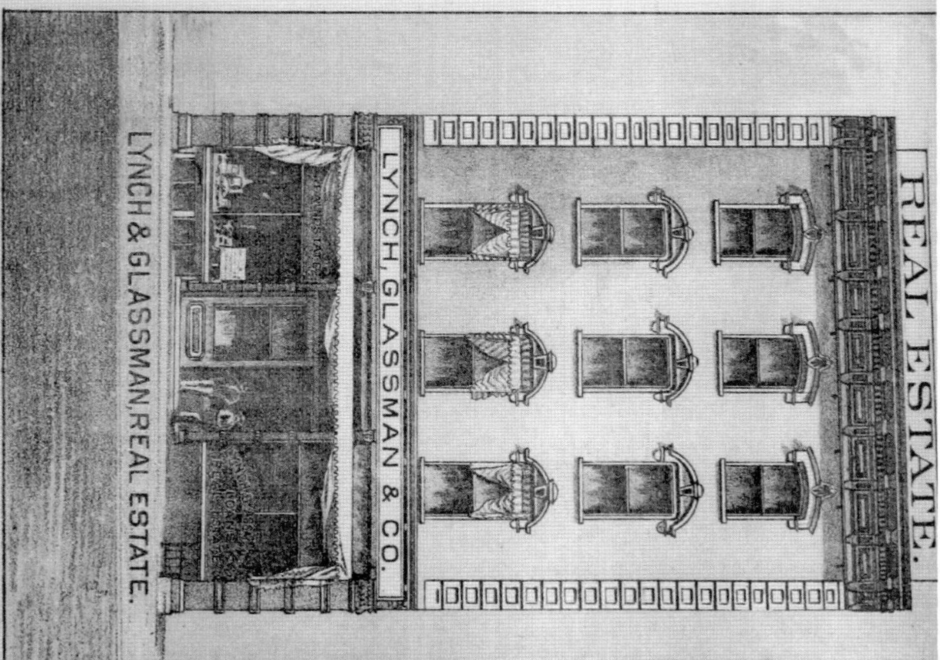

LYNCH & GLASSMAN.

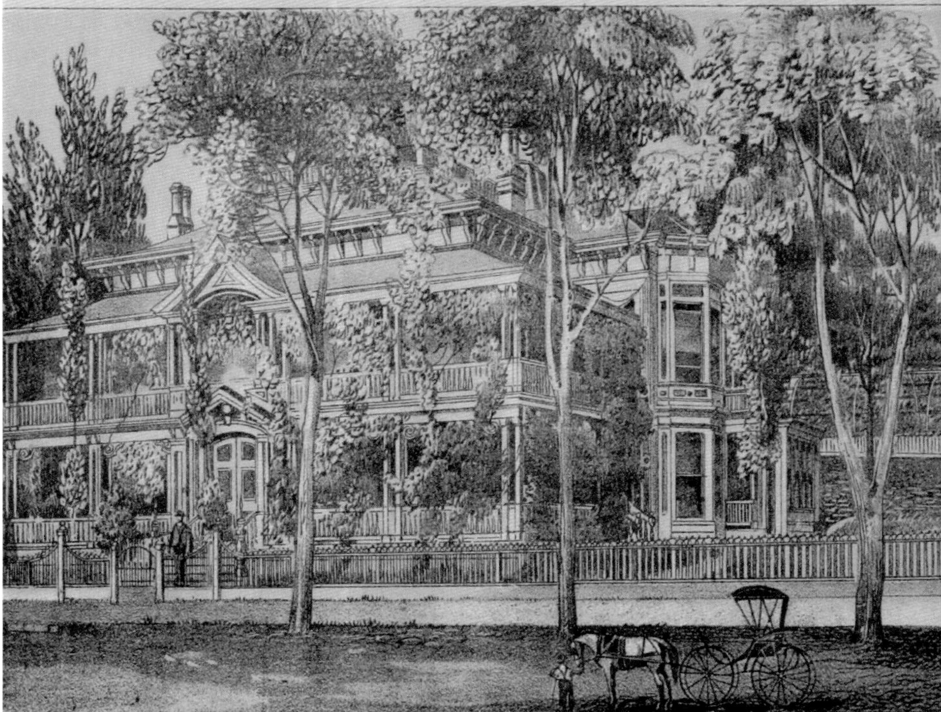

RESIDENCE OF THE LATE HON. W. H. HOOPER.

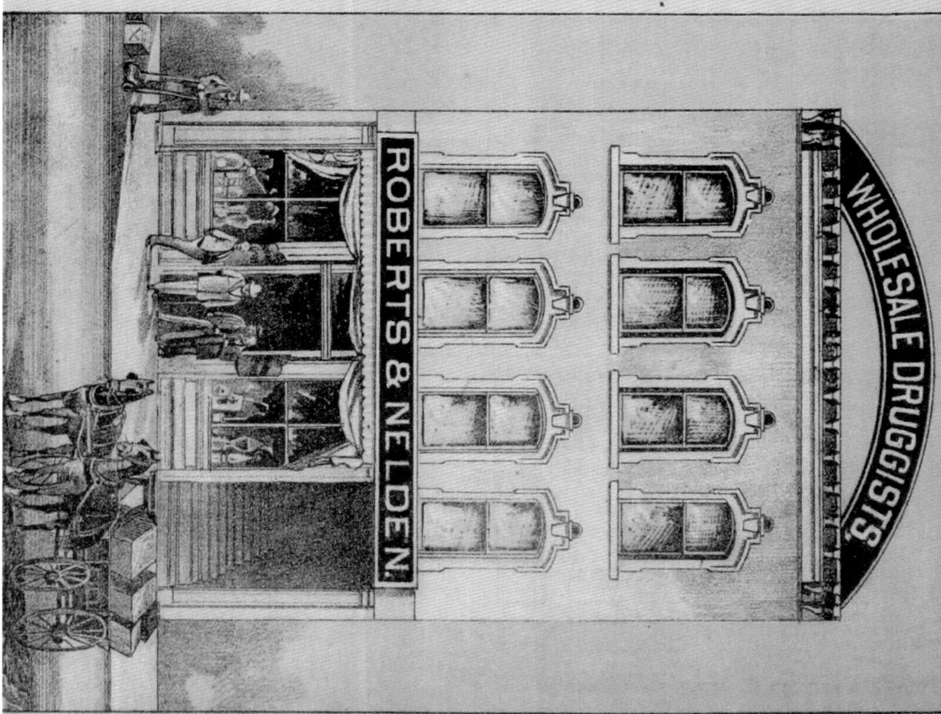

A. C. BRIXEN. Opened March 12th, 1887 M. BRIXEN.

LOCATION CENTRAL.

Electric Calls and Lights.

ath, Bar and Billiard Rooms.

Main Steet, near Walker House

SALT LAKE CITY.

CLIFT HOUSE

A. C. BRIXEN & BRO., PROPS.

Best Furnished House in the City

RATES, · $2.00 PER DAY.

Street Cars at Door.

CUISINE UNEXCELLED.

See View of CLIFT HOUSE in half-page lithograph; also in View of North Side, Third South St., from Main, looking West.

Geo. M. & John M. Cannon,

REAL ESTATE,

Loan and Collection Agents.

WE MEAN TO MAKE OUR FUTURE BUSINESS CAREER LIKE OUR PAST JUSTIFY OUR MOTTO:

"Moderate Charges. Fair Treatment. Reliability."

No. 39 MAIN STREET.

(2 Doors South of Z. C. M. I.)

SALT LAKE CITY, UTAH.

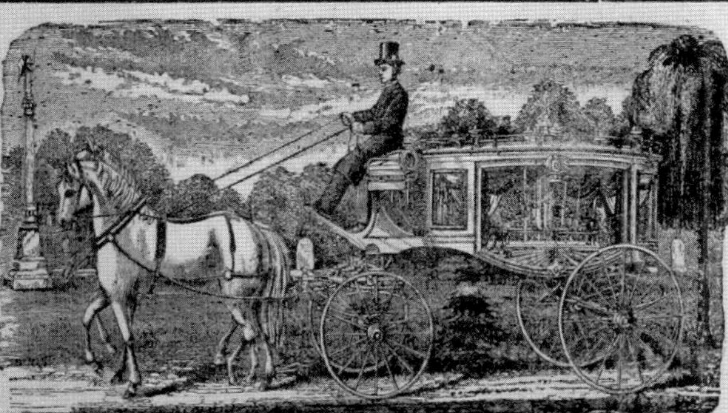

Joseph E. Taylor,

PIONEER UNDERTAKER OF UTAH

Having put in a Large Plant of Machinery, I now Manufacture my own Goods. Everything in the Undertaking Line furnished Wholesale or Retail at Prices that Defy Competition.

FACTORY AND WAREROOMS:

253 E. First South Street,

—*Telephone No. 70*— SALT LAKE CITY.

DIRECTORS AND OFFICERS:

F. W. JENNINGS, Pres't. and Mgr.
J. A. JENNINGS, Vice-President.
ISAAC JENNINGS.

JAS. E. JENNINGS, Sec'y. and Treas.

Post Office Box 262

Deseret Woolen Mills Co.,

(INCORPORATED)

SUCCESSORS TO WILLIAM JENNINGS & SONS

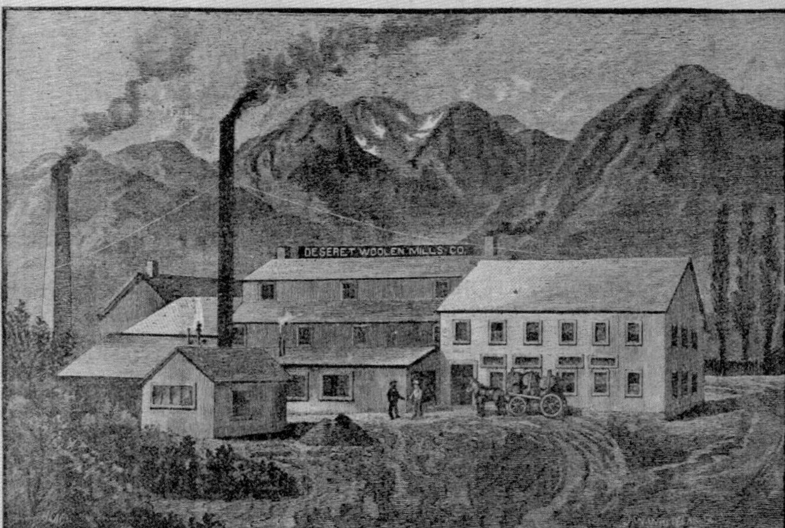

Manufacturers of

FLANNELS, DRESS GOODS, LINSEYS, YARNS,

ETC., ETC.,

HOSIERY AND KNIT GOODS.

SALT LAKE CITY, UTAH.

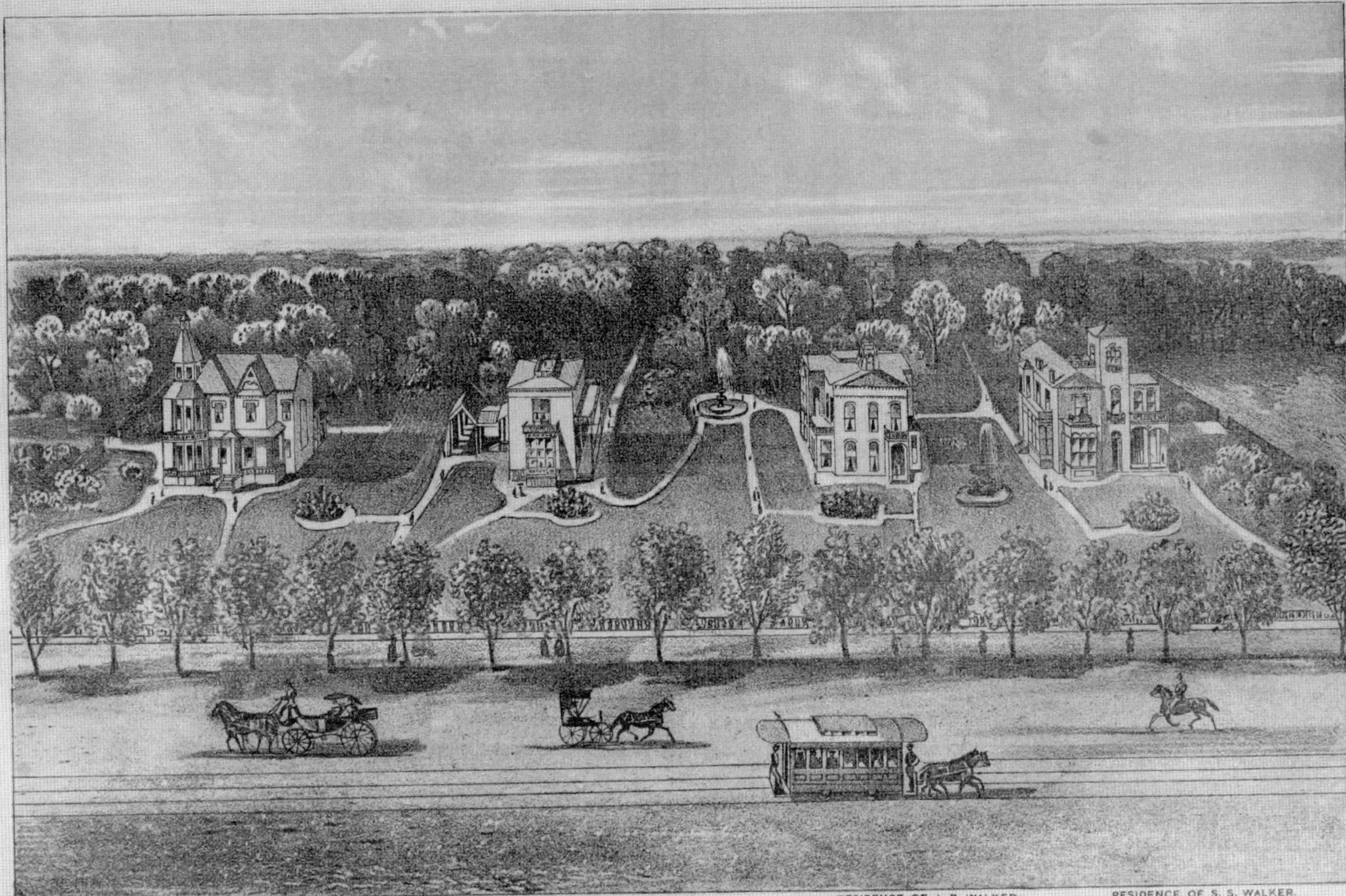

RESIDENCE OF BOYD PARK. RESIDENCE OF M. H. WALKER. RESIDENCE OF J. R. WALKER. RESIDENCE OF S. S. WALKER.

WALKER BROS. BLOCK.

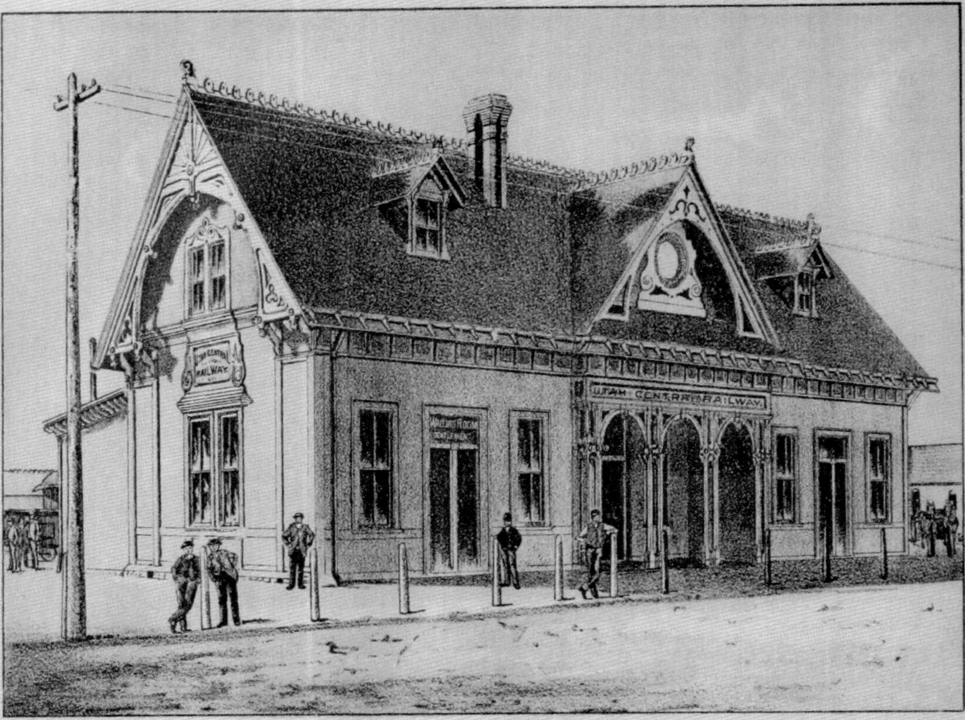

DEPOT OF THE UTAH CENTRAL RAILWAY.

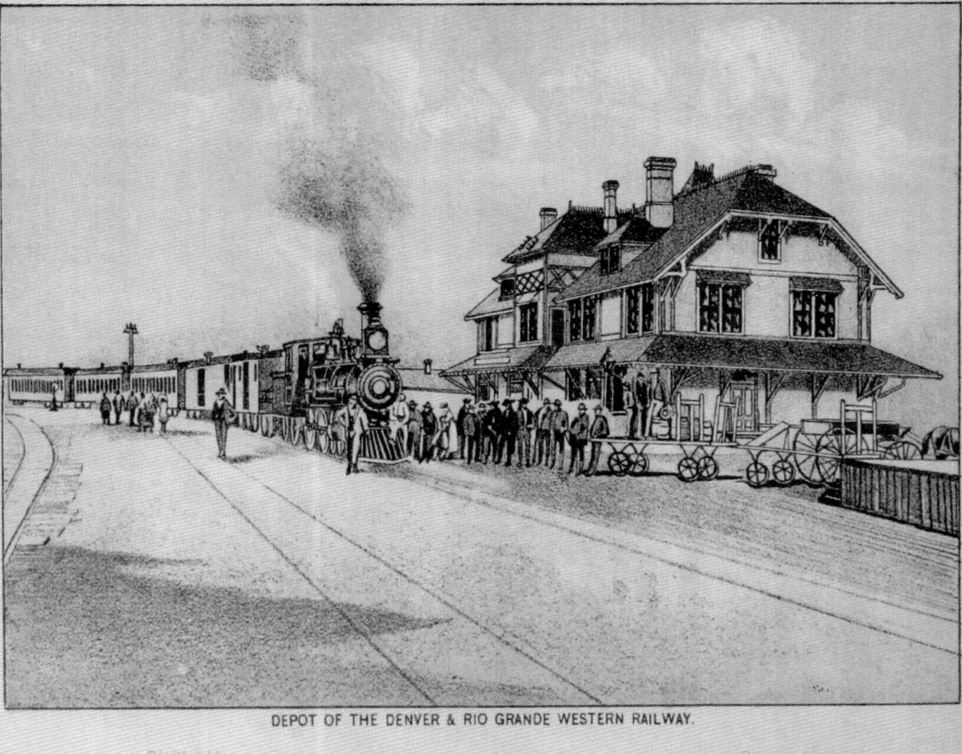

DEPOT OF THE DENVER & RIO GRANDE WESTERN RAILWAY.

ESTABLISHED 1855. INCORPORATED 1885.

GODBE, PITTS DRUG CO.,

WHOLESALE & RETAIL DRUGGISTS.

Importers of and Dealers in

Drugs, Chemicals, Paints, Oils, Varnishes, Assay Goods of all Kinds,

Druggists' Sundries, California Wines and Brandies, Imported Ales, Porters and Fine Liquors.

AGENTS FOR AMERICAN AND FOREIGN MANUFACTURERS OF ALL GOODS PERTAINING TO THE DRUG TRADE.

☞ See Our Building in View of Main Street, looking South from First South Street.

Spencer Clawson

Wholesale

DRY GOODS

SALT LAKE CITY.

(HOOPER & ELDREDGE BUILDING)

FACTORY, 171 MAIN STREET. SALT LAKE CITY.

SAM LEVY

Manufacturer of Fine

HAVANA HAND-MADE CIGARS

Nos. 171 and 173 S. Main Street,

P. O. BOX 576. SALT LAKE CITY, UTAH.

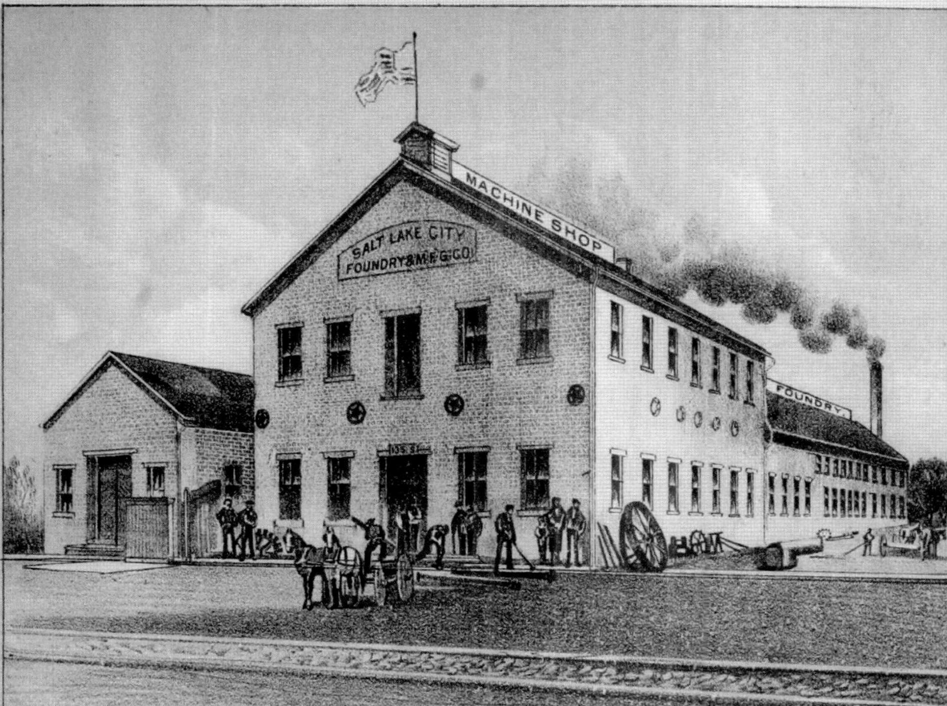

SALT LAKE FOUNDRY.

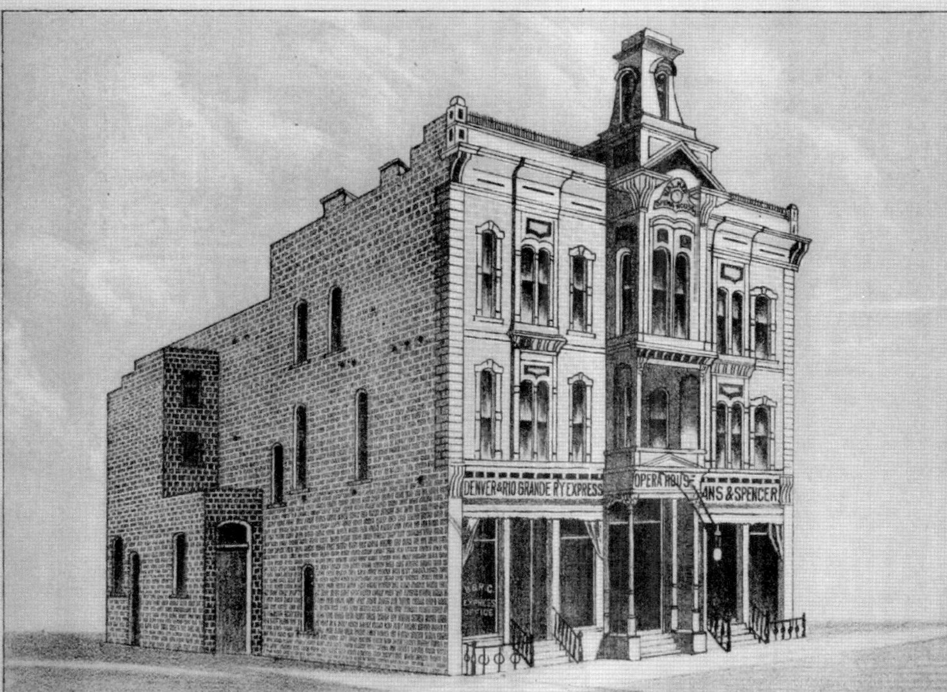

WALKER OPERA HOUSE

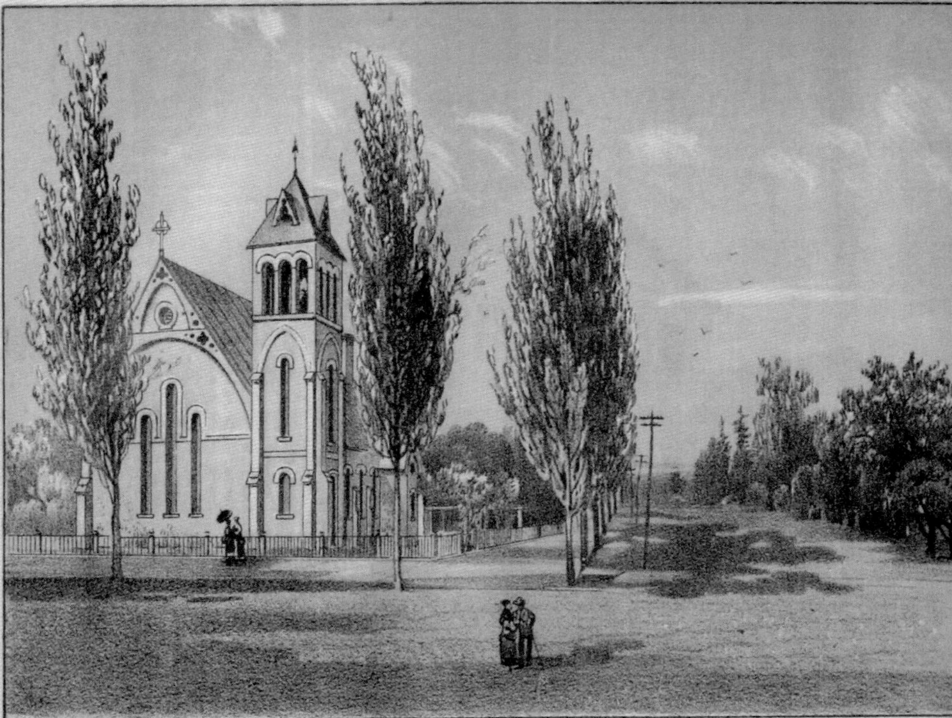

ST. PAUL'S CHAPEL.

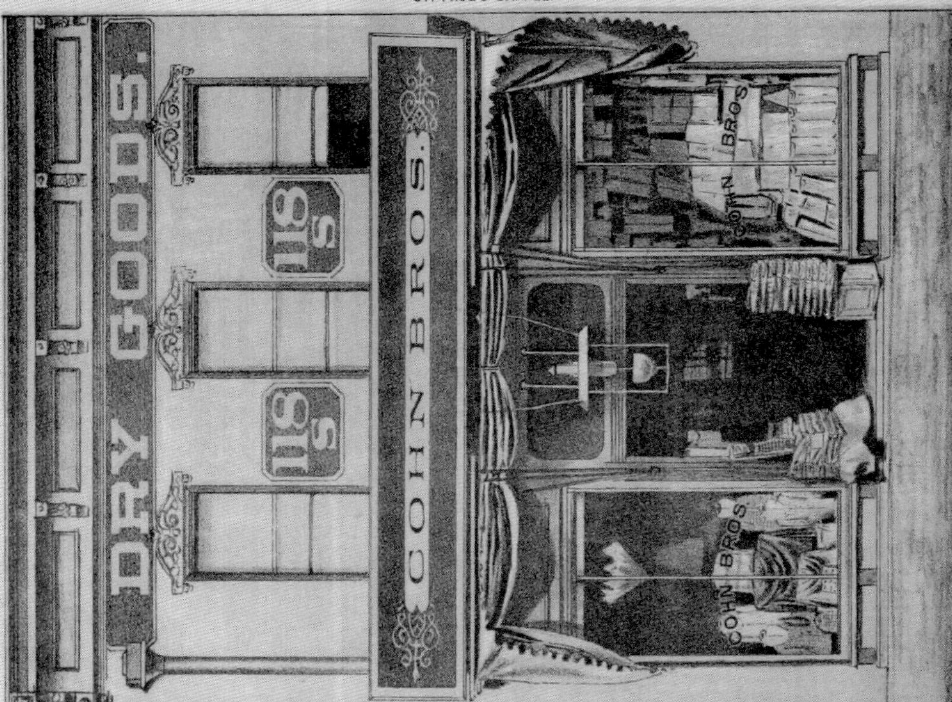

COHN BROS. STORE.

GEO. M. SCOTT,
President.

H. S. RUMFIELD,
Secretary.

JAS. GLENDINNING,
Vice-President and Treasurer.

GEO. M. SCOTT & CO.,

(INCORPORATED)

—Importers and Dealers in—

Hardware, Iron, Steel, Iron Pipe, Miners' Tools, Stoves,

TINWARE, METALS, ETC.,

And a General Assortment of Mine, Mill and Smelter Supplies.

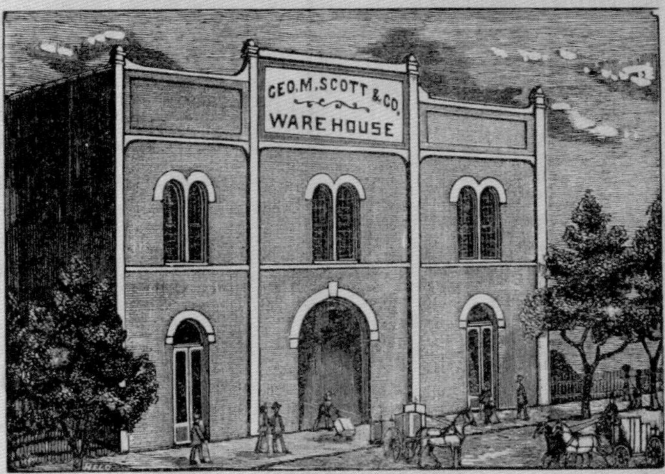

—Wholesale and Retail Dealers in—

BELTING, PULLEYS, GAS & WATER PIPE, POWDER, FUSE, CAPS, Etc.,
PACKING, SHAFTING, BRASS & IRON FITTINGS, VALVES, HOSE,
BABBIT METAL, PLUMBERS SUPPLIES, STOCKHOLM TAR, ROSIN, PITCH AND OAKUM.

Exclusive Agents for Blake Steam Pumps, Brilliant Engine and Cylinder Oil, Buffalo Scales, California Powder Co., Roebling's Steel Wire Rope, Dodge Wooden Pulley Co., Atlas Engines and Boilers.

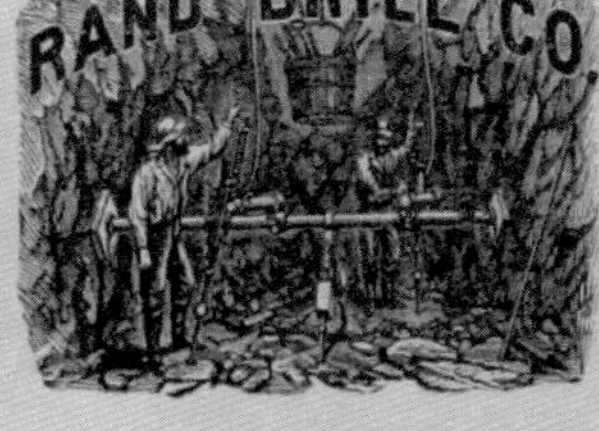

WE beg to announce to the mining community that we have secured the Agency of the Rand Rock Drill & Compressor Co., and carry constantly in stock a Full Line of Rock Drills, Air Compressors, Air Receivers, Steam and Air Hose, together with a Full Line of Duplicate Parts for Rand Drills.

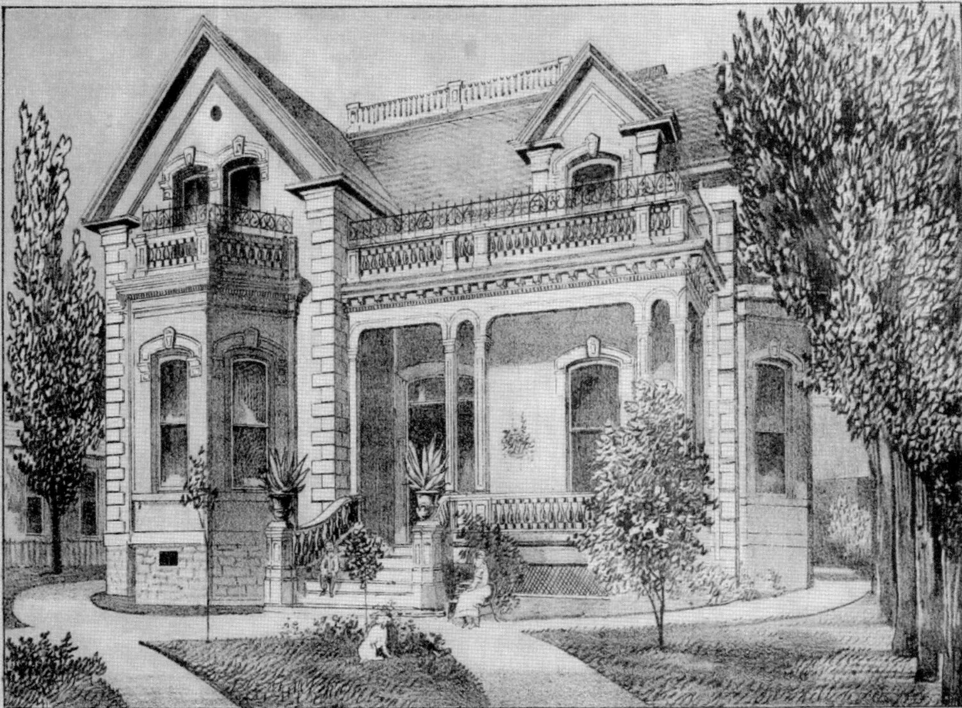

RESIDENCE OF JAMES GLENDINNING.

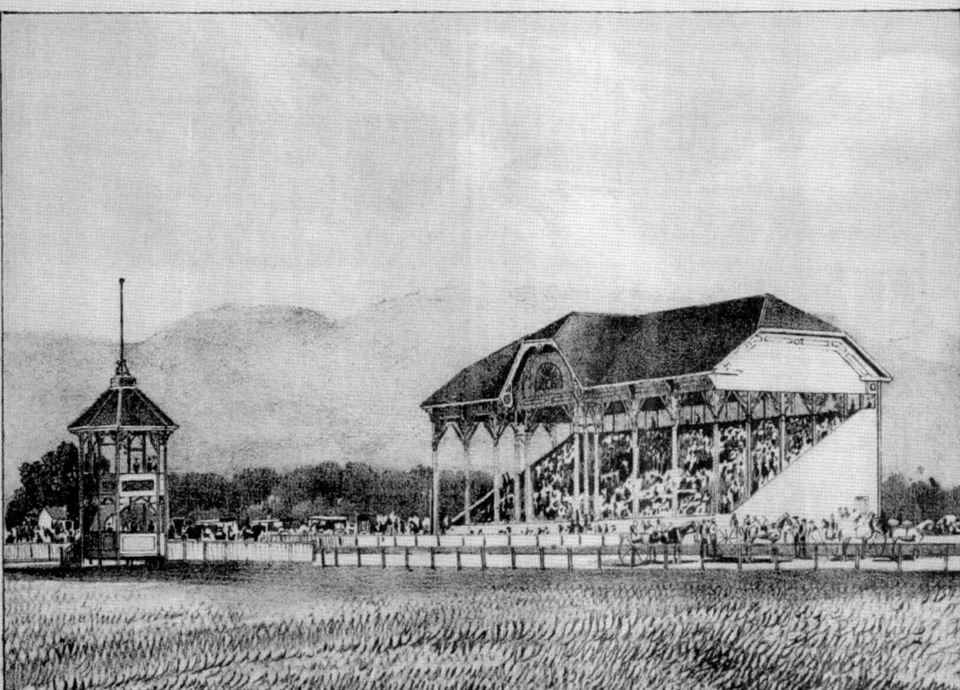

UTAH DRIVING PARK ASSOCIATION, TRACK AND GROUNDS.

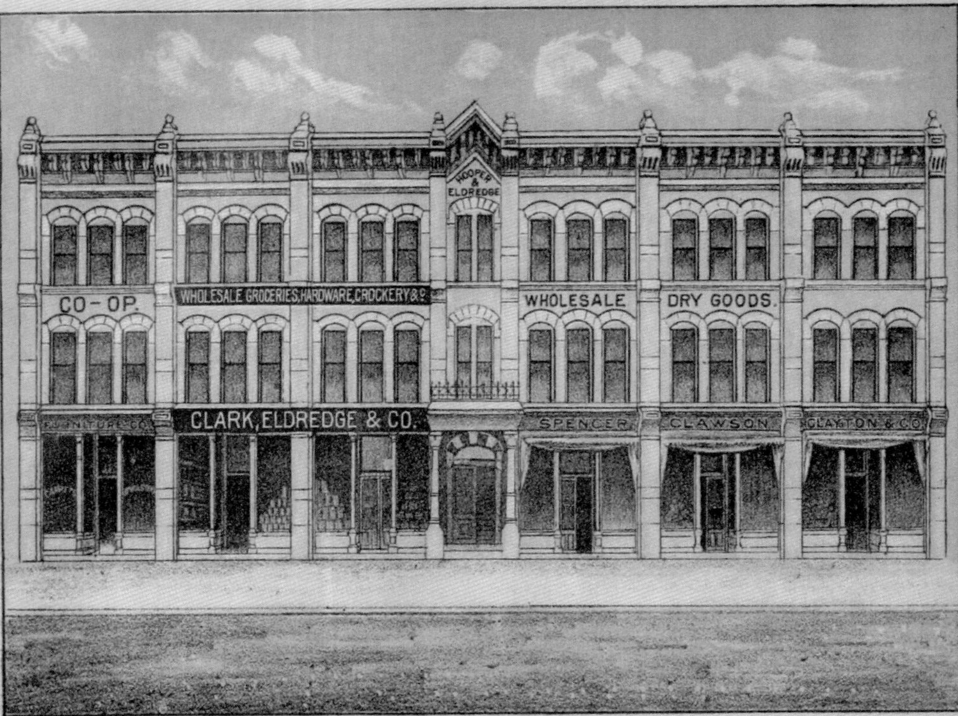

HOOPER & ELDREDGE BLOCK.

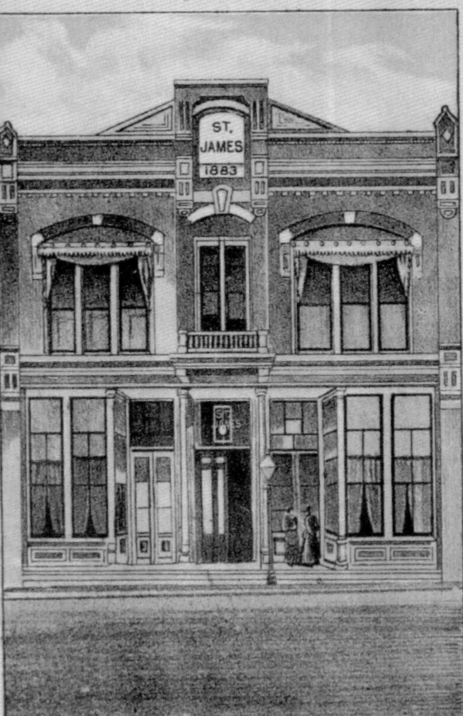

ST. JAMES HOTEL.

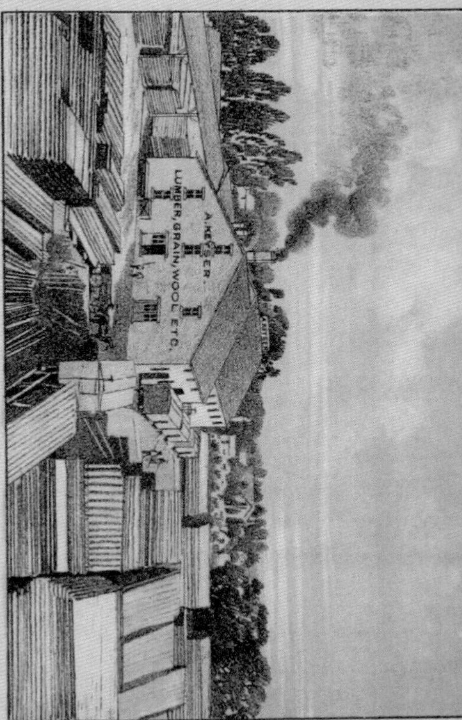

A. KEYSER'S WAREHOUSE.

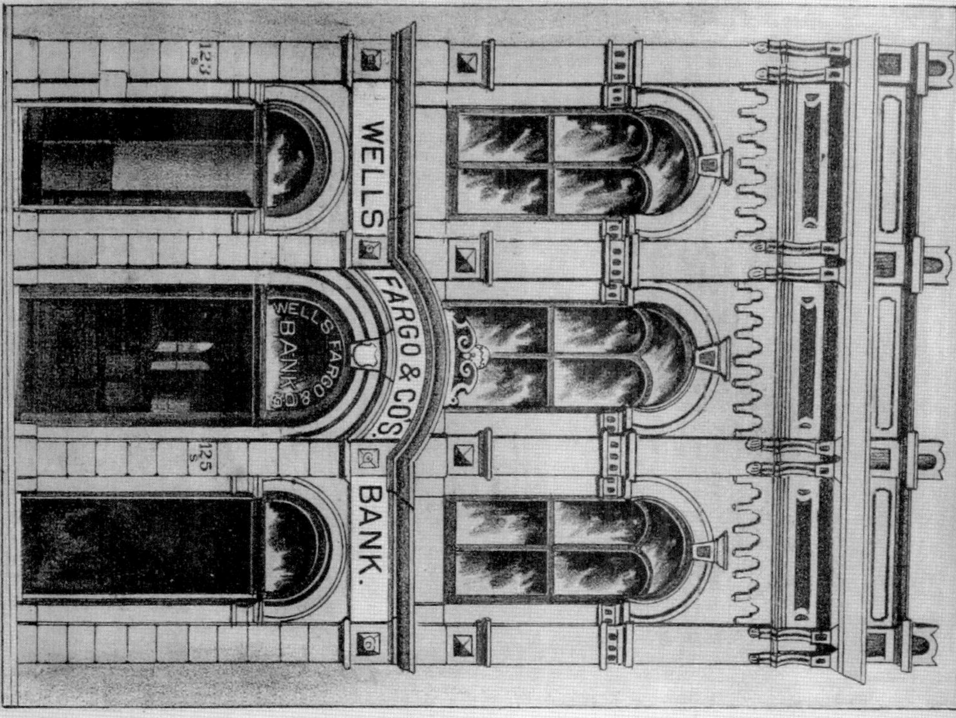

WELLS, FARGO & CO.'S BANK.

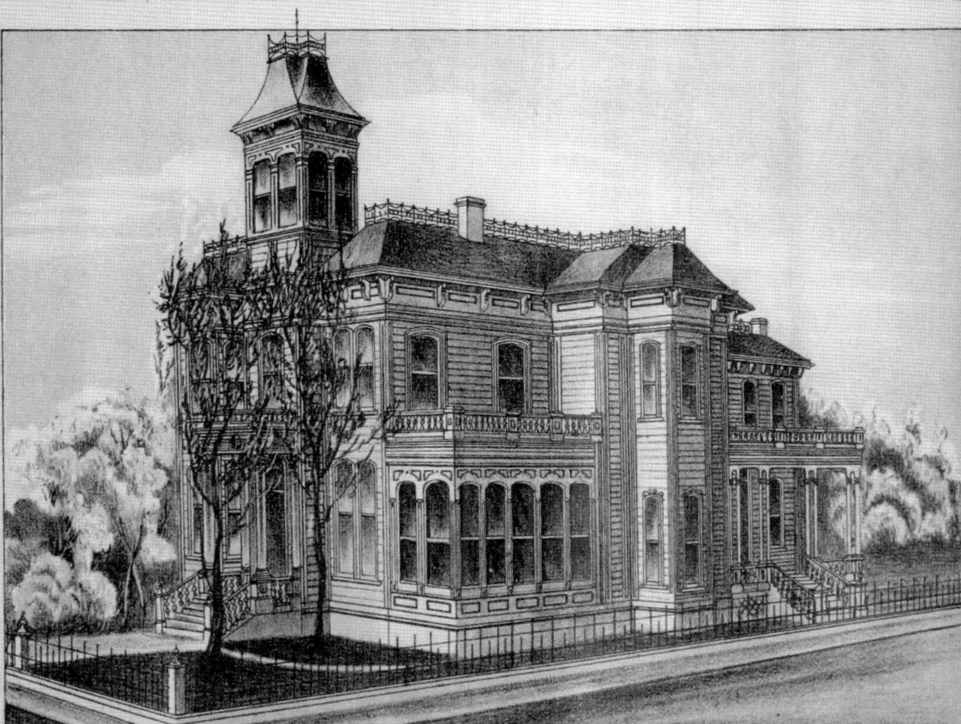

RESIDENCE OF J. E. DOOLY.

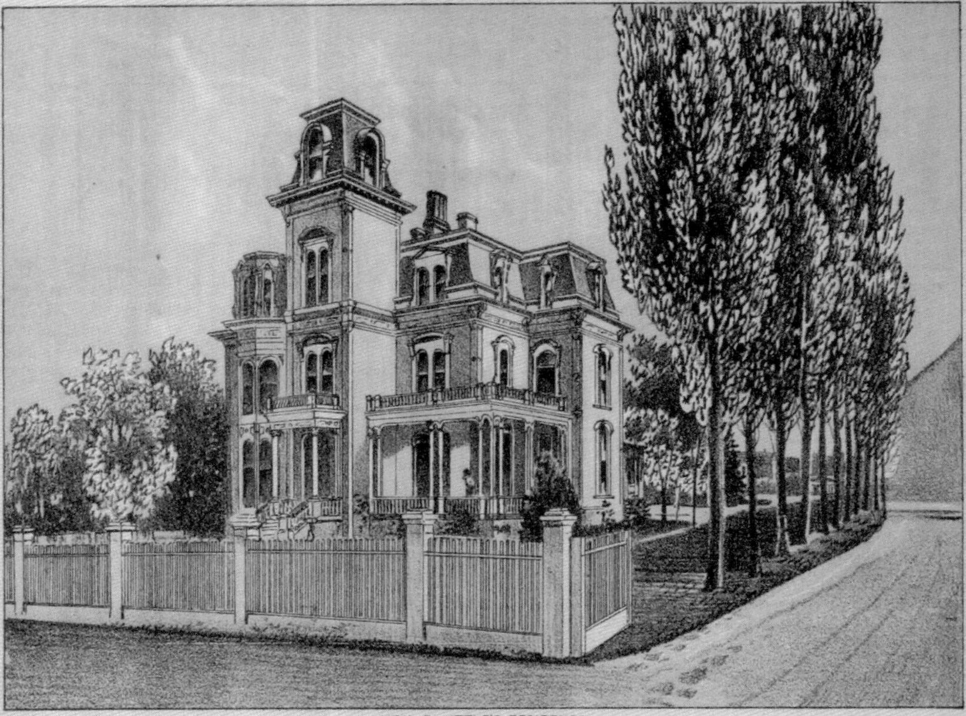

HON. F. LITTLE'S RESIDENCE.

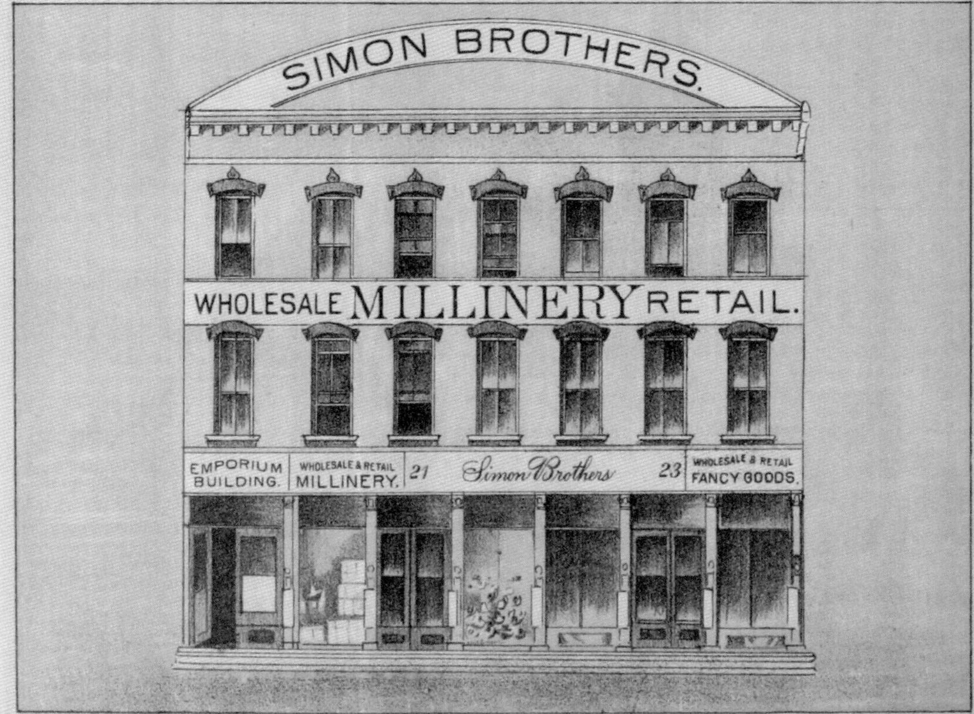

SIMON BROS., STORE.

COAL DEPARTMENT, UNION PACIFIC RAILWAY.

Rock Spring, **COAL** Red Canyon,

Pleasant Valley.

ROCK SPRING.—The Best Coal West of the Missouri River.
RED CANYON.—The Cheapest Coal in the Market.
PLEASANT VALLEY.—From the Well-known Utah Central Mines.

For Domestic and Steam Purposes, and in all Sizes—LUMP, EGG, STOVE, NUT and SLACK.

CLEAN COAL and PROMPT DELIVERIES, by the Ton or Car Load.

OFFICE: 201 S. MAIN ST., WASATCH CORNER. — **A. J. GUNNELL,** General Agent.

YARDS: OPP. UTAH CENTRAL DEPOT, TELEPHONE 240. — **F. B. SHELLY,** Manager Yard.

A. C. SMITH & CO.,

** Wholesale and Retail Dealers in **

DRUGS & CHEMICALS.

* * *

A Full Assortment of Acids, Dyes, Paints, Oils and Varnishes, Trusses, Toilet Articles, Imported and Domestic Perfumeries.

Agents for the Celebrated HOLDFAST 5c. CIGAR

N. E. Corner Main and Second South Streets, Salt Lake City, Utah.

The Pioneer Sporting Goods House of Utah.

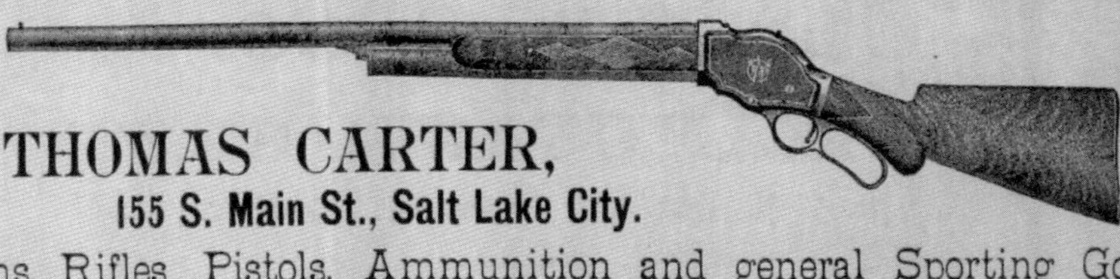

THOMAS CARTER,

155 S. Main St., Salt Lake City.

Guns, Rifles, Pistols, Ammunition and general Sporting Goods.

AGENT FOR DUPONT'S SPORTING & BLASTING POWDER.

The Only Genuine Thomson Waterproof Boot. *Illustrated Catalogue for 1887* *Free on Application.*

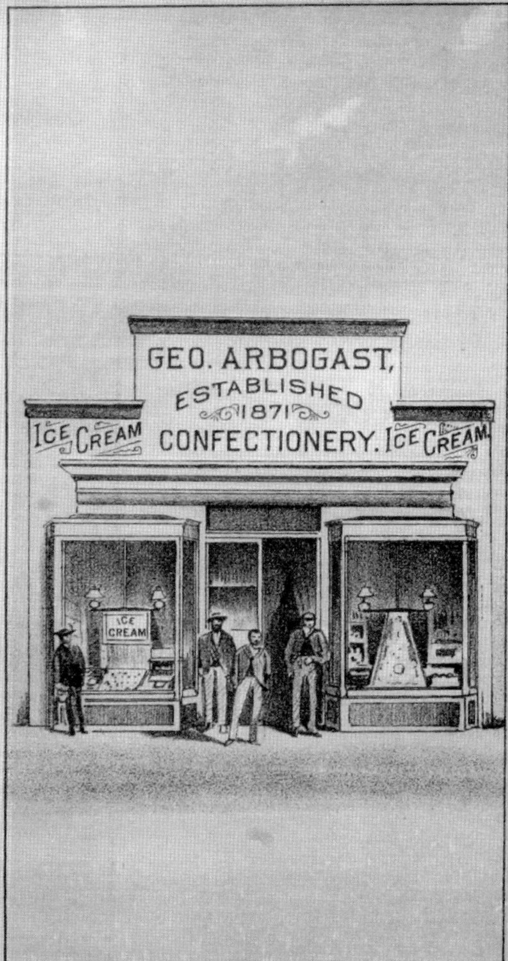

OYSTER GROTTO.

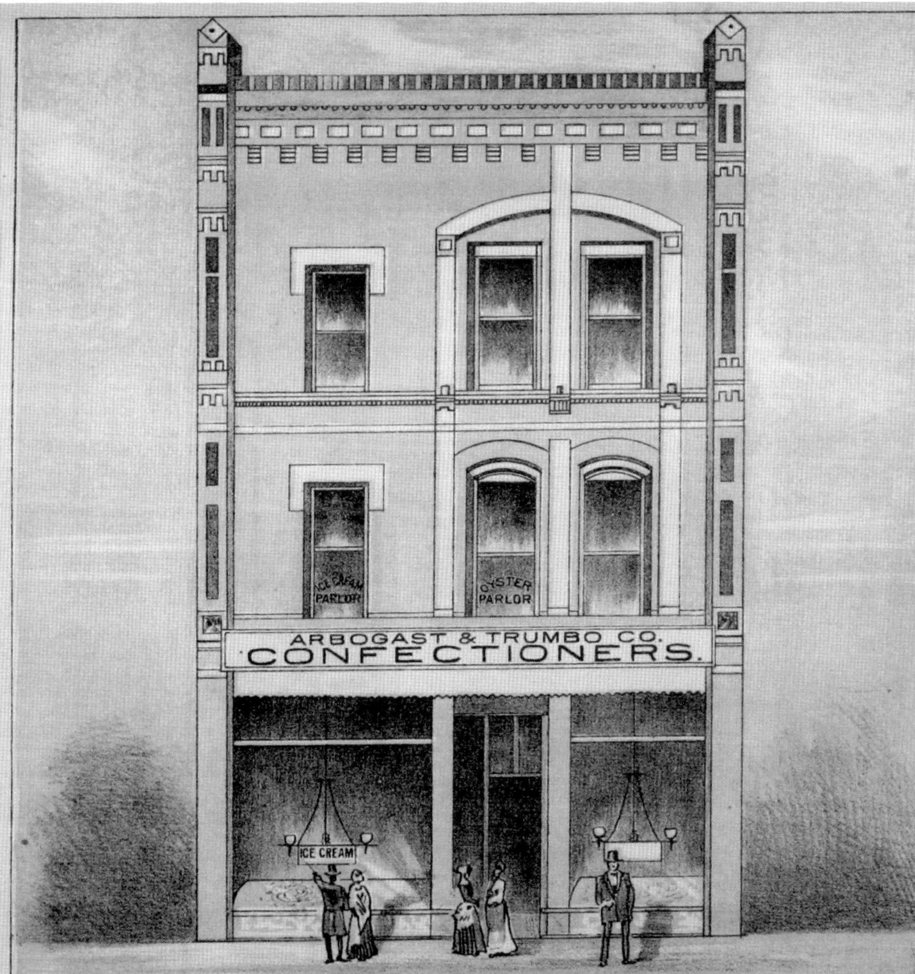

ARBOGAST & TRUMBO'S STORE.

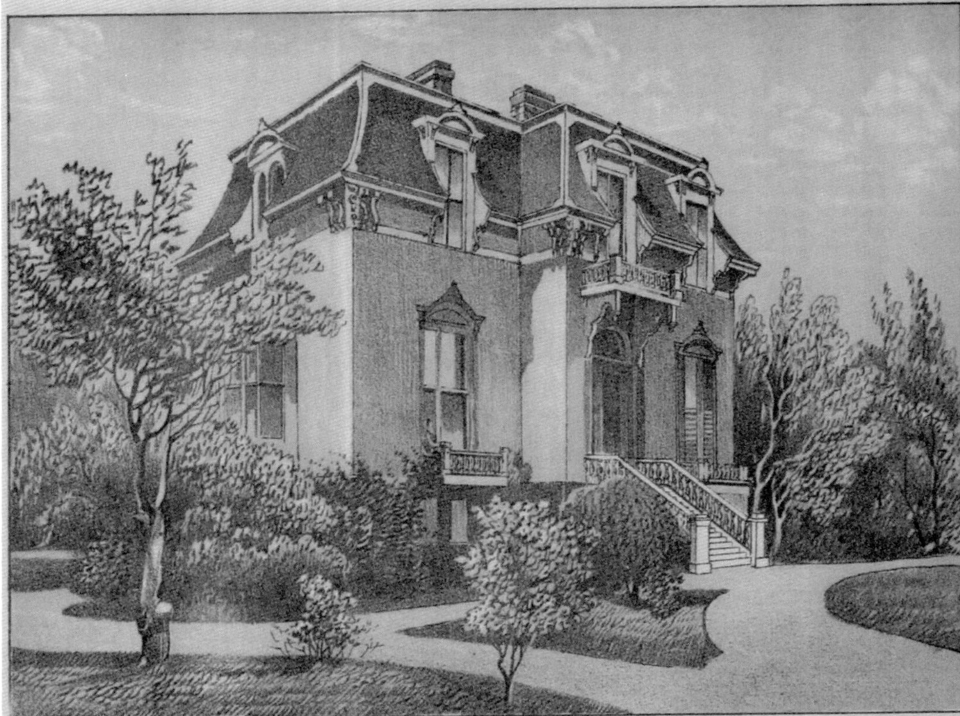

RESIDENCE OF HON. JOHN T. CAINE.

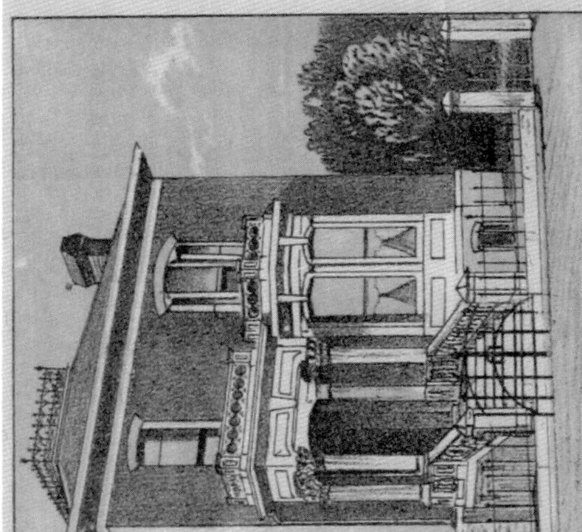

RESIDENCE OF F. A. PASCOE.

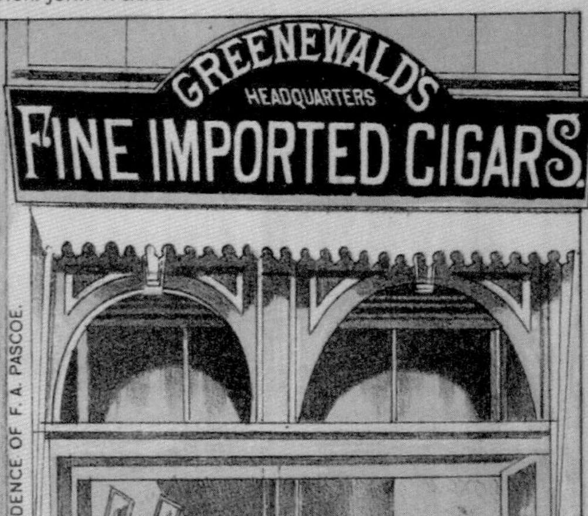

GREENEWALD'S STORE.

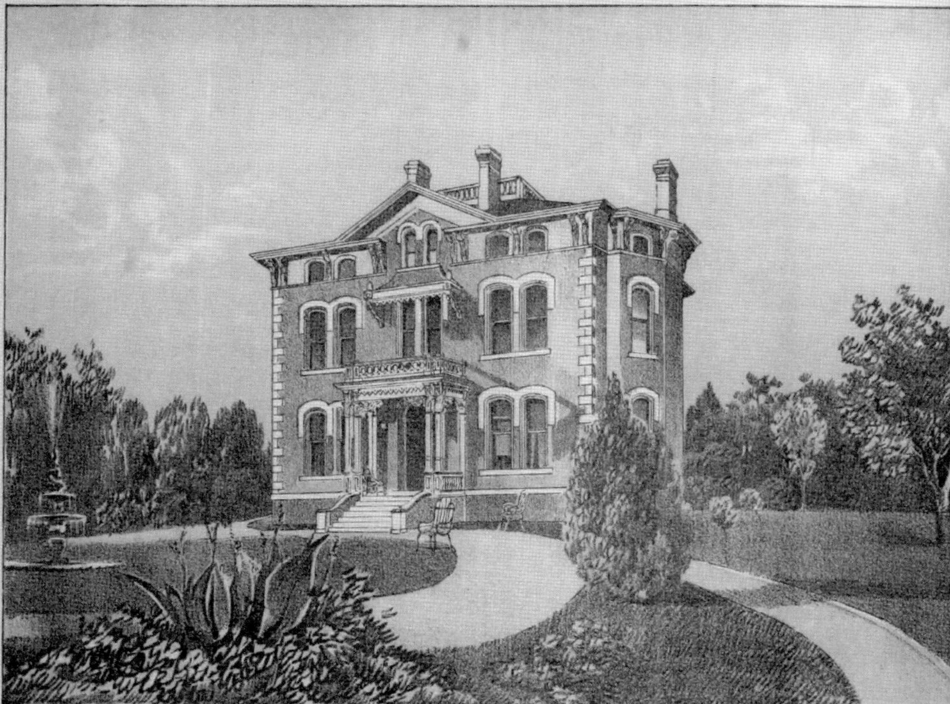

RESIDENCE OF EX-MAYOR JAMES SHARP.

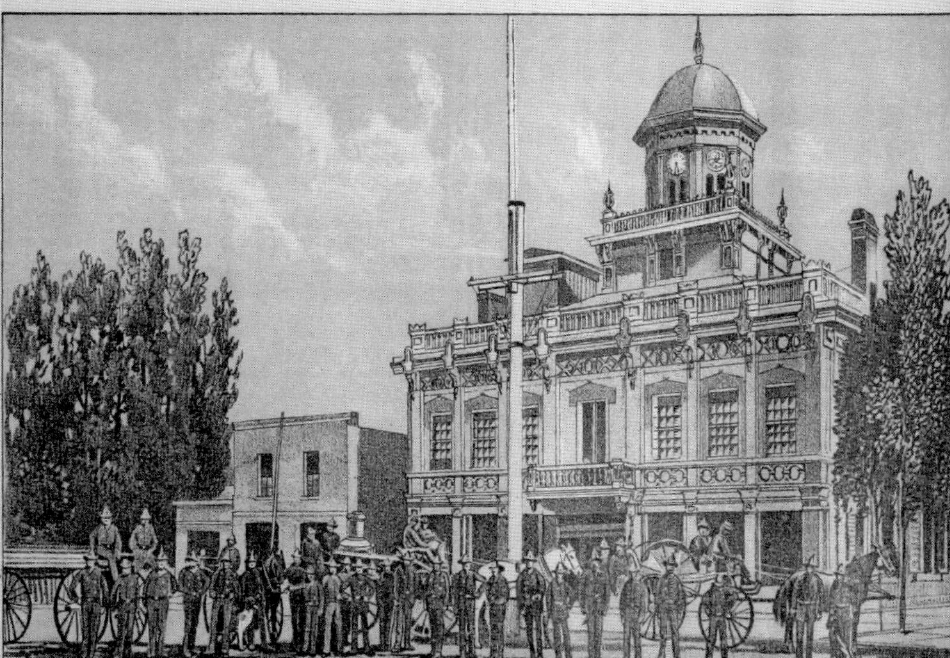

SALT LAKE CITY FIRE DEPARTMENT.

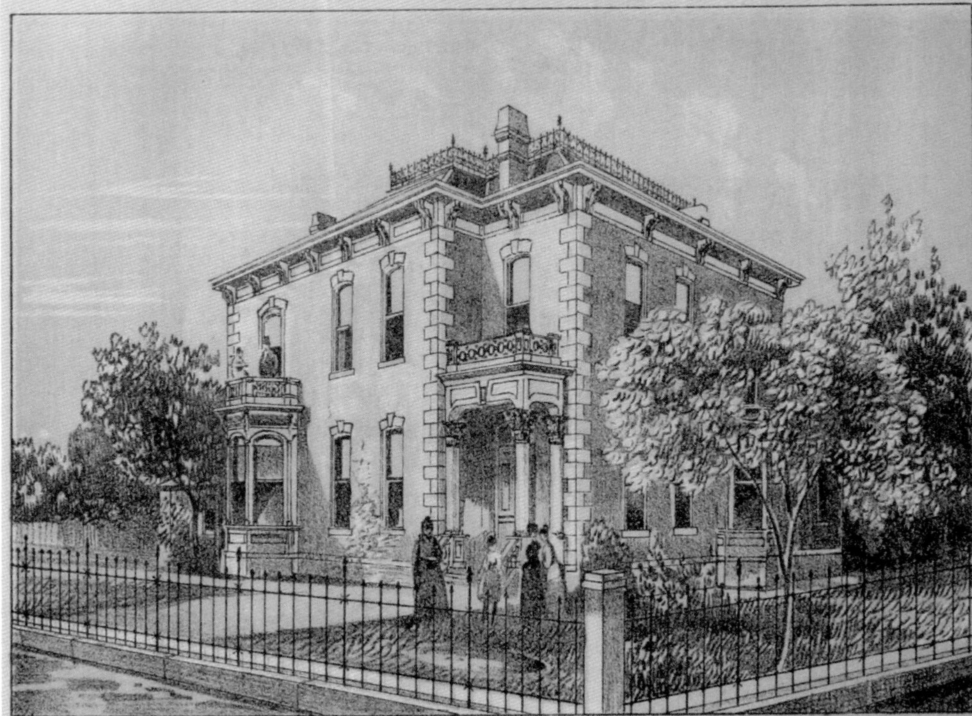

RESIDENCE OF F. J. P. PASCOE.

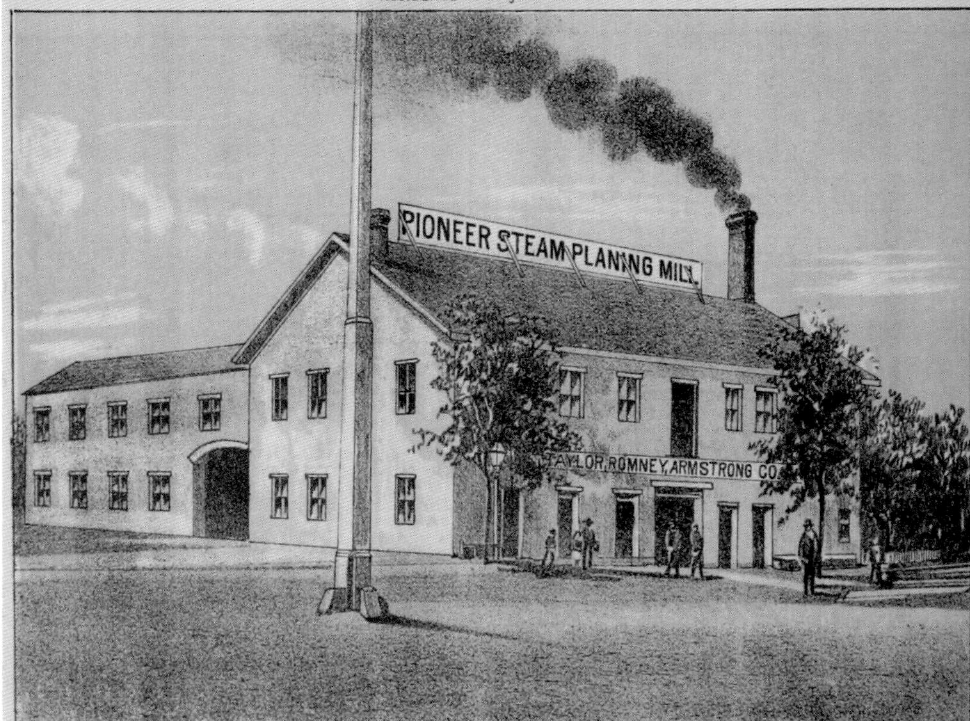

TAYLOR, ROMNEY, ARMSTRONG CO.

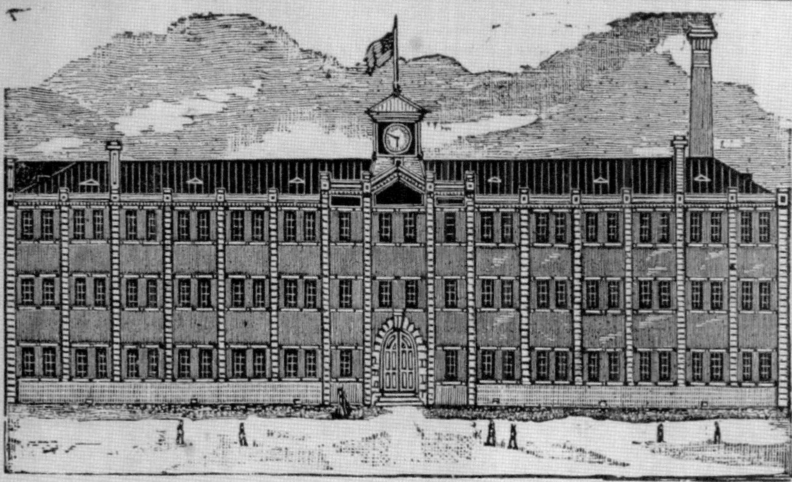

THE above View represents the large POWER BUILDING now in course of erection at North Salt Lake—Kinney & Gourlay's new city addition—size 50 x 200 feet, three stories high, built of cut brown stone, iron and cement, and guaranteed to be fire-proof. The building will contain six rooms, each 50x100 feet, which will be fitted up and especially designed for light manufacturing, the heat, power and electric light being furnished by the promoter.

NORTH SALT LAKE

The new manufacturing and residence addition to Salt Lake City, is located adjoining the famous Hot Springs Lake, one of the most beautiful sheets of water in the country. The entire Kinney & Gourlay plat lies within the city limits, and is only two miles from Main Street, the principal business thoroughfare. Now is the time for Eastern

Speculators, Home-Buyers & Manufacturers

To invest. Salt Lake City is certain to catch the great Western boom in a very short time, and such a chance for investment may not occur again.

Maps and all necessary information furnished promptly on application. Correspondence especially solicited from home-buyers and manufacturers.

I Will GIVE AWAY a Number of FACTORY SITES

To Manufacturers Who will Start Industries Thereon.

L. D. KINNEY, PROP.

—SEND FOR—

"THE SALT LAKE ENTERPRISE,"

An Eight-Page Weekly, Published by The Enterprise Publishing Co., Devoted to the Resources of Utah,

If you wish to get correct information in regard to the richest and most beautiful country in the United States.

HEBER J. GRANT, President.
J. F. GRANT, Vice-President and Manager
GEO. T. ODELL, Assistant Manager and Treasurer.
R. S. WELLS, Secretary.

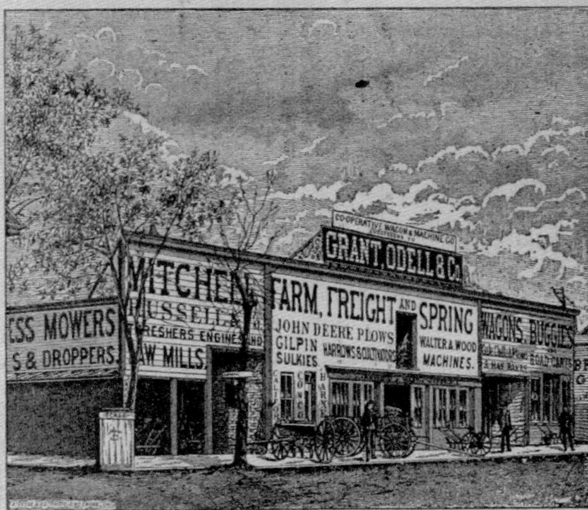

DIRECTORS:

Heber J. Grant.
J. F. Grant.
G. T. Odell.
F. M. Lyman.
John Henry Smith.
Orson A. Woolley.
C. S. Burton.
W. W. Riter.
J. F. Wells.
Jos. F. Smith.
Geo. Romney.

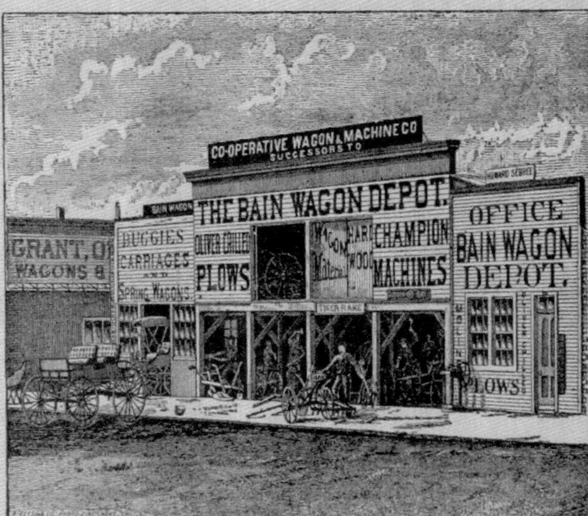

MASSILLON OR RUSSELL THRESHERS.

MITCHELL

AND

BAIN

WAGONS.

JOHN DEERE

AND

Oliver Chilled

PLOWS.

WOOD

AND

CHAMPION

MACHINES.

BUGGIES

AND

SPRING

WAGONS.

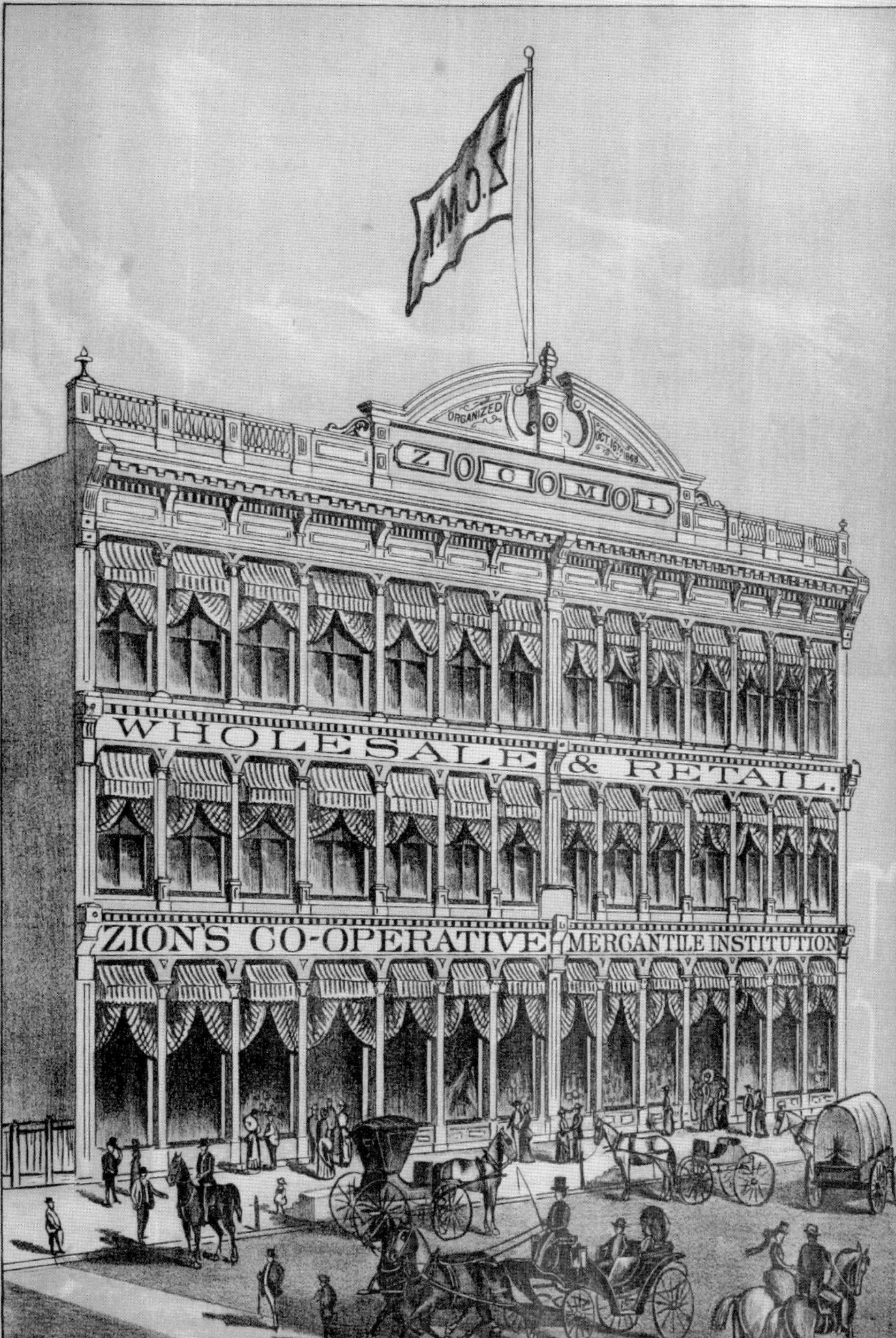
ORGANIZED
Z C M I
WHOLESALE & RETAIL.
ZION'S CO-OPERATIVE MERCANTILE INSTITUTION

Z. C. M. I. STORE.

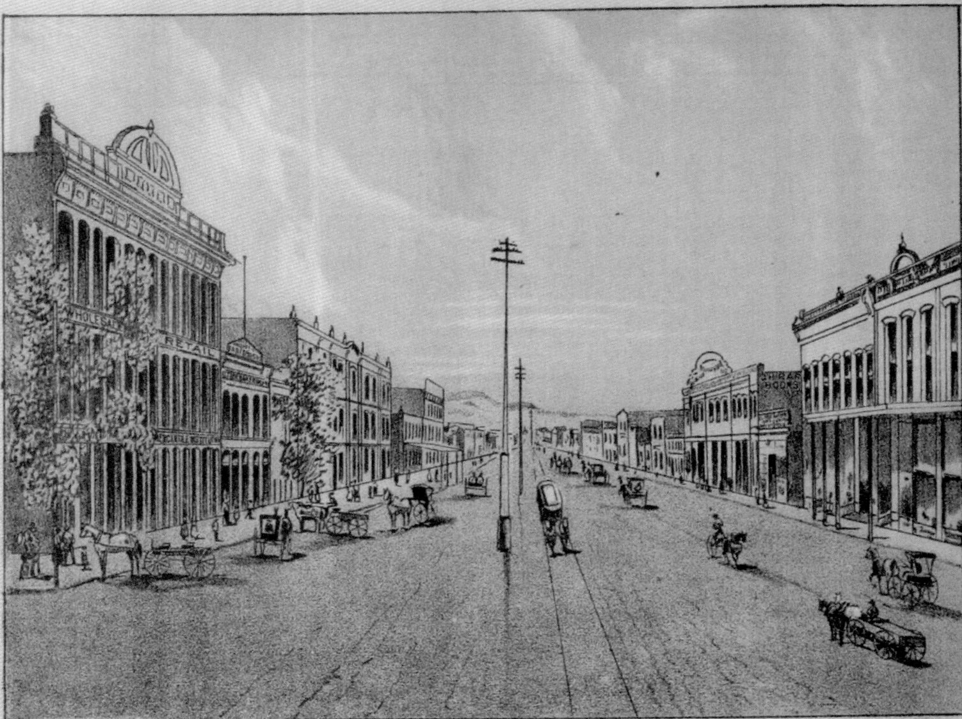

MAIN ST., FROM SOUTH TEMPLE, LOOKING SOUTH.

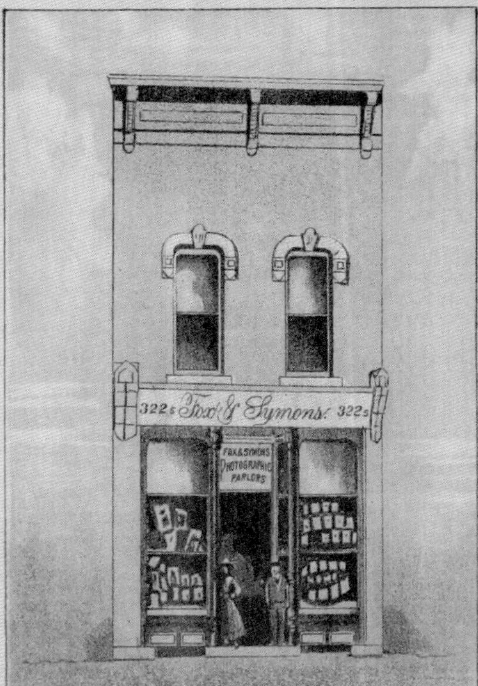

FOX & SYMONS' PHOTOGRAPHIC PARLORS.

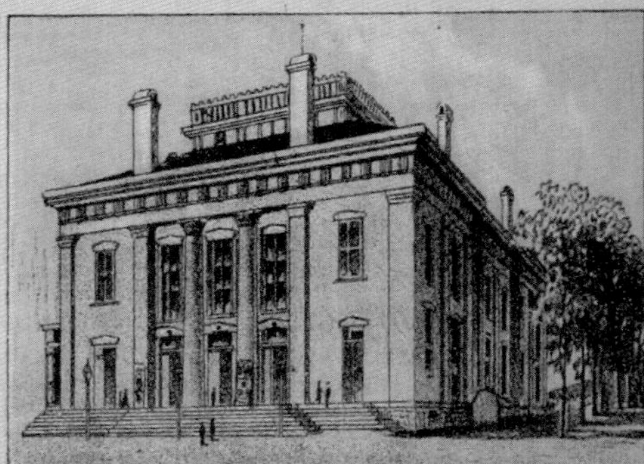

SALT LAKE THEATRE.

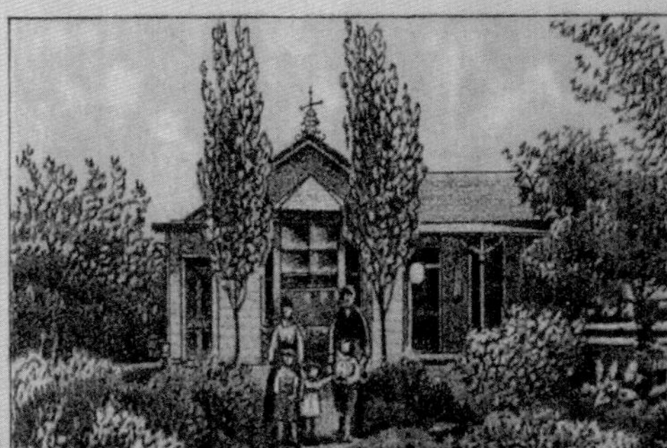

RESIDENCE OF E. A. FOLLAND.

ESTABLISHED 1846

Now Occupies over 500 ACRES IN CULTIVATION of

FRUIT AND ORNAMENTAL TREES, ROSES, SHRUBS, ETC.

We claim great advantages for the soil of Geneva and vicinity in the production of Healthy Long-Lived Trees. This is a matter of great importance to every planter. Not a year passes that we do not receive additional testimony of the fact that trees grown upon our heavy, strong, rich, well-drained soil are healthier, longer-lived, less liable to injury from extreme cold, and more productive than when taken from a light soil. Another very important fact is that being furnished with a more abundant supply of healthy, well-ripened and fibrous roots, they bear transplanting to a different soil and climate much better.

TESTIMONIAL.

I have for the last two years purchased Fruit Trees from the Geneva Nursery, and on my visit of late through the various settlements to Brigham City and return, saw the orchards of fruit trees sold by Samuel Smith and agents of the Geneva Nursery, the past three years, which were very fine, and far surpassed my expectations; and by enquiring of the owners I found they were well satisfied with their trees and fruit. I am pleased to find a company that can be relied upon for first-class fruit, as a long looked for necessity.

TERRITORIAL ENQUIRER, PROVO CITY, UTAH, Aug. 30, 1887.

CHARLES E. DAVIES

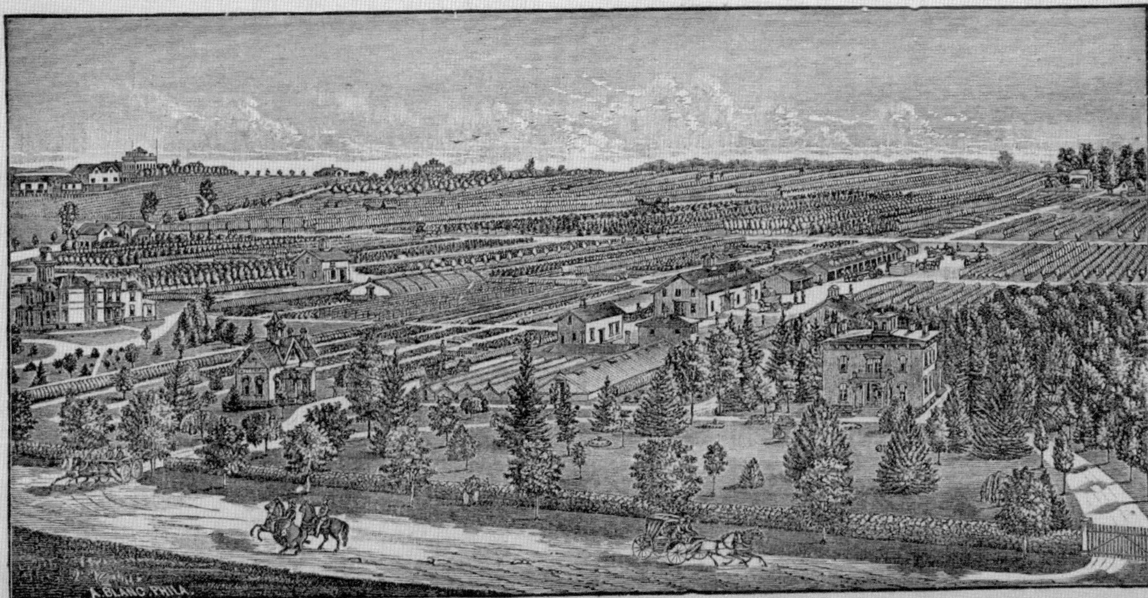

HOME GROUNDS OF THE GENEVA NURSERY

GENEVA, N. Y. —— W. & T. SMITH, Proprietors.

UTAH NURSERY COMPANY, (**J. A. GOODHUE, President.**)

P. O. Box 453. GENERAL WESTERN AGENTS,

SALT LAKE CITY.

J. J. SNELL & CO.,

Real Estate Agents,

POSTOFFICE BUILDING, SALT LAKE CITY, UTAH.

HOUSES, LOTS & FARMS FOR SALE.

HOUSES FOR RENT. RENTS COLLECTED.
COURT SCRIPT BOUGHT. MONEY TO LOAN.

Thirty Years on the Ground.

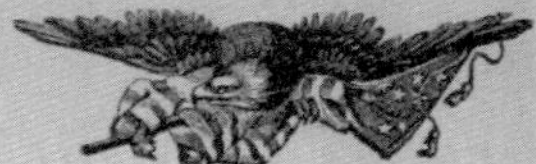

EAGLE CRACKER BAKERY,

MRS. S. R. STANLEY, PROPRIETOR.

Manufacturer of Staple & Fancy Crackers,

Cor. Second West and Seventh South Sts.,

P. O. Box 297. SALT LAKE CITY.

All Orders Promptly Attended to.

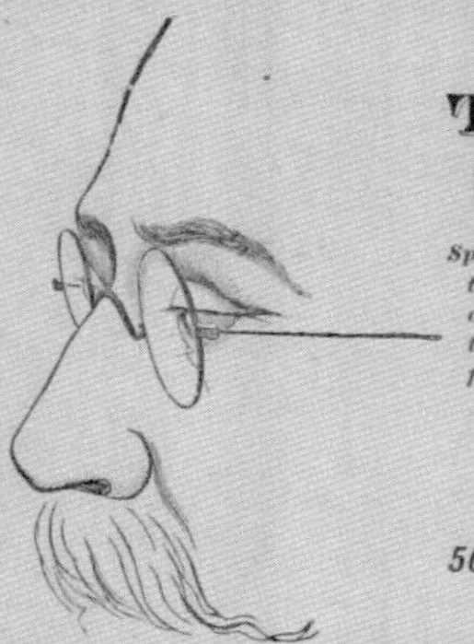

DR. REED,

THE EYE

Chronic & Special Diseases.

Spectacles and Eye Glasses fitted to Order. Lenses in Ocean Blue and London Smoke. Special Attention Paid to Fitting Artificial Eyes. Consultation Free.

—The Sign of—

THE BIG EYES,

50 E. Second South Street,

SALT LAKE CITY.

D. JAMES & CO.,

PLUMBERS,

Tinners, Gas and Steam Fitters,

No. 67 Main Street,

P. O. BOX 306. SALT LAKE CITY.

W. G. BROWN, GEN. AGT., Denver, Colorado. H. E. SPRAGUE, PRESIDENT, New York City. A. H. DANFORTH, V. P. AND GEN. MGR., South Pueblo, Colorado.

THE COLORADO COAL & IRON COMPANY,

Blast Furnaces, Steel Works & Rolling Mills, Located at South Pueblo, Colo.

Gas and Blacksmithing Coals and Coke, Steel Rails, Blooms and Billets, Mining Rails, Splice Bars, Spikes, Bolts and Nuts, Steel Nails, Pig Iron, Bar Iron, Cast Iron Pipe for Water and Gas.

WESTERN SALES AGENCY, SALT LAKE CITY. ***W. A. WETMORE, Agt.***

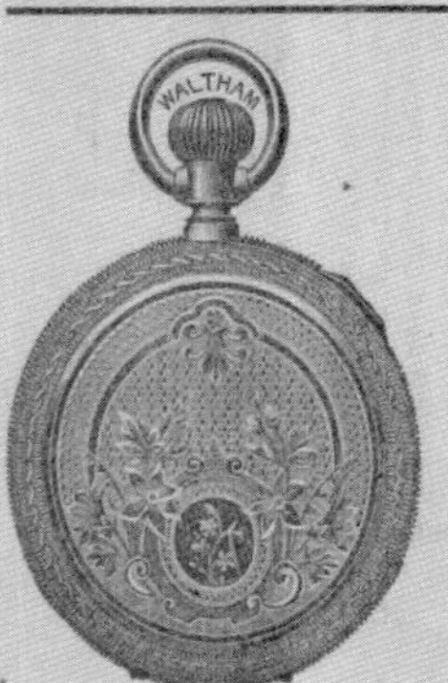

JOSLIN & PARK,

THE LEADING JEWELERS,

Salt Lake City, Utah, and Leadville, Colorado.

Importers and Manufacturers, Headquarters for Everything in the Line of Watches, Diamonds, Jewelry, Silverware, Fancy Goods and Novelties.

Orders for Medals, Badges and Prize Cups Filled at Short Notice.

WATCHES DE-MAGNETIZED.

JOSLIN & PARK, 170 S. Main Street, Salt Lake City.

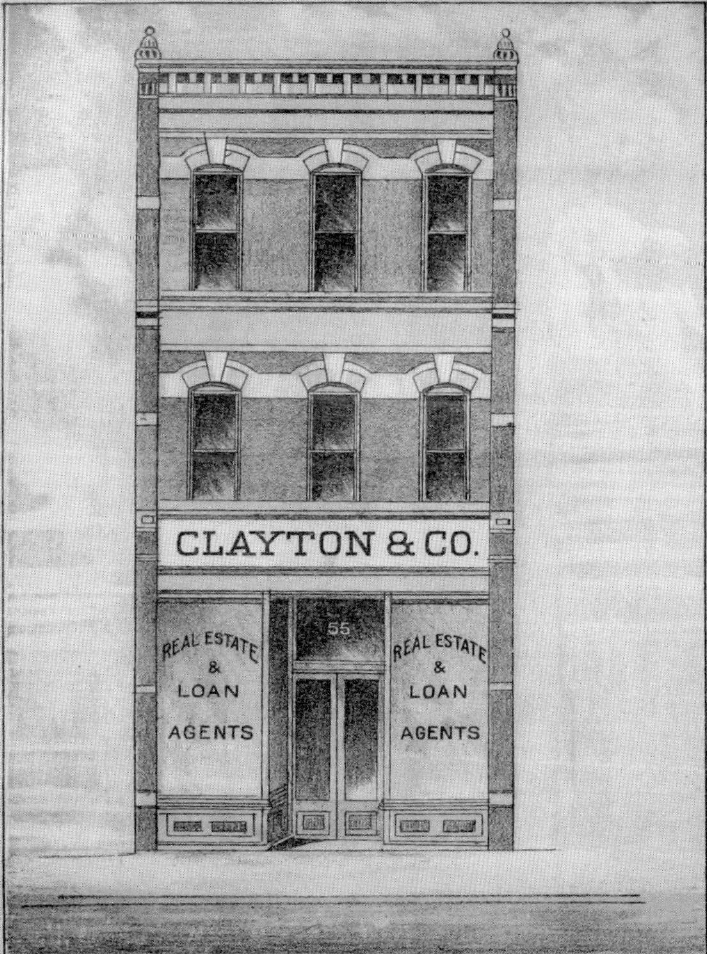

CLAYTON & CO.'S OFFICE.

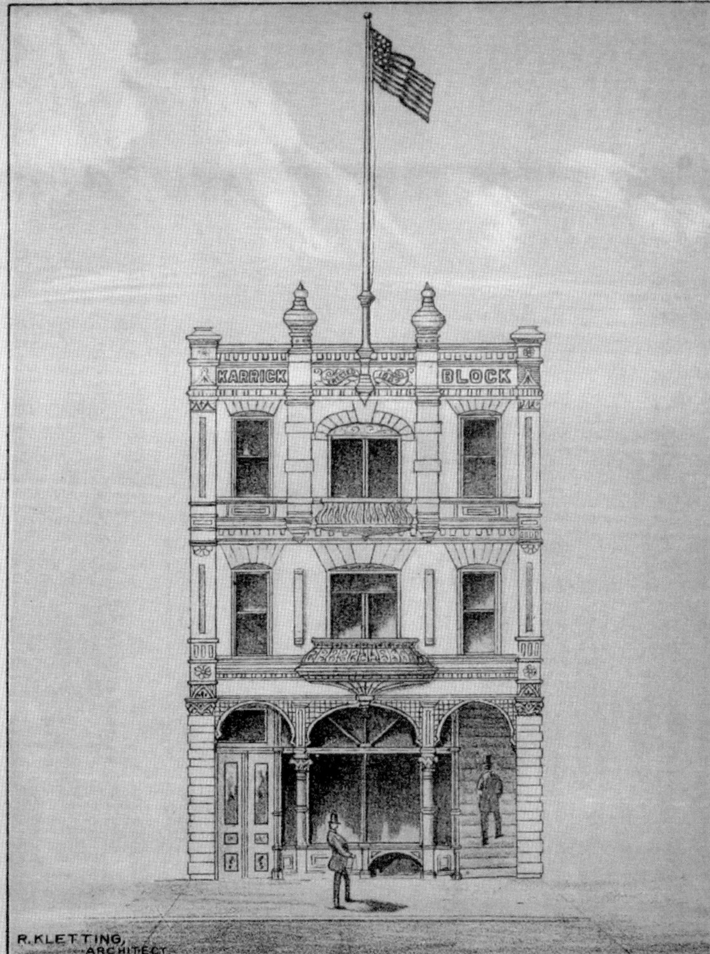

KARRICK BLOCK.

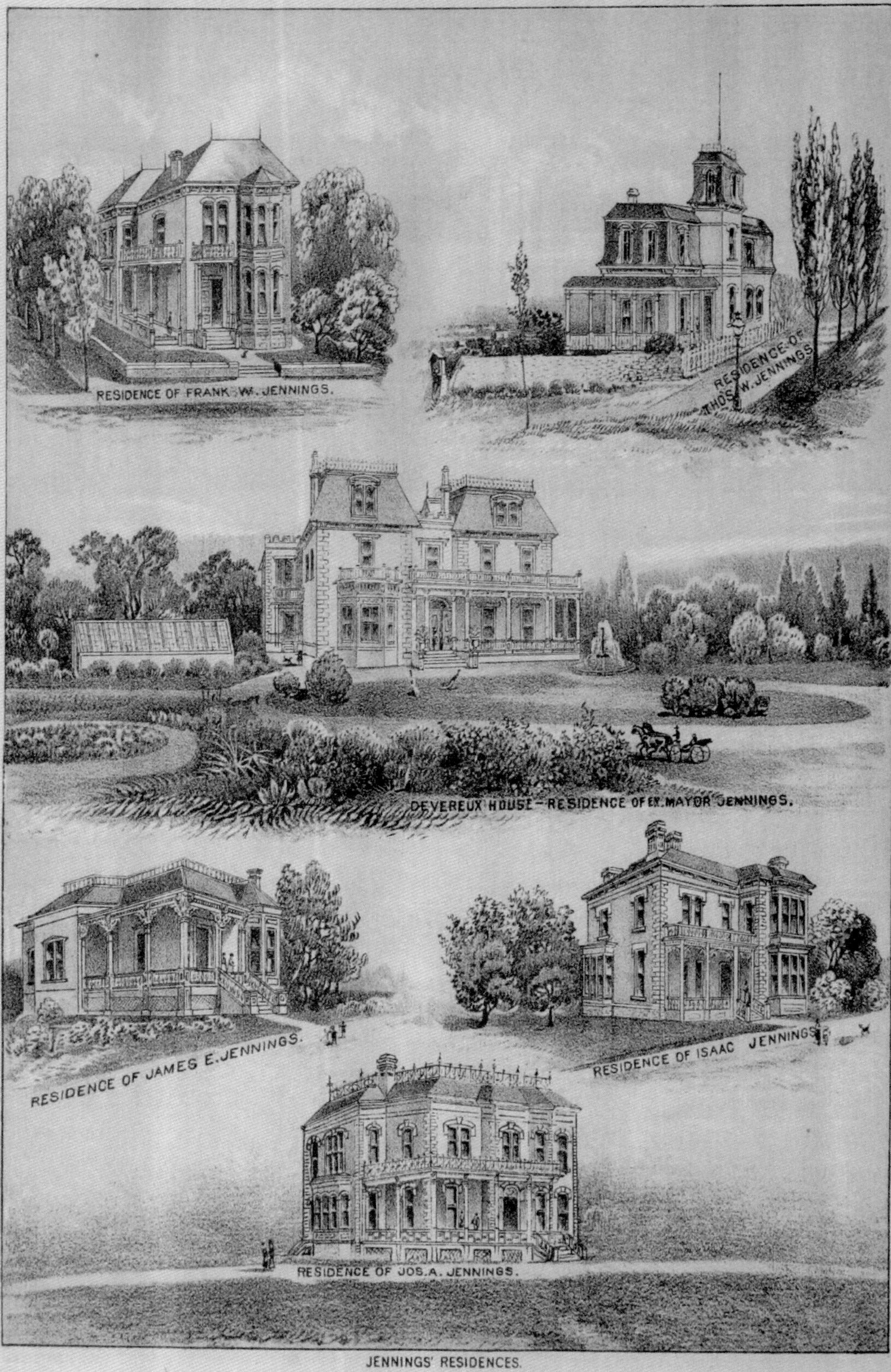

JENNINGS' RESIDENCES.

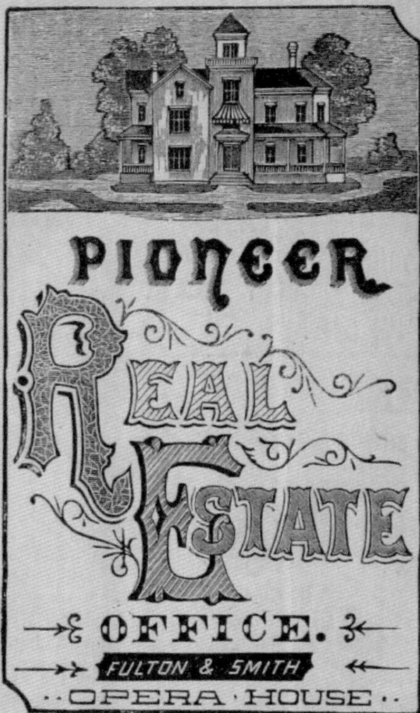

—WE ARE THE—

PIONEER REAL ESTATE FIRM

And have a thorough knowledge of all Properties, and their value, in and around SALT LAKE CITY. We have Choice Homes, we have Rich Farms and Farming Land, we have Improved and Unimproved Lots, we have Lands in Small and Large Tracts adjoining and in the immediate vicinity of this City. We respectfully invite the attention of those wishing to Purchase or Sell REAL ESTATE in this vicinity; also those wishing to BORROW or LOAN MONEY. Please call on or correspond with us at your earliest convenience, as Property is steadily advancing

FULTON & SMITH,

SALT LAKE CITY.

MOORE, ALLEN & CO.,

—Importers and—

Wholesale Druggists

SALT LAKE CITY,

Respectfully invite attention to their Large and Complete Stock of

Drugs, Medicines, Chemicals, Assay Goods

BALANCES, FURNACES, MORTARS, TEST LEAD WEIGHTS, CRUCIBLES, TONGS & GLASSWARE,

Comprising Everything Wanted in the Trade.

Write for Prices. Are Headquarters. And Never Undersold.

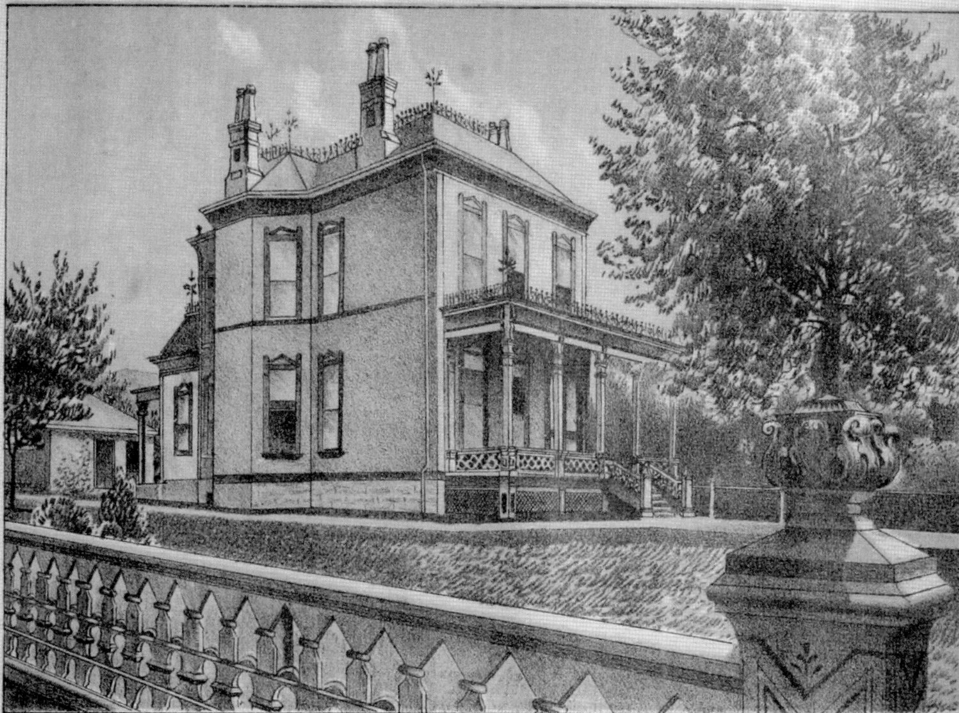

RESIDENCE OF W. E. SMEDLEY.

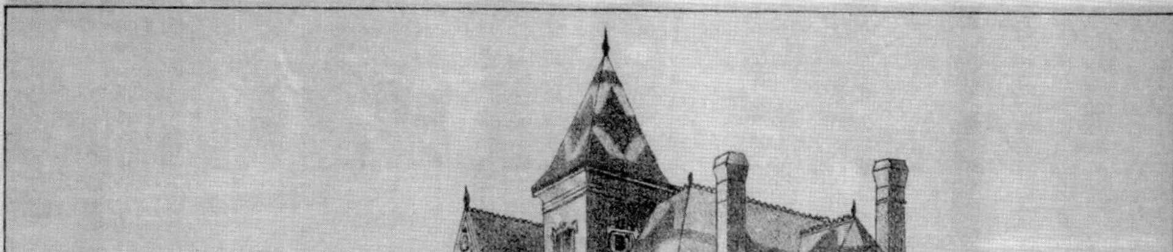

RESIDENCE OF J. C. CONKLIN.

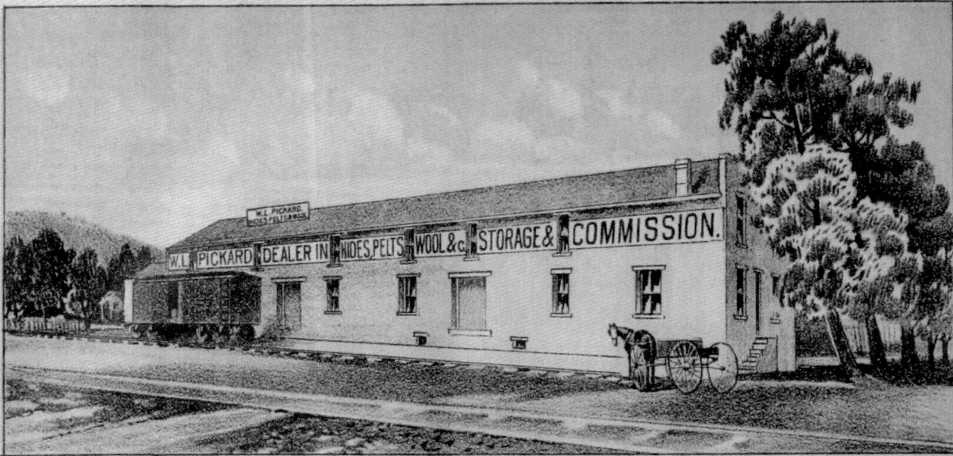

W. L. PICKARD'S WAREHOUSE.

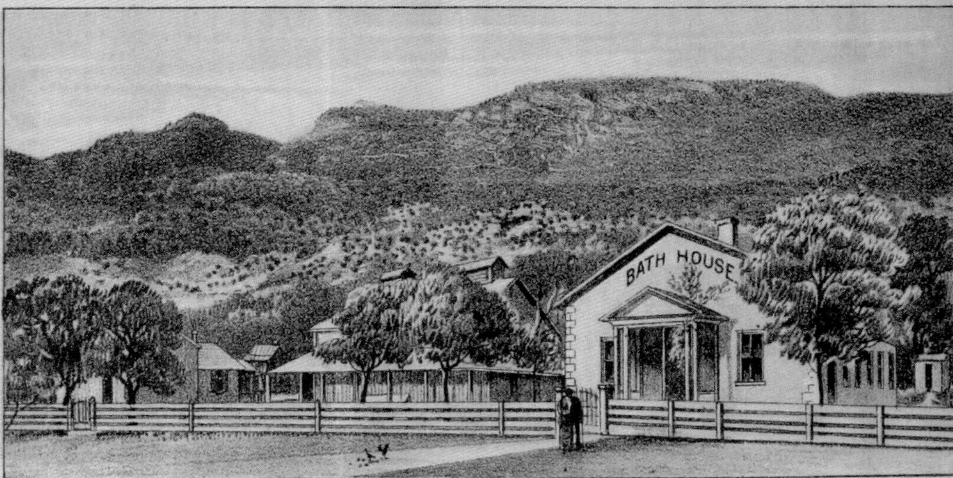

WARM SPRINGS BATH HOUSE.

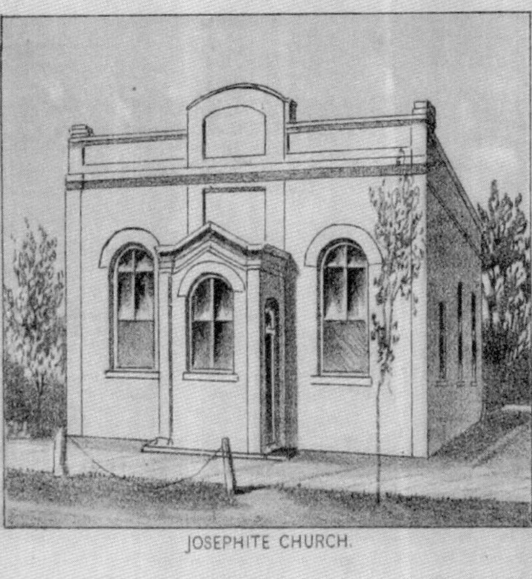

JOSEPHITE CHURCH.

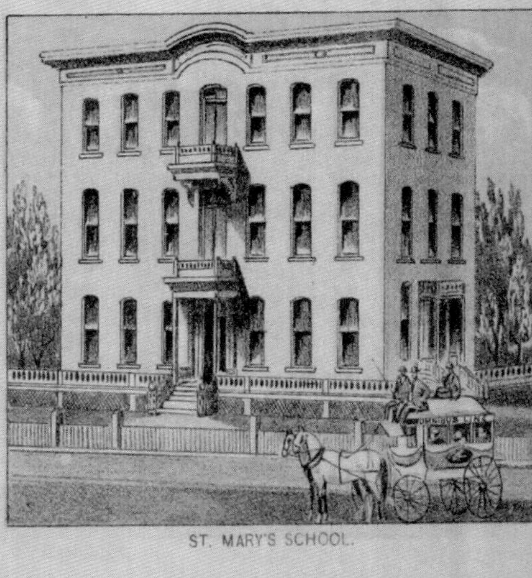

ST. MARY'S SCHOOL.

L. C. Parke, *President.* B. T. Lacy, *Vice-President.* C. P. Mason, *Manager.*

UTAH & MONTANA MACHINERY CO.,

(INCORPORATED)

Successor to PARKE, LACY & CO.

Agency Union Iron Works, San Francisco, California.

The Leading Machinery Establishment of the West.

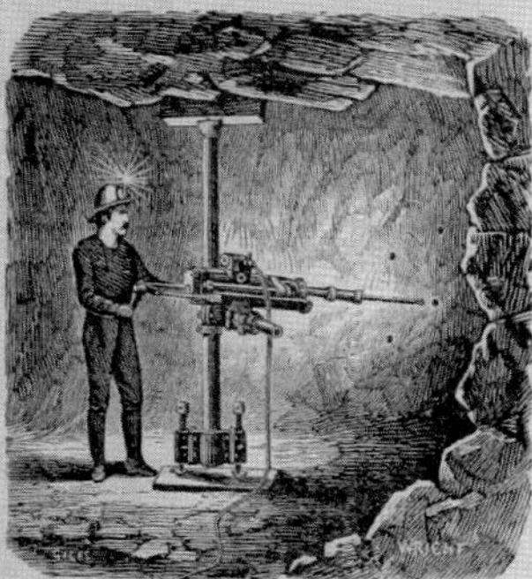

INGERSOLL "ECLIPSE" ROCK DRILL.

Carrying in stock for immediate shipment: *Lidgerwood Hoisting Engines, Ingersoll Air Compressors and Rock Drills, Knowles Steam Pumps, Boilers, Vertical and Horizontal Engines, Horse Whims, Wire Rope, Westinghouse Automatic Engines, Best Lubricating Oils, Powder, Fuse, Caps, Gas and Water Pipe, Brass and Iron Fittings, Packing, Latest Improved Wooden Pulleys, Miners' Tools, Sight-Feed Lubricators, Fairbanks' Standard Scales, Blowers and Fans, Mine, Mill and Smelter Supplies, Best Octagon and Grooved Drill Steel.*

Contractors for furnishing and erecting Stamp Mills, Smelters, Concentrating Plants, Etc., Etc. Exclusive Agency for Wall's Patent Corrugated Rolls and Vanning Jigs.

Office and Warehouse, 259 S. Main Street, Union Block,

SALT LAKE CITY.

Agency, Butte, Montana.

See View of our Establishment in half page Engraving of Union Block, Main St.

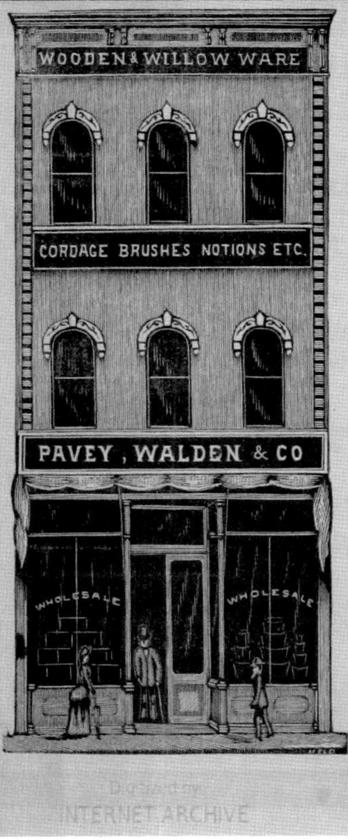

PAVEY, WALDEN & CO.,

WHOLESALE

Wooden and Willowware,

Grocers' and Hardware Sundries.

74 WEST SECOND SOUTH STREET,

SALT LAKE CITY.

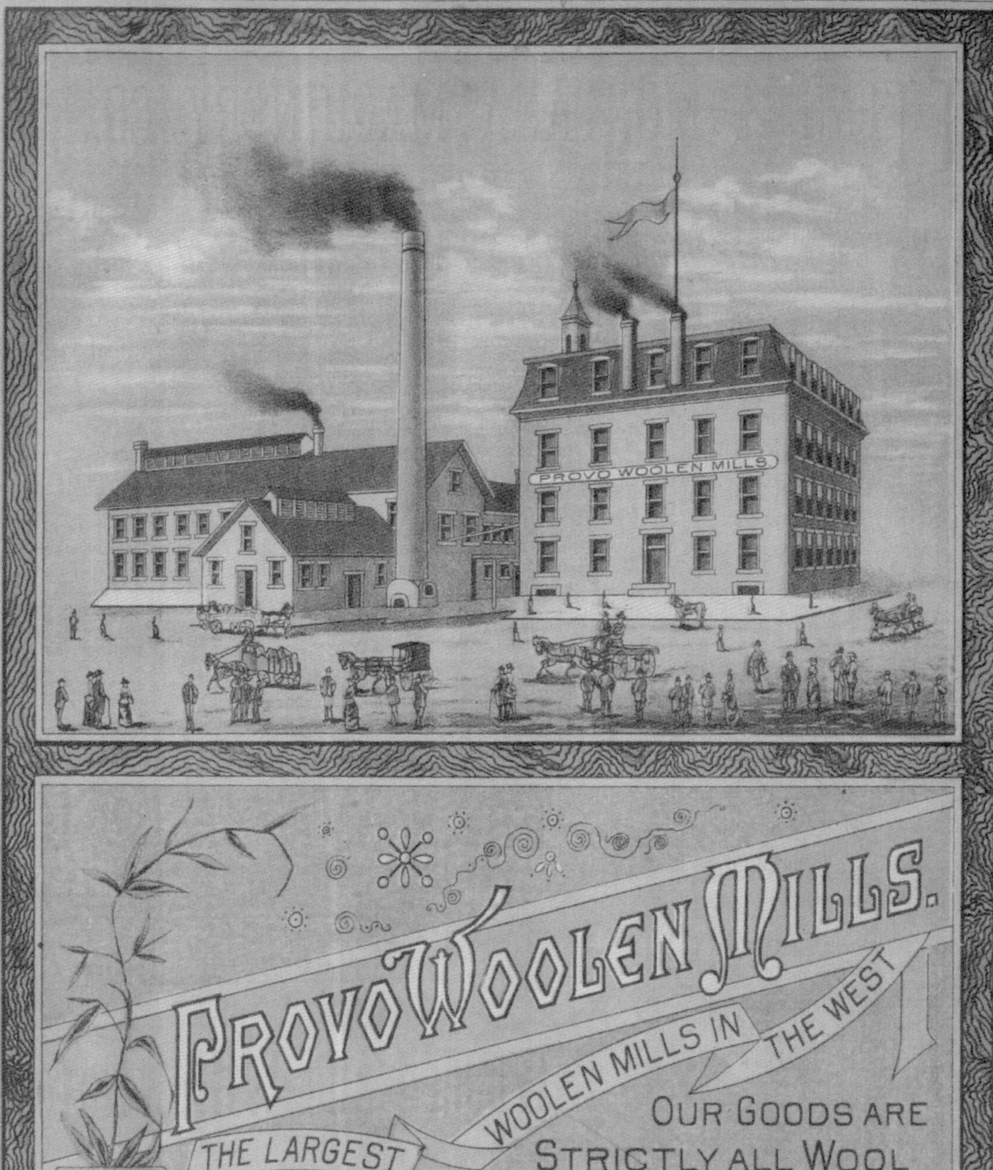

AUG. GAST BANK NOTE & LITHO CO - ST. LOUIS & N.Y.